D1288511

THE
ILLUSTRATED
TREASURY OF
POETRY
FOR
CHILDREN

THE ILLUSTRATED TREASURY OF POETRY FOR CHILDREN

Edited and with Commentary by DAVID ROSS

With an Introduction by MARK VAN DOREN

*Illustrated by Burmah Burris, Mel Klapholz, Ursula
Landshoff, and Roy McKie and by Gyo Fujikawa, Sir
John Tenniel, W. S. Gilbert, Edward Lear and others*

Grosset & Dunlap • NEW YORK
A NATIONAL GENERAL COMPANY

With love to
Beatrice and Jonathan

1973 Printing
COPYRIGHT © 1970 BY GROSSET & DUNLAP, INC.
ALL RIGHTS RESERVED.
PUBLISHED SIMULTANEOUSLY IN CANADA.
LIBRARY OF CONGRESS CATALOG CARD NUMBER: 76-86680.
ISBN: 0-448-02828-X (REGULAR EDITION)
ISBN: 0-448-04114-6 (DELUXE EDITION)
ISBN: 0-448-03116-7 (LIBRARY EDITION)
THE SELECTIONS REPRINTED IN THIS COLLECTION ARE USED BY
PERMISSION OF AND SPECIAL ARRANGEMENT WITH THE PROPRI-
ETORS OF THEIR RESPECTIVE COPYRIGHTS AND ARE INDIVIDUALLY
ACKNOWLEDGED ON PAGE 330.
PRINTED IN THE UNITED STATES OF AMERICA.
BOOK DESIGN BY ERLE YAHN.

Foreword

THIS BOOK IS FOR CHILDREN. However, since "men and women are but children of a larger growth" it is for them too. This then is a book for children of all ages. A book for all seasons of the heart: for the child who cannot yet read, but is read to; and for all those other children to whom poetry is like opening up a magical window to the world.

In this book you will find old favorites, still radiantly alive. You will discover with delight and excitement new poems to grow fond of as you get to know them better. And one way of getting to know a poem better is by reading it aloud. In that way you release its music, so that you and those about you can hear the poem sing.

No one can say why we cherish this or that poem, or what assures it of a long life. But this much may be said, that before a poem can endure, it must first endear itself to us. Or to say it another way; when a poem is deeply loved, it is never outlived. The child's pleasure in nonsense jingles and counting-out rhymes is that starting point that can eventually lead to the enjoyment of Shakespeare. What justifies a poem is the delight it gives, the sense of wonder and enchantment it communicates.

In compiling this anthology, it was my purpose to gather the poems and songs that "every child may joy to hear."

DAVID ROSS

Contents

Introduction
MARK VAN DOREN xii

The Seasons 3

The Garden Year
SARA COLERIDGE 4
The Going of the Snow
LOUISE TOWNSEND NICHOLL ... 4
Spring Night
THOMAS WESTWOOD 5
Spring
WILLIAM BLAKE 5
Four Little Foxes
LEW SARETT 6
Spring Quiet
CHRISTINA ROSSETTI 6
In Just-
E. E. CUMMINGS 7
Pippa's Song
ROBERT BROWNING 7
Written in March
WILLIAM WORDSWORTH 8
The Wind
ANONYMOUS 9
April
ANONYMOUS 9
On May Morning
JOHN MILTON 10
June, from The Vision of
  Sir Launfall
JAMES RUSSELL LOWELL 11
Summer Is Coming
ANONYMOUS 11
The Throstle
ALFRED, LORD TENNYSON 12
Fourth of July
EDMUND PENNANT 12
Sumer Is Icumen In
ANONYMOUS 13
Summer Is A-coming In
ANONYMOUS 13
Summer Storm
JAMES RUSSELL LOWELL 14
Scythe Song
ANDREW LANG 15
The Last Chrysanthemum
THOMAS HARDY 15
Autumn
WALTER DE LA MARE 16
September
HELEN HUNT JACKSON 16
Autumn
EMILY DICKINSON 16

Old October
THOMAS CONSTABLE 17
November
THOMAS HOOD 18
Thanksgiving Day
LYDIA MARIA CHILD 18
First Thanksgiving of All
NANCY BYRD TURNER 19
The Snow-storm
RALPH WALDO EMERSON 20
Blow, Blow, Thou Winter
  Wind
WILLIAM SHAKESPEARE 21
Winter
CHRISTINA ROSSETTI 21
Velvet Shoes
ELINOR WYLIE 21
To a Snowflake
FRANCIS THOMPSON 22
Now Winter Nights Enlarge
THOMAS CAMPION 22
Snow-flakes
HENRY WADSWORTH
  LONGFELLOW 23
When Icicles Hang by the
  Wall
WILLLIAM SHAKESPEARE 23
Our Window Is Stained
ALFRED KREYMBORG 24
Stopping by Woods on a
  Snowy Evening
ROBERT FROST 24
Lines from Snowbound
JOHN GREENLEAF WHITTIER 25
The Old Year
JOHN CLARE 26
The New Year
DINAH MARIA MULOCK CRAIK 27
Ring Out, Wild Bells
ALFRED, LORD TENNYSON 27

CHRISTMAS

Christ's Nativity
THE BIBLE 28
I Heard the Bells on
  Christmas Day
HENRY WADSWORTH
  LONGFELLOW 29
Twelfth Night Carol
ANONYMOUS 29
December Music
WINFIELD TOWNLEY SCOTT .. 30
Jingle Bells
JAMES PIERPONT 31

Long, Long Ago
ANONYMOUS 32
Old Winter
THOMAS NOEL 32
Our Joyful Feast
GEORGE WITHER 33
The Friendly Beasts
ANONYMOUS 33
We Wish You a Merry
  Christmas
ANONYMOUS 34
Christmas Is A-comin'
ANONYMOUS 34
Kriss Kringle
THOMAS BAILEY ALDRICH 35
Three Acres of Land
ANONYMOUS 35
Christmas at Sea
ROBERT LOUIS STEVENSON 36

The Tide Rises,
The Tide Falls 39

The Sea
GEORGE GORDON, LORD
  BYRON 40
They That Go Down
THE BIBLE 40
Crossing the Bar
ALFRED, LORD TENNYSON 41
The Noise of Waters
JAMES JOYCE 41
The Secret of the Sea
HENRY WADSWORTH
  LONGFELLOW 42
A Wet Sheet and a Flowing
  Sea
ALLAN CUNNINGHAM 43
The Sailor's Consolation
CHARLES DIBDIN 43
Heart's Content
ANONYMOUS 44
The Sea
BARRY CORNWALL 45
Little Billee
WILLIAM MAKEPEACE
  THACKERAY 46
The Tide River
CHARLES KINGSLEY 47
The Mermaid
ALFRED, LORD TENNYSON 48
The Mermaid
ANONYMOUS 48

The Tide Rises, the Tide
  Falls
HENRY WADSWORTH
  LONGFELLOW 50
Dover Beach
MATTHEW ARNOLD 50
To Sea!
THOMAS LOVELL BEDDOES 51
Villanelle of the Sea
A. M. SULLIVAN 52
The Golden Vanity
ANONYMOUS 52
How's My Boy?
SIDNEY DOBELL· 54
The Tempest
JAMES THOMAS FIELDS 55
The Wreck of the Hesperus
HENRY WADSWORTH
  LONGFELLOW 55
The Yarn of the "Nancy Bell"
W. S. GILBERT 57

Creatures of the Sea and Sky 61

Crickets
CONRAD AIKEN 62
Solomon and the Bees
JOHN GODFREY SAXE 63
The Nightingale and Glow-
  Worm
WILLIAM COWPER 64
Julius Caesar and the Honey-
  Bee
CHARLES TENNYSON TURNER 64
On a Fly Drinking from His
  Cup
WILLIAM OLDYS 65
Clock-a-Clay
JOHN CLARE 65
The Man and the Fish
LEIGH HUNT 66
The Frog
ANONYMOUS 67
The Little Turtle
VACHEL LINDSAY 67
To a Fish of the Brook
JOHN WOLCOT 67
Seaside Poems:
Do Fishes Go to School?
RUTH WHITMAN 68
The Horses of the Sea
CHRISTINA ROSSETTI 68
Dame Duck's Lecture
ANONYMOUS 69
The Chickens
ANONYMOUS 70

The Sandpiper
CELIA THAXTER 70
To a Waterfowl
WILLIAM CULLEN BRYANT 71
The Cuckoo
ANONYMOUS 72
To the Cuckoo
WILLIAM WORDSWORTH 72
To an Oriole
EDGAR FAWCETT 73
Song: The Owl
ALFRED, LORD TENNYSON 73
The Owl
BARRY CORNWALL 74
What Does Little Birdie Say?
ALFRED, LORD TENNYSON 75
Answer to a Child's Question
SAMUEL TAYLOR COLERIDGE 75
Song
JOHN KEATS 76
A Bird Came Down the Walk
EMILY DICKINSON 76
The Skylark
CHRISTINA ROSSETTI 76
The Thrush's Nest
JOHN CLARE 77
The Darkling Thrush
THOMAS HARDY 77
The Winged Worshippers
CHARLES SPRAGUE 78
Crow
FRANCES MINTURN HOWARD 78
The Pheasant
ALEXANDER POPE 79
Titwillow
W. S. GILBERT 80
The Eagle
ALFRED, LORD TENNYSON 81
The Eagle and the Mole
ELINOR WYLIE 82
Robin Redbreast
ANONYMOUS 82
Stay Near Me
WILLIAM WORDSWORTH 83
I've Watched You Now
WILLIAM WORDSWORTH 83

In Search of the Horizon 85

I Saw a Man Pursuing the
  Horizon
STEPHEN CRANE 86
A Book
EMILY DICKINSON 86
The Ballad of Sir Patrick
  Spens
ANONYMOUS 87

A Vagabond Song
BLISS CARMAN 88
The Land of Story-Books
ROBERT LOUIS STEVENSON 88
My Bed Is a Boat
ROBERT LOUIS STEVENSON 89
As I Float
DAVID ROSS 89
Verses
WILLIAM COWPER 90
Follow the Gleam
ALFRED, LORD TENNYSON 91
Reveille
A. E. HOUSMAN 92
Eldorado
EDGAR ALLAN POE 92
Home Thoughts from Abroad
ROBERT BROWNING 93
The Sea Gypsy
RICHARD HOVEY 93
The Sunset City
HENRY SYLVESTER CORNWELL 94
Singing through the Forests
JOHN GODFREY SAXE 95
The Crescent Boat
WILLIAM WORDSWORTH 96
The Children's Hour
HENRY WADSWORTH
  LONGFELLOW 98
One, Two, Three
HENRY CUYLER BUNNER 99
Kubla Khan
SAMUEL TAYLOR COLERIDGE 100
Requiem
ROBERT LOUIS STEVENSON 101

Spells and Enchantments 103

Vision of Belshazzar
GEORGE GORDON, LORD
  BYRON 104
The Song of Wandering
  Aengus
WILLIAM BUTLER YEATS 105
La belle Dame sans Merci
JOHN KEATS 106
The Ballad of the Harp
  Weaver
EDNA ST. VINCENT MILLAY .. 107
Little Orphant Annie
JAMES WHITCOMB RILEY 110
The Witch's House
LAURA BENÉT 111
The Raven
EDGAR ALLAN POE 112
To Morfydd
LIONELL JOHNSON 115

Miracles 117

Miracles
WALT WHITMAN 118
The Light Is Sweet
THE BIBLE 119
Morning
EMILY DICKINSON 119
I See the Moon
ANONYMOUS 120
Washed in Silver
JAMES STEPHENS 120
The Man in the Moon
ANONYMOUS 120
The Moon
ANONYMOUS 121
Escape at Bedtime
ROBERT LOUIS STEVENSON 121
When I Heard the Learn'd
    Astronomer
WALT WHITMAN 122
Who Has Seen the Wind
CHRISTINA ROSSETTI 122
The West Wind
JOHN MASEFIELD 123
The Wind
ROBERT LOUIS STEVENSON 124
Clouds
CHRISTINA ROSSETTI 125
Laughing Song
WILLIAM BLAKE 125
The Rhodora
RALPH WALDO EMERSON 125
What Is the Grass?
WALT WHITMAN 126
The Year
COVENTRY PATMORE 127
To Jane
PERCY BYSSHE SHELLEY 127
The First Dandelion
WALT WHITMAN 128
Single Majesty
MARK VAN DOREN 129
My Heart Leaps Up
WILLIAM WORDSWORTH 129
Baby Seeds
ANONYMOUS 129
Leisure
W. H. DAVIES 130
Pied Beauty
GERARD MANLEY HOPKINS 130
Moment of Visitation
GUSTAV DAVIDSON 131
Give Me the Splendid Silent
    Sun
WALT WHITMAN 132
Meditation
THOMAS TRAHERNE 132

A Thing of Beauty from
    Endymion
JOHN KEATS 133

Miniatures 135

The Chair
THEODORE ROETHKE 136
A Centipede Was Happy Quite
ANONYMOUS 136
The Rain
ANONYMOUS 137
Suffolk Epitaph
ANONYMOUS 137
If
ANONYMOUS 137
Epigram (Sir I Admit)
ALEXANDER POPE 137
Epigram (I Am His Highness'
    Dog)
ALEXANDER POPE 137
You Fancy Wit
ALEXANDER POPE 137
Epitaph
ANONYMOUS 137
Epitaph Intended for Sir Isaac
    Newton
ALEXANDER POPE 138
Riddle
ANONYMOUS 138
An Epitaph and a Reply
ANONYMOUS 138
Riddle
ANONYMOUS 138
What Can't Be Cured
ANONYMOUS 138
In the Dumps
ANONYMOUS 138
A Man in the Wilderness
ANONYMOUS 139
Man Is a Fool
ANONYMOUS 139
The Giant Fisherman
W. KING 139
For Want of a Nail
ANONYMOUS 139
The Hands of Toil
JAMES RUSSELL LOWELL 139
Work Is Love
ANONYMOUS 140
Jolly Red Nose
FRANCIS BEAUMONT AND
    JOHN FLETCHER 140
The Human Heart
WILLIAM WORDSWORTH 140
After Many a Summer from
    Tithonus
ALFRED, LORD TENNYSON 140

The Man of Thessaly
ANONYMOUS 141
I Met a Man
ANONYMOUS 141

Music 143

I Hear America Singing
WALT WHITMAN 144
The Crow Doth Sing
WILLIAM SHAKESPEARE 144
Music
WILLIAM SHAKESPEARE 145
Ode
ARTHUR O'SHAUGHNESSY 146
A Song of Enchantment
WALTER DE LA MARE 146
Song's Eternity
JOHN CLARE 147
Bugle Song
ALFRED, LORD TENNYSON 148
Song for Boys and Girls
CHARLES ANGOFF 149
The Rivals
JAMES STEPHENS 149
A Swing Song
WILLIAM ALLINGHAM 150
Look at Six Eggs
CARL SANDBURG 150
Music
RALPH WALDO EMERSON 151
There's Music in a Hammer
ANONYMOUS 151
Song in the Songless
GEORGE MEREDITH 151
The Song of Hiawatha
HENRY WADSWORTH
    LONGFELLOW 152
Lean Out of the Window
JAMES JOYCE 154
A Time for Singing
GUSTAV DAVIDSON 154
Ariel's Song
WILLIAM SHAKESPEARE 155
Song—Tell Me Where Is
    Fancy Bred
WILLIAM SHAKESPEARE 155
Under the Greenwood Tree
WILLIAM SHAKESPEARE 155
Merry Are the Bells
ANONYMOUS 156
Song
JOHN FLETCHER 156
Choric Song from The Lotos
    Eaters
ALFRED, LORD TENNYSON 156
Afton Water
ROBERT BURNS 157

To Music
ROBERT HERRICK 158
Psalm 150
THE BIBLE 158
The Flowers That Bloom in
the Spring
W. S. GILBERT 159
The Day Is Done
HENRY WADSWORTH
LONGFELLOW 160
Neither Spirit nor Bird
MARY AUSTIN 161
I, Too
LANGSTON HUGHES 161

Nonsense! 163

The Moon Is Up
ANONYMOUS 164
I Saw a Peacock
ANONYMOUS 165
The Great Panjandrum
SAMUEL FOOTE 165
Rhyme for a Simpleton
ANONYMOUS 166
Counting-Out Rhymes
ANONYMOUS 166
The Walloping Window-Blind
CHARLES E. CARRYL 167
The Jumblies
EDWARD LEAR 168
Jabberwocky
LEWIS CARROLL 171
The Voice of the Lobster
LEWIS CARROLL 172
The Dinkey-Bird
EUGENE FIELD 172
Incidents in the Life of My
Uncle Arly
EDWARD LEAR 173
Ways and Means
LEWIS CARROLL 175
Father William
ANONYMOUS 176
A Chronicle
ANONYMOUS 177
The Twins
HENRY S. LEIGH 178

LIMERICKS

There Was An Old Man Who
Said, "Do
ANONYMOUS 179
The Reverend Henry Ward
Beecher
OLIVER WENDELL HOLMES 179
A Fly and a Flea in a Flue
ANONYMOUS 179

A Briton Who Swore at
His King
DAVID ROSS 179
An Indolent Vicar of Bray
ANONYMOUS 179
The Bottle of Perfume That
Willie Sent
ANONYMOUS 179
A Yak Who Was New to
the Zoo
DAVID ROSS 180
An Epicure Dining at Crewe
ANONYMOUS 180
There Was a Young Lady of
Niger
ANONYMOUS 180
There Was an Old Lady of
Steen
ANONYMOUS 180
There Was a Young Woman
Named Bright
ANONYMOUS 180
There Was a Faith Healer
of Deal
ANONYMOUS 180
There Was an Old Man
from Peru
ANONYMOUS 180
There Was an Old Man with
a Beard
ANONYMOUS 180
There Once Was a Young
Man Named Hall
ANONYMOUS 181
A Maiden at College Named
Breeze
ANONYMOUS 181
There Was a Young Lady of
Crete
ANONYMOUS 181
There Was an Old Looney of
Rhyme
ANONYMOUS 181
A Clergyman Told from His
Text
ANONYMOUS 181
There Was an Old Man in
a Tree
EDWARD LEAR 181
There Was an Old Man from
St. Bees
W. S. GILBERT 181

Present Mirth 183

Abdul Abulbul Amir
ANONYMOUS 184

The Georges
WALTER SAVAGE LANDOR 186
The Riddling Knight
ANONYMOUS 186
A Riddle
CATHERINE FANSHAWE 188
A Riddle
ANONYMOUS 188
Lines to a Young Lady
EDWARD LEAR 189
Lord Chancellor's Song
W. S. GILBERT 189
It Chanced to Be Our Washing
Day
OLIVER WENDELL HOLMES .. 191
When Father Carves the Duck
E. V. WRIGHT 192
Methuselah
ANONYMOUS 192
The Deacon's Masterpiece or,
The Wonderful "One-Hoss
Shay"
OLIVER WENDELL HOLMES .. 193
The Ploughboy in Luck
ANONYMOUS 195
An Expostulation
ISAAC BICKERSTAFF 195
Morning
CHARLES STUART CALVERLEY 196
The Nose and the Eyes
WILLIAM COWPER 196
Mr. Nobody
ANONYMOUS 197
Robinson Crusoe's Island
CHARLES E. CARRYL 198
Changed
CHARLES STUART CALVERLEY 200
The Confession
RICHARD HARRIS BARHAM 200
A Farmer's Boy
ANONYMOUS 201
There Was a Little Girl
HENRY WADSWORTH
LONGFELLOW 201
The Naughty Boy
JOHN KEATS 202
The Elderly Gentleman
GEORGE CANNING 202
The Height of the Ridiculous
OLIVER WENDELL HOLMES .. 203
The Milkmaid
JEFFREYS TAYLOR 204
The Rum Tum Tugger
T. S. ELIOT 205
The Old Man Who Lived in
the Woods
ANONYMOUS 206

Sweet William, His Wife, and
  the Sheepskin
ANONYMOUS 207

Creatures on Land 209

I Think I Could Turn and
  Live with Animals
WALT WHITMAN 210
Variation on a Sentence
LOUISE BOGAN 210
Theatre Mouse
CHARLES A. WAGNER 211
The City Mouse
CHRISTINA ROSSETTI 212
Three Wishes
ANONYMOUS 212
The Kitten and the Falling
  Leaves
WILLIAM WORDSWORTH 213
My Cat Jeoffry
CHRISTOPHER SMART 214
That Cat
BEN KING 215
Cure for a Pussy Cat
ANONYMOUS 215
The Cats of Kilkenny
ANONYMOUS 215
On a Spaniel Called Beau
  Killing a Young Bird
WILLIAM COWPER 216
Beau's Reply
WILLIAM COWPER 216
Epitaph to a Newfoundland
  Dog
GEORGE GORDON, LORD
  BYRON 217
Elegy on the Death of a Mad
  Dog
OLIVER GOLDSMITH 218
Dapple Gray
ANONYMOUS 219
The Horse
THE BIBLE 219
The Horse from Henry V
WILLIAM SHAKESPEARE 219
Donkeys
EDWARD FIELD 220
The Cow
ROBERT LOUIS STEVENSON 221
The Lamb
WILLIAM BLAKE 221
The Ram
ANONYMOUS 222
The God of Sheep
JOHN FLETCHER 222
The Goat
ANONYMOUS 223

The Goat Paths
JAMES STEPHENS 223
The Sloth
THEODORE ROETHKE 224
The Tiger
WILLIAM BLAKE 225
Grizzly Bear
MARY AUSTIN 225
The Bear Hunt
ABRAHAM LINCOLN 226
Hunting Song
SAMUEL TAYLOR COLERIDGE .. 227
The Ballad of the Fox
ANONYMOUS 228
The Squirrel
ANONYMOUS 229
The Little Animal
JOSEPH TUSIANI 229
To Miss Georgiana Shipley
BENJAMIN FRANKLIN 230
To a Squirrel at Kyle-Na-No
WILLIAM BUTLER YEATS 231
On a Squirrel Crossing the
  Road in Autumn, in New
  England
RICHARD EBERHART 231
The Blind Men and the
  Elephant
JOHN GODFREY SAXE 232
Brown and Furry
CHRISTINA ROSSETTI 233
Animal Fair
ANONYMOUS 233
Bed-Time Story
MELVILLE CANE 234
The Snail
ANONYMOUS 234
Nursery Snail
RUTH HERSCHBERGER 235
The Snail
WILLIAM COWPER 235
The Housekeeper
CHARLES LAMB 236
Remonstrance with the Snails
ANONYMOUS 236

Cast of Characters 239

The Village Schoolmaster
OLIVER GOLDSMITH 240
The Ballad of William Syca-
  more
STEPHEN VINCENT BENÉT 241
The Ox-Tamer
WALT WHITMAN 243
King Solomon and King David
ANONYMOUS 244

Parson Gray
OLIVER GOLDSMITH 244
The Fiddler of Dooney
WILLIAM BUTLER YEATS 245
Quoits
MARY EFFIE LEE NEWSOME .. 245
The Leprachaun; or, Fairy
  Shoemaker
WILLIAM ALLINGHAM 246
The Shepherd
WILLIAM BLAKE 248
Maud Muller
JOHN GREENLEAF WHITTIER 248
One More River
ANONYMOUS 251
Pocahontas
WILLIAM MAKEPEACE
  THACKERAY 252
We Are Seven
WILLIAM WORDSWORTH 253
The Watch
MAY SWENSON 254
For Children if They'll Take
  Them
X. J. KENNEDY 255
Skipper Ireson's Ride
JOHN GREENLEAF WHITTIER .. 255
The Gardener
ROBERT LOUIS STEVENSON 257
Old Meg
JOHN KEATS 258
I Think Continually of Those
  Who Were Truly Great
STEPHEN SPENDER 259
He Bloomed among Eagles
DAVID ROSS 260
Anne Rutledge from The
  Spoon River Anthology
EDGAR LEE MASTERS 260
Song of the Western Men
ROBERT STEPHEN HAWKER ... 261
O Captain! My Captain!
WALT WHITMAN 262
Lincoln Was a Tall Man
ELIAS LIEBERMAN 263
Song for Unbound Hair
GENEVIEVE TAGGARD 264
Adventures with My Grand-
  father
ANNE MARX 265
The Solitary Reaper
WILLIAM WORDSWORTH 266
An Old Woman of the Roads
PADRAIC COLUM 267
Cockles and Mussels
ANONYMOUS 267
The Ahkond of Swat
EDWARD LEAR 268

To Thomas Moore
GEORGE GORDON, LORD
  BYRON 269

LOVE POEMS
The Bailiff's Daughter of
  Islington
ANONYMOUS 270
I Will Make You Brooches
ROBERT LOUIS STEVENSON 271
John Anderson, My Jo
ROBERT BURNS 272
The Passionate Shepherd to
  His Love
CHRISTOPHER MARLOWE 272
Reply to the Passionate Shep-
  herd
SIR WALTER RALEIGH 273
Music I Heard with You from
  Discordants
CONRAD AIKEN 273

Men at Arms 275

Old Ironsides
OLIVER WENDELL HOLMES .. 276
The Charge of the Light Bri-
  gade
ALFRED, LORD TENNYSON 277
Bonnie George Campbell
ANONYMOUS 278
The Soldier's Dream
THOMAS CAMPBELL 278
The Blue and the Gray
FRANCIS MILES FINCH 280
Johnny Has Gone for a
  Soldier
ANONYMOUS 281
Battle-Hymn of the Republic
JULIA WARD HOWE 281
Horatius at the Bridge
THOMAS BABINGTON
  MACAULAY 282
Soldier Rest!
SIR WALTER SCOTT 287
The Paper in the Meadow
OSCAR WILLIAMS 287

Recollections 289

The Sands o' Dee
CHARLES KINGSLEY 290
I Remember, I Remember
THOMAS HOOD 290
My Early Home
JOHN CLARE 292
The Oak and the Ash
ANONYMOUS 292

Song
ALFRED, LORD TENNYSON 293
Martha
WALTER DE LA MARE 293
The Little Girl I Used to Be
MARGUERITE HARRIS 294
Time, You Old Gipsy Man
RALPH HODGSON 294
Sing Me a Song
ROBERT LOUIS STEVENSON 295
Aladdin
JAMES RUSSELL LOWELL 295
The Old Song
CHARLES KINGSLEY 295
My Lost Youth
HENRY WADSWORTH
  LONGFELLOW 296
All That's Past
WALTER DE LA MARE 299
A Memory
WILLIAM ALLINGHAM 299
Mountain Road
MARY OLIVER 300
Having New England Fathers
JOHN HOLMES 300
Jenny Kissed Me
LEIGH HUNT 301
Tears, Idle Tears from *The
  Princess*
ALFRED, LORD TENNYSON 302
Annabel Lee
EDGAR ALLAN POE 303
With Rue My Heart Is Laden
A. E. HOUSMAN 304
Love and Age
THOMAS LOVE PEACOCK 304
Memory
THOMAS BAILEY ALDRICH 305
Home No More
ROBERT LOUIS STEVENSON 306
The Noise That Time Makes
MERRILL MOORE 307
The House on the Hill
EDWIN ARLINGTON ROBINSON 308
The Time of Roses
THOMAS HOOD 308
The Harp That Once through
  Tara's Halls
THOMAS MOORE 309
The Tropics in New York
CLAUDE MCKAY 309
Chapter Two
WINFIELD TOWNLEY SCOTT .. 310
Blue Girls
JOHN CROWE RANSOM 311
The Ballad of Bouillabaisse
WILLIAM MAKEPEACE
  THACKERAY 311

Wisdom 315

Psalm 23
THE BIBLE 316
The Noble Nature
BEN JONSON 316
Lines Written in Early Spring
WILLIAM WORDSWORTH 317
Once in a Saintly Passion
JAMES THOMSON 317
How Many
CHRISTINA ROSSETTI 317
The Glories of Our Blood and
  State
JAMES SHIRLEY 318
Proprietor
A. M. SULLIVAN 318
The Fool's Prayer
EDWARD ROWLAND SILL 319
My Mind to Me a Kingdom Is
EDWARD DYER 320
Patriotism
SIR WATER SCOTT 320
Content
ROBERT GREENE 321
The Character of a Happy
  Life
SIR HENRY WOTTON 321
Sweet Content
THOMAS DEKKER 322
Gladness of Heart
ECCLESIASTES 322
Fetters
LOUIS GINSBERG 323
Invictus
WILLIAM ERNEST HENLEY 323
Solitude
ALEXANDER POPE 324
Ozymandias
PERCY BYSSHE SHELLEY 325
To Get Thine Ends
ROBERT HERRICK 326
Success Is Counted Sweetest
EMILY DICKINSON 326
The Road Not Taken
ROBERT FROST 327
The Little Cares
ELIZABETH BARRETT
  BROWNING 327
Abou Ben Adhem
LEIGH HUNT 328
Auguries of Innocence
WILLIAM BLAKE 329

Index 332

Introduction

"CHILDREN'S POETRY." That could mean poetry by children, poetry about children, or poetry for them. In the pages that follow it is for them as readers. And if they read some of these poems, or all of them, in company with older persons, their parents or otherwise, so much the better. For they are true poems, and as such are not intended to be limited in their appeal. Doubtless there will be young readers who neither want nor need an elder by them as they go through the book, and that too would be good. But the best thing of all would be for them to share the experience with others whose interest, whose delight, was at least equal to their own. Poetry gains by being read aloud and talked about by those who like it. And to the best poetry this happens over and over again. "Listen to this." "Remember how it goes?" "Yes, and the next line too." Poetry, except for those who have mastered it and made it their whole life, is neither a solitary nor a silent art. Master poets, like master musicians, can absorb everything that is there without moving their lips or fingers. Short of this, however, it is natural, indeed it is necessary, for poetry to be shared.

No true poem was ever for children only. Poetry is one world, and ideally there is no end to the number, or the kind, or the age, of its inhabitants. This is not saying that every poet, and every reader of poetry, is a child at heart. Perhaps it is more like saying that every child, even while he remains a child, is an adult at heart. Children are older than they seem, just as adults are younger than they look. And poetry, like play, can bring them close together. Poetry in fact *is* play—the play of the mind over and among all things, strange or familiar, that exist. Poetry comes out of the mind as it reports and reflects upon feeling. Feeling must be there, but it cannot act alone; it has to be measured, it has to be given form, by an intellect cultivated toward this end. The matter at hand may be trivial or immense, it may be as little as mice or as big as all the world, it may call for sense or nonsense in the poem to be written. There is no difference finally. All good poetry, whatever the size of its subject, is both serious and light. It is light, that is to say, because it carries itself without apparent effort; at any rate it is not heavy, it does not burden the ground. And it is serious because it sings or says things to us that we remember. We do not remember the utterances of a shallow mind, however silly or however solemn its deportment.. Beneath every poem worthy of the name there is understanding, and it goes deeper than sometimes we suppose.

The clearest sign of its depth is that it makes our own minds happy. And at the depth where it does this it cares not how old or young we are. It desires only to engage our full attention—which, to be sure, we may not have learned yet how to give. And there are those who never in their lives will want to give it. And that is quite all right. Nobody has to like poetry; it is not a duty to be done. Only a minority of mankind loves words that much. And this minority, as it happens, never announces that it "loves poetry." It certainly does not love all poetry, for most poetry is poor. It loves good poems. And it wishes there were more good poems than in fact there are. But the ones it does find good it can love without limit, as we love our friends. A good poem is a good friend; and so, it may be, is some other person, old or young, who loves it too. Sooner or later good poems make good friends. And it is a fortunate thing when these friends are parents and children. It is not necessary, though it is desirable, that parents should have had the experience first; if they have not, their children may educate them. There was a time when they both loved Mother Goose, which is perfect poetry of its kind. But it is only one of many kinds; the rest remain to be discovered.

If the present volume does not offer specimens of all the kinds there are, that need not be surprising, for the list is long. But it offers God's plenty; its range is wide. Shakespeare, the greatest of poets, is here of course, though chiefly in his songs. So is Milton, and so are Wordsworth, Whitman, Emily Dickinson, Blake, Emerson, Tennyson, Keats, Shelley, Burns, Hardy, Yeats, Frost, Longfellow, Lewis Carroll, and Browning; and so is the Bible, whose poetry has never been surpassed in any language. But this is only the beginning. There are riddles, there are nonsense verses; there is one of T. S. Eliot's famous cat poems in doggerel rhythm and rhyme; there are limericks; there are fantasies and diversions by Edward Lear; and inescapably there is Longfellow's demonstration of how "forehead" should be pronounced:

> *There was a little girl*
> *Who had a little curl*
> *Right in the middle of her forehead;*
> *And when she was good*
> *She was very, very good,*
> *But when she was bad she was horrid.*

These six immortal lines may have had a further purpose; legend tells us that they were written one day when Longfellow's small daughter Edith was refusing to have her hair curled; but they do make it clear that "horrid" and "forehead" rhyme, and so they serve our memories somewhat as do the lines that begin:

Thirty days hath September.

The feast before the reader is very rich, with main dishes and side dishes; and who is to say which dishes are the more important? No seasoned adult reader will care, and neither will a young reader who is in the process of being seasoned. Not that any reader will like all of the poems equally. That never happens in any comparable collection. Nor will there be agreement among the readers' choices. What is it that determines such choices? Nobody knows. They are usually made, however, at first glance. A poem that strikes us as good strikes us immediately; it leaps forth from the page; it sounds in our ears; it penetrates to the center of our understanding. It is a case of love at first sight, which philosophers have said is the only love that matters. This is how we choose our friends; we do not prove to ourselves that we should like them, we simply do like them from the start. So with paintings and pieces of music. And the clearest conclusion with respect to very famous poems—or anything else—is that all readers, or at least most readers, have fallen in love with them for good. That is how they have become classics. But again, the reason is mysterious. Blake's "The Tiger," Hopkins' "Pied Beauty," Frost's "Stopping by Woods on a Snowy Evening," Smart's "My Cat Jeoffry," the twenty-third Psalm, Wordsworth's "The Solitary Reaper," Stevenson's "Requiem," Carroll's "Jabberwocky," Riley's "Little Orphant Annie," Hood's "I Remember, I Remember"—who can explain the success these poems have had? Who can measure the satisfaction, line after line, that Shakespeare gives us in "When Icicles Hang by the Wall"? For better or worse it cannot be done. And perhaps this is just as well.

David Ross, who chose the poems for this book, has long been beloved as a reader of poetry over the radio and elsewhere. "I have selected poetry," he says, "which adults will enjoy reading to children, and to which children should be exposed. I have also included poetry that a child can read himself. This, I hope, will lead to discussion of the poem between the adult and the child." It is a wise hope, and the contents of the volume justify it in advance. These poems will make many friends, both for themselves and among their readers.

MARK VAN DOREN

We have been careful that they that will read may have delight, and that they that are desirous to commit to memory might have ease, and that all into whose hands it comes might have profit.

II MACCABEES 2:25

The Seasons

ALL OF US are impressed—and quite rightly—with the stately spaceships that carry men beyond the atmosphere and into orbits that were, until recent times, possible only in stories of science fiction. Yet few of us stop to consider what a magnificent space vehicle we ourselves inhabit. Few of us realize what a splendid journey we are on as our earth swings in its vast orbit around the sun. Since its birth, the earth has made this journey with clocklike regularity, and in so doing has brought earth its seasons. Poets, of course, have always been aware of this journey through space, of these predictably changing seasons, and of the wonders that they bring, and have sung them in songs of description, celebration, and awe.

The Garden Year

SARA COLERIDGE

January brings the snow,
Makes our feet and fingers glow.

February brings the rain,
Thaws the frozen lake again.

March brings breezes, loud and shrill,
To stir the dancing daffodil.

April brings the primrose sweet,
Scatters daisies at our feet.

May brings flocks of pretty lambs
Skipping by their fleecy dams.

June brings tulips, lilies, roses,
Fills the children's hands with posies.

Hot July brings cooling showers,
Apricots, and gillyflowers.

August brings the sheaves of corn,
Then the harvest home is borne.

Warm September brings the fruit;
Sportsmen then begin to shoot.

Fresh October brings the pheasant;
Then to gather nuts is pleasant.

Dull November brings the blast;
Then the leaves are whirling fast.

Chill December brings the sleet,
Blazing fire, and Christmas treat.

The Going of the Snow

LOUISE TOWNSEND NICHOLL

Through the open doors
I hear waters rushing.
The streams of March go full again and start
As I lie listening in the dark
To hear the Spring beginning.

This is the going of the snow.
After the thick white silent months
There comes a black night, sheer and thin and wet,
Filled full again with sound.

It was so easy for the snow to come,
So hard to go—
Therefore should Spring be proud.
The snow was gentle when it fell,
Weaving a soundless, mystic spell—
But going snow is loud, loud.

At last, at last
I hear the full brook rushing past.

Spring Night

THOMAS WESTWOOD

Slow, horses, slow,
As thro' the wood we go—
We would count the stars in heaven,
Hear the grasses grow:

Watch the cloudlets few
Dappling the deep blue,
In our open palms outspread
Catch the blessed dew.

Slow, horses, slow,
As thro' the wood we go—
We would see fair Dian rise
With her huntress bow:

We would hear the breeze
Ruffling the dim trees,
Hear its sweet love-ditty set
To endless harmonies.

Slow, horses, slow,
As thro' the wood we go—
All the beauty of the night
We would learn and know!

Spring

WILLIAM BLAKE

Sound the flute!
Now it's mute.
Birds delight
Day and Night;
Nightingale
In the dale,
Lark in Sky,
Merrily,
Merrily, merrily, to welcome in the Year.

Little Boy,
Full of joy;
Little Girl,
Sweet and small;
Cock does crow,
So do you;
Merry voice,
Infant noise,
Merrily, merrily, to welcome in the Year.

Little Lamb,
Here I am;
Come and lick
My white neck;
Let me pull
Your soft Wool;
Let me kiss
Your soft face;
Merrily, merrily, we welcome in the Year.

5

Spring Quiet

CHRISTINA ROSSETTI

Gone were but the winter,
  Come were but the spring,
I would go to a covert
  Where the birds sing;

Where in the whitethorn
  Singeth the thrush,
And a robin sings
  In the holly-bush.

Full of fresh scents
  Are the budding boughs
Arching high over
  A cool green house;

Full of sweet scents,
  And whispering air
Which sayeth softly:
  "We spread no snare;

"Here dwell in safety,
  Here dwell alone,
With a clear stream
  And a mossy stone.

"Here the sun shineth
  Most shadily;
Here is heard an echo
  Of the far sea,
    Though far off it be."

Four Little Foxes

LEW SARETT

Speak gently, Spring, and make no sudden sound;
For in my windy valley, yesterday I found
New-born foxes squirming on the ground—
  Speak gently.

Walk gently, March; forbear the bitter blow;
Her feet within a trap, her blood upon the snow,
The four little foxes saw their mother go—
  Walk softly.

Go lightly, Spring; oh, give them no alarm;
When I covered them with boughs to shelter them from harm,
The thin blue foxes suckled at my arm—
  Go lightly.

Step softly, March, with your rampant hurricane;
Nuzzling one another, and whimpering with pain,
The new little foxes are shivering in the rain—
  Step softly.

E. E. CUMMINGS' spring poem may look strange on the page, but his manner of breaking the lines and running together the names of the children gives the effect of the breathlessness of children at play. Cummings has also concocted such novel words as "mud-luscious" and "puddle-wonderful," words that graphically convey the joyful squishiness of spring. Toward the end of the poem he describes the balloonman as "goatfooted." This may be a reference to the goatfooted Greek god Pan, who embodied the spirit of youth and gaity. According to the ancient Greeks, the music Pan made on his reed pipes was so compelling that everyone who heard—even the gods—came running and followed him wherever he led.

In Just-

e. e. cummings

In Just-
spring   when the world is mud-
luscious the little
lame balloonman

whistles   far   and wee

and eddieandbill come
running from marbles and
piracies and it's
spring

when the world is puddle-wonderful

the queer
old balloonman whistles
far   and   wee
and bettyandisbel come dancing

from hop-scotch and jump-rope and

it's
spring
and
     the

          goat-footed

balloonMan   whistles
far
and
wee

Pippa's Song

ROBERT BROWNING

The year's at the spring,
And day's at the morn;
Morning's at seven;
The hill-side's dew-pearl'd;
The lark's on the wing;
The snail's on the thorn;
God's in His heaven—
All's right with the world!

For lo, the winter is past;
The rain is over and gone.

These lines from "The Song of Songs" celebrate the coming of spring. William Wordsworth also welcomes the spring with a torrent of words and word-pictures. His last line is the same as the Old Testament quotation above—perhaps to emphasize how we are linked even to ancient Biblical times by our love for the spring season.

Written in March

While resting on the Bridge at the Foot of Brother's Water

WILLIAM WORDSWORTH

The cock is crowing,
The stream is flowing,
The small birds twitter,
The lake doth glitter,
The green field sleeps in the sun;
The oldest and youngest
Are at work with the strongest;
The cattle are grazing,
Their heads never raising;
There are forty feeding like one!

Like an army defeated
The snow hath retreated,
And now doth fare ill
On the top of the bare hill;
The ploughboy is whooping—anon—anon:
There's joy in the mountains;
There's life in the fountains;
Small clouds are sailing,
Blue sky prevailing;
The rain is over and gone!

The Wind

ANONYMOUS

I come to work as well as play;
    I'll tell you what I do;
I whistle all the live-long day,
    "Woo-oo-oo-oo! Woo-oo!"

I toss the branches up and down
    And shake them to and fro,
I whirl the leaves in flocks of brown,
    And send them high and low.

I strew the twigs upon the ground,
    The frozen earth I sweep;
I blow the children round and round
    And wake the flowers from sleep.

April

ANONYMOUS

Two little clouds one April day
    Went sailing across the sky.
They went so fast that they bumped their heads,
    And both began to cry.

The big round sun came out and said,
    "Oh, never mind, my dears,
I'll send all my sunbeams down
    To dry your fallen tears."

JOHN MILTON (1608–1674), looking back over his early years, reported: "From twelve years of age I hardly ever left my studies, or went to bed before midnight." No wonder his learning was prodigious. He knew the Bible and the Talmud, was proficient in Latin, Greek, and Hebrew, and was at least conversant with several European languages. Although most renowned for his powerful and stately epics, he could also write joyous, dancing lines, such as these from his poem to mirth, "L'Allegro."

> *Haste thee, Nymph, and bring with thee*
> *Jest and youthful Jollity,*
> *Quips and Cranks and wanton Wiles*
> *Nods and Becks and wreathèd Smiles,*
> *Sport, that wrinkled Care derides,*
> *And Laughter holding both his sides.*
> *Come and trip it as you go*
> *On the light fantastic toe;* . . .

And he could, as in the following poem, sing with warmth and freshness of a May morning.

On May Morning

JOHN MILTON

Now the bright morning Star, Daye's harbinger,
Comes dancing from the East, and leads with her
The Flowery May, who from her green lap throws
The yellow Cowslip, and the pale Primrose.
 Hail, bounteous May! that dost inspire
 Mirth, and youth, and warm desire;
 Woods and Groves are of thy dressing;
 Hill and Dale doth boast thy blessing.
Thus we salute thee with our early Song,
And welcome thee, and wish thee long.

June

JAMES RUSSELL LOWELL

And what is so rare as a day in June?
    Then, if ever, come perfect days;
Then Heaven tries earth if it be in tune,
    And over it softly her warm ear lays;
Whether we look, or whether we listen,
We hear life murmur, or see it glisten;
Every clod feels a stir of might,
    An instinct within it that reaches and towers,
And, groping blindly above it for light,
    Climbs to a soul in grass and flowers;
The flush of life may well be seen
    Thrilling back over hills and valleys;
The cowslip startles in meadows green,
    The buttercup catches the sun in its chalice,
And there's never a leaf nor a blade too mean
    To be some happy creature's palace;
The little bird sits at his door in the sun,
    Atilt like a blossom among the leaves,
And lets his illumined being o'errun
    With the deluge of summer it receives;
His mate feels the eggs beneath her wings,
And the heart in her dumb breast flutters and sings;
He sings to the wide world, and she to her nest,—
In the nice ear of Nature which song is the best?

Summer Is Coming

ANONYMOUS

Summer is coming! Summer is coming!
    How do you think I know?
I found some pussy willows
    So I know it must be so.

The Throstle

ALFRED, LORD TENNYSON

"Summer is coming, summer is coming,
   I know it, I know it, I know it.
Light again, leaf again, life again, love again,"
   Yes, my wild little Poet.

Sing the new year in under the blue.
   Last year you sang it as gladly.
"New, new, new, new!" Is it then so new
   That you should carol so madly?

"Love again, song again, nest again, young again,"
   Never a prophet so crazy!
And hardly a daisy as yet, little friend,
   See, there is hardly a daisy.

"Here again, here, here, here, happy year!"
   O warble unchidden, unbidden!
Summer is coming, is coming, my dear,
   And all the winters are hidden.

Throstle—thrush

Fourth of July

EDMUND PENNANT

Hold my hand, look away
the explosion is coming;
disagreeable play
   like soldiers drumming.

Hush, hold me, hold tight,
it's mere paper and powder:
the touch of a light
   and the dragon is chowder.

Then hurry with Dad
to a brook, and let's linger
where the jewelweed pod
   explodes to the finger!

THE EARLIEST KNOWN FLOWER of English song dates from the 13th century and celebrates the arrival of summer. Here are two versions of it, the original poem with its distinctive language and spelling, and a modern rendering of it. In both versions, the word "verteth" in the second stanza means "looks for green shoots." Vert is French for "green."

Sumer Is Icumen In

ANONYMOUS

Sumer is icumen in,
Lhude sing cuccu!
Groweth sed, and bloweth med,
And springeth the wude nu—
    Sing cuccu!

Awe bleteth after lomb,
Lhouth after calve cu;
Bulluc sterteth, bucke verteth,
    Murie sing cuccu!

Cuccu, cuccu, well singes thu, cuccu:
Ne swike thu naver nu;
Sing cuccu, nu, sing cuccu,
Sing cuccu, sing cuccu, nu!

Summer Is A-coming In

ANONYMOUS

Summer is a-coming in,
Loud sing cuckoo;
Groweth seed and bloweth mead,
And springeth the wood new,
    Sing cuckoo!

Ewe bleateth after lamb,
Loweth after calf the cow;
Bullock starteth, buck verteth,
    Merry sing cuckoo.

Cuckoo, cuckoo, well singeth thou cuckoo,
Thou art never silent now.
Sing cuckoo, now, sing cuckoo
    Sing cuckoo, sing cuckoo, now!

Summer Storm

JAMES RUSSELL LOWELL

Suddenly all the sky is hid
  As with the shutting of a lid,
One by one great drops are falling
    Doubtful and slow;
Down the pane they are crookedly crawling,
    And the wind breathes low;
Slowly the circles widen on the river,
    Widen and mingle, one and all;
Here and there the slenderer flowers shiver,
    Struck by an icy rain-drop's fall.

Now on the hills I hear the thunder mutter,
    The wind is gathering in the west;
The upturned leaves first whiten and flutter,
    Then droop to a fitful rest;
Up from the stream with sluggish flap
    Struggles the gull and floats away;
Nearer and nearer rolls the thunder-clap,—
    We shall not see the sun go down to-day:
Now leaps the wind on the sleepy marsh,
    And tramples the grass with terrified feet,
The startled river turns leaden and harsh,
    You can hear the quick heart of the tempest beat.

    Look! look! that livid flash!
And instantly follows the rattling thunder,
As if some cloud-crag, split asunder,
    Fell, splintering with a ruinous crash,
On the Earth, which crouches in silence under;

And now a solid gray of rain
Shuts off the landscape, mile by mile;
  For a breath's space I see the blue wood again,
And, ere the next heart-beat, the wind-hurled pile,
    That seemed but now a league aloof,
    Bursts crackling o'er the sun-parched roof;
Against the windows the storm comes dashing,
Through tattered foliage the hail tears crashing,
      The blue lightning flashes,
      The rapid hail clashes,
    The white waves are tumbling,
      And, in one baffled roar,
    Like the toothless sea mumbling
      A rock-bristled shore,
    The thunder is rumbling
    And crashing and crumbling,—
Will silence return nevermore?

    Hush! Still as death,
    The tempest holds his breath
As from a sudden will;
The rain stops short, but from the eaves
You see it drop, and hear it from the leaves,
    All is so bodingly still;
    Again, now, now, again
    Plashes the rain in heavy gouts,
      The crinkled lightning
      Seems ever brightening,

And loud and long
Again the thunder shouts
His battle-song, —
One quivering flash,
One wildering crash,
Followed by silence dead and dull,
As if the cloud, let go,
Leapt bodily below
To whelm the earth in one mad overthrow,
And then a total lull.

Gone, gone, so soon!
No more my half-crazed fancy there
Can shape a giant in the air,
No more I see his streaming hair,
The writhing portent of his form;—
The pale and quiet moon
Makes her calm forehead bare,
And the last fragments of the storm,
Like shattered rigging from a fight at sea,
Silent and few, are drifting over me.

Scythe Song

ANDREW LANG

Mowers, weary and brown, and blithe,
What is the word methinks you know,
Endless over-word that the Scythe
Sings to the blades of grass below?
Scythes that swing in the grass and clover,
Something, still, they say as they pass;
What is the word, that over and over,
Sings the Scythe to the flowers and grass?

Hush, ah hush, the Scythes are saying,
Hush, and heed not, and fall asleep;
Hush, they say to the grasses swaying,
Hush, they sing to the clover deep!
Hush, 'tis a lullaby Time is singing—
Hush, and heed not, for all things pass,
Hush, ah hush! and the Scythes are swinging
Over the clover, over the grass.

The Last Chrysanthemum

THOMAS HARDY

Why should this flower delay so long
    To show its tremulous plumes?
Now is the time of plaintive robin-song,
    When flowers are in their tombs.

Through the slow summer, when the sun
    Called to each frond and whorl
That all he could for flowers was being done,
    Why did it not uncurl?

It must have felt that fervid call
    Although it took no heed,
Waking but now, when leaves like corpses fall,
    And saps all retrocede.

Too late its beauty, lonely thing,
    The season's shine is spent,
Nothing remains for it but shivering
    In tempests turbulent.

Had it a reason for delay,
    Dreaming in witlessness
That for a bloom so delicately gay
    Winter would stay its stress?

—I talk as if the thing were born
    With sense to work its mind;
Yet it is but one mask of many worn
    By the Great Face behind.

September

HELEN HUNT JACKSON

The goldenrod is yellow,
  The corn is turning brown,
The trees in apple orchards
  With fruit are bending down.

The gentian's bluest fringes
  Are curling in the sun,
In dusty pods the milkweed
  Its hidden silk has spun.

The sedges flaunt their harvest
  In every meadow nook,
And asters by the brookside
  Make asters in the brook.

By all these lovely tokens
  September days are here,
With summer's best of weather
  And autumn's best of cheer.

Autumn

WALTER DE LA MARE

There is wind where the rose was;
Cold rain where sweet grass was;
  And clouds like sheep
  Stream o'er the steep
Grey skies where the lark was.

Nought gold where your hair was;
Nought warm where your hand was;
  But phantom, forlorn,
  Beneath the thorn,
Your ghost where your face was.

Sad winds where your voice was;
Tears, tears where my heart was;
  And ever with me,
  Child, ever with me,
Silence where hope was.

Autumn

EMILY DICKINSON

The morns are meeker than they were,
  The nuts are getting brown;
The berry's cheek is plumper,
  The rose is out of town.

The maple wears a gayer scarf,
  The field a scarlet gown.
Lest I should be old-fashioned,
  I'll put a trinket on.

SHAKESPEARE opens his historical play *Richard III* with the memorable line "Now is the winter of our discontent," a line that the winter-loving Thomas Constable questions in his "Old October," as he proceeds to make clear some of the joys he finds in winter.

Old October

THOMAS CONSTABLE

Hail, old October, bright and chill,
First freedman from the summer sun!
Spice high the bowl, and drink your fill!
Thank heaven, at last the summer's done!

Come, friend, my fire is burning bright,
A fire's no longer out of place,
How clear it glows! (there's frost to-night,)
It looks white winter in the face.

You've been to "Richard." Ah! you've seen
A noble play: I'm glad you went;
But what on earth does Shakespeare mean
By "*winter* of our *discontent*"?

Be mine the tree that feeds the fire!
Be mine the sun knows when to set!
Be mine the months when friends desire
To turn in here from cold and wet!

The sentry sun, that glared so long
O'erhead, deserts his summer post;
Ay, you may brew it hot and strong:
"The joys of winter"—come, a toast!

Shine on the kangaroo, thou sun!
Make far New Zealand faint with fear!
Don't hurry back to spoil our fun,
Thank goodness, old October's here!

17

WITH A TWINKLE in his eye, the nineteenth-century poet Thomas Hood leads his reader by the No's to pull a surprise in the very last line.

November

THOMAS HOOD

No sun—no moon!
No morn—no noon!
No dawn—no dusk—no proper time of day—
No sky—no earthly view—
No distance looking blue—
No road—no street—no "t'other side the way"—
No end to any Row—
No indications where the Crescents go—
No top to any steeple—
No recognitions of familiar people—

No courtesies for showing 'em—
No knowing 'em!
No mail—no post—
No news from any foreign coast—
No park—no ring—no afternoon gentility—
No company—no nobility—
No warmth, no cheerfulness, no healthful ease,
No comfortable feel in any member—
No shade, no shine, no butterflies, no bees,
No fruits, no flowers, no leaves, no birds,
November!

Thanksgiving Day

LYDIA MARIA CHILD

Over the river and through the wood,
   To Grandfather's house we go,
      The horse knows the way
      To carry the sleigh
Through the white and drifted snow.

Over the river and through the wood,
   Oh, how the wind does blow!
      It stings the toes,
      And bites the nose,
As over the ground we go.

Over the river and through the wood,
   To have a first rate play,
      Hear the bells ring,
      "Ting-a-ling-ling"!
Hurrah for Thanksgiving day!

Over the river and through the wood,
   Trot fast my dapple gray!
      Spring over the ground,
      Like a hunting hound!
For this is Thanksgiving Day.

Over the river and through the wood,
   And straight through the barnyard gate,
      We seem to go
      Extremely slow,
It is so hard to wait!

Over the river and through the wood—
   Now Grandmother's cap I spy!
      Hurrah for the fun
      Is the pudding done?
Hurrah for the pumpkin pie!

First Thanksgiving of All

NANCY BYRD TURNER

Peace and Mercy and Jonathan,
And Patience (very small),
Stood by the table giving thanks
The first Thanksgiving of all.
There was very little for them to eat,
Nothing special and nothing sweet;
Only bread and a little broth,
And a bit of fruit (and no tablecloth);
But Peace and Mercy and Jonathan
And Patience, in a row,
Stood up and asked a blessing on
Thanksgiving, long ago.

Thankful they were their ship had come
Safely across the sea;
Thankful they were for hearth and home,
And kin and company;
They were glad of broth to go with their bread,
Glad their apples were round and red,
Glad of mayflowers they would bring
Out of the woods again next spring.
So Peace and Mercy and Jonathan,
And Patience (very small),
Stood up gratefully giving thanks
The first Thanksgiving of all.

The Snow-storm

RALPH WALDO EMERSON

Announced by all the trumpets of the sky,
Arrives the snow, and, driving o'er the fields,
Seems nowhere to alight: the whited air
Hides hills and woods, the river, and the heaven,
And veils the farm-house at the garden's end.
The sled and traveller stopped, the courier's feet
Delayed, all friends shut out, the housemates sit
Around the radiant fireplace, enclosed
In a tumultuous privacy of storm.

Come see the north wind's masonry.
Out of an unseen quarry evermore
Furnished with tile, the fierce artificer
Curves his white bastions with projected roof
Round every windward stake, or tree, or door.

Speeding, the myriad-handed, his wild work
So fanciful, so savage, nought cares he
For number or proportion. Mockingly,
On coop or kennel he hangs Parian wreaths;
A swan-like form invests the hidden thorn;
Fills up the farmer's lane from wall to wall,
Maugre the farmer's sighs; and, at the gate,
A tapering turret overtops the work.

And when his hours are numbered, and the world
Is all his own, retiring, as he were not,
Leaves, when the sun appears, astonished Art
To mimic in slow structures, stone by stone,
Built in an age, the mad wind's night-work,
The frolic architecture of the snow.

Parian—like the fine marble quarried on the Greek island of Paros.
Maugre—despite

Blow, Blow, Thou Winter Wind

WILLIAM SHAKESPEARE

Blow, blow, thou winter wind,
Thou art not so unkind
   As man's ingratitude;
Thy tooth is not so keen,
Because thou art not seen,
   Although thy breath be rude.
Heigh-ho! sing heigh-ho! unto the green holly;
Most friendship is feigning, most loving mere folly:
   Then, heigh-ho, the holly!
   This life is most jolly!

Freeze, freeze, thou bitter sky,
Thou dost not bite so nigh
   As benefits forgot:
Though thou the waters warp,
Thy sting is not so sharp
   As friend remembered not.
Heigh-ho! sing heigh-ho! unto the green holly;
Most friendship is feigning, most loving mere folly:
   Then, heigh-ho, the holly!
   This life is most jolly!

Winter

CHRISTINA ROSSETTI

Bread and milk for breakfast,
   And woolen frocks to wear,
And a crumb for robin redbreast
   On the cold days of the year.

Velvet Shoes

ELINOR WYLIE

Let us walk in the white snow
In a soundless space;
With footsteps quiet and slow,
At a tranquil pace,
Under veils of white lace.

I shall go shod in silk,
And you in wool,
White as a white cow's milk,
More beautiful
Than the breast of a gull.

We shall walk through the still town
In a windless peace;
We shall step upon white down,
Upon silver fleece,
Upon softer than these.

We shall walk in velvet shoes:
Wherever we go
Silence will fall like dews
On white silence below.
We shall walk in the snow.

Francis Thompson, who died in 1907, is known for having written some of the finest religious poems in the English language. In this poem, his question to the snowflake "Who hammered you, wrought you?" is similar to the question asked by William Blake in "The Tiger": "Did He who made the lamb make thee?" In both poems the answer is summed up in the snowflake's response: "God wrought me." Nothing is too great, nothing too insignificant for God's notice.

To a Snowflake

Francis Thompson

What heart could have thought you?—
Past our devisal
(O filigree petal!)
Fashioned so purely,
Fragilely, surely,
From what Paradisal
Imagineless metal,
Too costly for cost?
Who hammered you, wrought you,
From argentine vapor?—
"God was my shaper.
Passing surmisal,
He hammered, He wrought me,
From curled silver vapor,
To lust of His mind:—
Thou could'st not have thought me!
So purely, so palely,
Tinily, surely,
Mightily, frailly,
Insculped and embossed,
With His hammer of wind,
And His graver of frost."

Now Winter Nights Enlarge

Thomas Campion

Now winter nights enlarge
  The number of their hours,
And clouds their storms discharge
  Upon the airy towers.
Let now the chimneys blaze
  And cups o'erflow with wine;
Let well-tuned words amaze
  With harmony divine.
Now yellow waxen lights
  Shall wait on honey love,
While youthful revels, masques, and courtly sights
  Sleep's leaden spells remove.

This time doth well dispense
  With lovers' long discourse;
Much speech hath some defence,
  Though beauty no remorse.
All do not all things well;
  Some measures comely tread,
Some knotted riddles tell,
  Some poems smoothly read.
The summer hath his joys,
  And winter his delights;
Though love and all his pleasures are but toys,
  They shorten tedious nights.

Snow-flakes

Henry Wadsworth Longfellow

Out of the bosom of the Air,
  Out of the cloud-folds of her garments shaken,
Over the woodlands brown and bare,
  Over the harvest-fields forsaken,
    Silent and soft and slow
    Descends the snow.

Even as our cloudy fancies take
  Suddenly shape in some divine expression,
Even as the troubled heart doth make
  In the white countenance confession,
    The troubled sky reveals
    The grief it feels.

This is the poem of the air,
  Slowly in silent syllables recorded;
This is the secret of despair,
  Long in its cloudy bosom hoarded,
    Now whispered and revealed
    To wood and field.

When Icicles Hang by the Wall

William Shakespeare

When icicles hang by the wall,
  And Dick the shepherd blows his nail,
And Tom bears logs into the hall,
  And milk comes frozen home in pail,
When blood is nipped, and ways be foul,
Then nightly sings the staring owl,
    To-who;
To-whit, to-who, a merry note,
While greasy Joan doth keel the pot.

When all aloud the wind doth blow,
  And coughing drowns the parson's saw,
And birds sit brooding in the snow,
  And Marian's nose looks red and raw,
When roasted crabs hiss in the bowl,
Then nightly sings the staring owl,
    To-who;
To-whit, to-who a merry note,
While greasy Joan doth keel the pot.

23

Keel—clean.

Stopping by Woods on a Snowy Evening

ROBERT FROST

Whose woods these are I think I know.
His house is in the village though;
He will not see me stopping here
To watch his woods fill up with snow.

My little horse must think it queer
To stop without a farmhouse near
Between the woods and frozen lake
The darkest evening of the year.

He gives his harness bells a shake
To ask if there is some mistake.
The only other sound's the sweep
Of easy wind and downy flake.

The woods are lovely, dark and deep.
But I have promises to keep,
And miles to go before I sleep,
And miles to go before I sleep.

Our Window Is Stained

ALFRED KREYMBORG

Our window is stained
with the figures she has blown on it.
Our window is stained
with the figures she has blown on it
with her breath.
Our window is stained
with the figures she has blown on it
with her breath.
on which a spirit has blown—
A spirit? a saint? a sprite?
who was it
blew figures on her breath
that our window is stained
with the figures she has blown on it?

JOHN GREENLEAF WHITTIER spent his boyhood on his father's New England farm, where winters are long and can be harsh. In his small masterpiece *Snowbound*, from which the following selection is taken, Whittier depicts the rigors, the sights, the stark landscape, and the simple country pleasures of an old-fashioned New England winter.

Lines from Snowbound

John Greenleaf Whittier

The sun that brief December day
Rose cheerless over hills of gray,
And, darkly circled, gave at noon
A sadder light than waning moon.
Slow tracing down the thickening sky
Its mute and ominous prophecy,
A portent seeming less than threat,
It sank from sight before it set.
A chill no coat, however stout,
Of homespun stuff could quite shut out,
A hard, dull bitterness of cold,
That checked, mid-vein, the circling race
Of life-blood in the sharpened face,
The coming of the snow-storm told.
The wind blew east: we heard the roar
Of Ocean on his wintry shore,
And felt the strong pulse throbbing there
Beat with low rhythm our inland air.

Meanwhile we did our nightly chores,—
Brought in the wood from out of doors,
Littered the stalls, and from the mows
Raked down the herd's-grass for the cows;
Heard the horse whinnying for his corn;
And, sharply clashing horn on horn,
Impatient down the stanchion rows
The cattle shake their walnut bows;
While, peering from his early perch
Upon the scaffold's pole of birch,
The cock his crested helmet bent
And down his querulous challenge sent.

Unwarmed by any sunset light
The gray day darkened into night,
A night made hoary with the swarm
And whirlwind of the blinding storm,
As zigzag, wavering to and fro,
Crossed and re-crossed the winged snow.
And ere the early bed-time came

The white drift piled the window frame,
And through the dark the clothes-line posts
Looked in like tall and sheeted ghosts.

So all night long the storm roared on;
The morning broke without a sun;
In tiny spherule traced with lines
Of Nature's geometric signs,
In starry flake, and pellicle,
All day the hoary meteor fell;
And when the second morning shone,
We looked upon a world unknown,
On nothing we could call our own.
Around the glistening wonder bent
The blue walls of the firmament,
No clouds above, no earth below,—
A universe of sky and snow!
The old familiar sights of ours
Took marvellous shapes; strange domes and towers
Rose up where sty or corn-crib stood,
Or garden wall, or belt of wood;
A smooth white mound the brush pile showed,
A fenceless drift what once was road;
The bridle-post an old man sat
With loose-flung coat and high cocked hat;
The well-curb had a Chinese roof;
And even the long sweep, high aloof,
In its slant splendor, seemed to tell
Of Pisa's leaning miracle.

25

Shut in from all the world without,
We sat the clean-winged hearth about,
Content to let the north wind roar
In baffled rage at pane and door,
While the red logs before us beat
The frost-line back with tropic heat;
And ever, when a louder blast
Shook beam and rafter as it passed,
The merrier up its roaring draught
The great throat of the chimney laughed.

The house-dog on his paws outspread
Laid to the fire his drowsy head,
The cat's dark silhouette on the wall
A couchant tiger's seemed to fall;
And, for the winter fireside meet,
Between the andirons' straddling feet,
The mug of cider simmered slow,
The apples sputtered in a row,
And close at hand the basket stood
With nuts from brown October's wood.

The Old Year

John Clare

The Old Year's gone away
  To nothingness and night:
We cannot find him all the day
  Nor hear him in the night:
He left no footstep, mark or place
  In either shade or sun:
The last year he'd a neighbour's face,
  In this he's known by none.

All nothing everywhere:
  Mists we on mornings see
Have more of substance when they're here
  And more of form than he.

He was a friend by every fire,
  In every cot and hall—
A guest to every heart's desire,
  And now he's nought at all.

Old papers thrown away,
  Old garments cast aside,
The talk of yesterday,
  Are things identified;
But times once torn away
  No voices can recall:
The eve of New Year's Day
  Left the Old Year lost to all.

Cot—cottage

The New Year

DINAH MARIA MULOCK CRAIK

Who comes dancing over the snow,
　His soft little feet all bare and rosy?
Open the door, though the wild winds blow,
　Take the child in and make him cozy.
Take him in and hold him dear
He is the wonderful glad New Year.

Ring Out, Wild Bells

ALFRED, LORD TENNYSON

Ring out, wild bells, to the wild sky,
　The flying cloud, the frosty light;
　The year is dying in the night;
Ring out, wild bells, and let him die.

Ring out the old, ring in the new,
　Ring, happy bells, across the snow;
　The year is going, let him go;
Ring out the false, ring in the true.

Ring out the grief that saps the mind,
　For those that here we see no more; ·
　Ring out the feud of rich and poor,
Ring in redress to all mankind.

Ring out a slowly dying cause,
　And ancient forms of party strife;
　Ring in the nobler modes of life,
With sweeter manners, purer laws.

Ring out the want, the care, the sin,
　The faithless coldness of the times;
　Ring out, ring out my mournful rhymes,
But ring the fuller minstrel in.

Ring out false pride in place and blood,
　The civic slander and the spite;
　Ring in the love of truth and right,
Ring in the common love of good.

Ring out old shapes of foul disease;
　Ring out the narrowing lust of gold;
　Ring out the thousand wars of old,
Ring in the thousand years of peace.

Ring in the valiant man and free,
　The larger heart, the kindlier hand;
　Ring out the darkness of the land,
Ring in the Christ that is to be.

CHRISTMAS

CHRISTMAS IS A DUAL HOLIDAY. As a holy day it is observed with hymns of thanksgiving and songs of adoration for the child born in a manger more than nineteen centuries ago. As a secular holiday it is a time for merriment, feasting, and the giving of gifts. Above all it is the children's season of joy, ushered in by Santa Claus and his spirited reindeer. And throughout its dual purposes, it is a time when men and women of all beliefs pray in their own ways for peace on earth and good will toward men. Perhaps this is the deepest meaning of Christmas.

Christ's Nativity

LUKE 2:1–7

And it came to pass in those days, that there went out a decree from Caesar Augustus, that all the world should be taxed. (And this taxing was first made when Cyrenius was governor of Syria.)

And all went to be taxed, every one into his own city.

And Joseph also went up from Galilee, out of the city of Nazareth, into Judea, unto the city of David, which is called Bethlehem (because he was of the house and lineage of David), to be taxed with Mary his espoused wife, being great with child.

And so it was, that, while they were there, the days were accomplished that she should be delivered. And she brought forth her firstborn son, and wrapped him in swaddling clothes, and laid him in a manger; because there was no room for them in the inn.

I Heard the Bells on Christmas Day

HENRY WADSWORTH LONGFELLOW

I heard the bells on Christmas Day
Their old, familiar carols play,
   And wild and sweet
   The words repeat
Of peace on earth, goodwill to men!

And thought how, as the day had come,
The belfries of all Christendom
   Had rolled along
   The unbroken song
Of peace on earth, goodwill to men!

And in despair I bowed my head;
"There is no peace on earth," I said;
   "For hate is strong
   And mocks the song
Of peace on earth, goodwill to men!"

Then pealed the bells more loud and deep.
"God is not dead; nor doth He sleep!
   The Wrong shall fail,
   The Right prevail,
With peace on earth, goodwill to men!"

Twelfth Night Carol

ANONYMOUS

Here we come a-whistling through the fields so green;
Here we come a-singing, so fair to be seen.
   God send you happy, God send you happy,
   Pray God send you a happy New Year!

Bring out your little table and spread it with a cloth,
Bring out your jug of milk, likewise your Christmas loaf.
   God send you happy, God send you happy,
   Pray God send you a happy New Year!

God bless the master of this house, God bless the mistress too;
And all the little children that round the table go.
   God send you happy, God send you happy,
   Pray God send you a happy New Year!

December Music

Winfield Townley Scott

As I went into the city, clattering chimes
Carolled December music over the traffic
And I remembered my childhood, the times
Of deep snow, the same songs.

Cars meshed in the rain, horns snarled, brakes
Cursed against trolleys, and the neon evening
Blurred past my cold spectacles, the flakes
Of the iron songs scattered.

I stood near a corner drugstore trying to hear,
While all the weather broke to pouring water,
The drowned phrases between those coming clear
Though of course I knew all.

The notes my mind sang over would not do
To knit the shattered song as I wanted it,
Wanted it bell to bell as it once rang through
To its triumphant end.

It was no matter what I had left to believe
On a flooded pavement under a battering sign,
Clutching my hat while rain ran in my sleeve
And my bifocals fogged.

It was only to think of my childhood, the deep snow
The same songs, and Christmas Eve in the air,
And at home everyone in the world I knew
All together there.

Jingle Bells

JAMES PIERPONT

Dashing thro' the snow,
In a one-horse open sleigh;
O'er the fields we go,
Laughing all the way;
Bells on bob-tail ring.
Making spirits bright;
Oh what sport to ride and sing
A sleighing song tonight.

REFRAIN: Jingle bells, jingle bells,
Jingle all the way;
Oh! What joy it is to ride
In a one-horse open sleigh.
Jingle bells, jingle bells,
Jingle all the way.
Oh! What joy it is to ride
In a one-horse open sleigh.

A day or two ago
I thought I'd take a ride,
And soon Miss Fannie Bright
Was seated by my side.
The horse was lean and lank;
Misfortune seemed his lot;
He got into a drifted bank,
And we, we got up-sot.   REFRAIN

A day or two ago
The story I must tell
I went out in the snow
And on my back I fell;
A gent was riding by
In a one-horse open sleigh
He laughed as there I sprawling lie,
And quickly drove away.   REFRAIN

Now the ground is white;
Go it while you're young;
Take the girls tonight,
And sing this sleighing song.
Just get a bob-tailed bay,
Two forty as his speed;
Hitch him to an open sleigh,
And crack, you'll take the lead.   REFRAIN

Long, Long Ago

ANONYMOUS

Winds through the olive trees
  Softly did blow,
Round little Bethlehem
  Long, long ago.

Sheep on the hillside lay
  Whiter than snow;
Shepherds were watching them,
  Long, long ago.

Then from the happy sky,
  Angels bent low,
Singing their songs of joy,
  Long, long ago.

For in a manger bed,
  Cradled we know,
Christ came to Bethlehem,
  Long, long ago.

Old Winter

THOMAS NOEL

Old Winter sad, in snow yclad,
  Is making a doleful din;
But let him howl till he crack his jowl,
  We will not let him in.

Ay, let him lift from the billowy drift
  His hoary, haggard form,
And scowling stand, with his wrinkled hand
  Outstretching to the storm.

And let his weird and sleety beard
  Stream loose upon the blast,
And, rustling, chime to the tinkling rime
  From his bald head falling fast.

Let his baleful breath shed blight and death
  On herb and flower and tree;
And brooks and ponds in crystal bonds
  Bind fast, but what care we?

Let him push at the door,—in the chimney roar,
  And rattle the window-pane;
Let him in at us spy with his icicle eye,
  But he shall not entrance gain.

Let him gnaw, forsooth, with his freezing tooth,
  On our roof-tiles, till he tire;
But we care not a whit, as we jovial sit
  Before our blazing fire.

Come, lads, let's sing, till the rafters ring;
  Come, push the can about;—
From our snug fire-side this Christmas-tide
  We'll keep old Winter out.

Yclad—dressed

Our Joyful Feast

GEORGE WITHER

So, now is come our joyful feast,
    Let every soul be jolly!
Each room with ivy leaves is drest,
    And every post with holly.
Though some churls at our mirth repine,
Round your brows let garlands twine,
Drown sorrow in a cup of wine,
    And let us all be merry!

Now all our neighbors' chimneys smoke,
    And Christmas logs are burning;
Their ovens with baked meats do choke,
    And all their spits are turning.
Without the door let sorrow lie,
And if for cold it hap to die,
We'll bury it in Christmas pie,
    And evermore be merry!

The Friendly Beasts

ANONYMOUS

Jesus our brother, kind and good,
Was humbly born in a stable rude,
And the friendly beasts around Him stood;
Jesus our brother, kind and good.

"I," said the donkey, shaggy and brown,
"I carried His mother up hill and down,
I carried her safely to Bethlehem town;
I," said the donkey, shaggy and brown.

"I," said the cow, all white and red,
"I gave Him my manger for His bed,
I gave Him my hay to pillow His head;
I," said the cow, all white and red.

"I," said the sheep, with the curly horn,
"I gave Him my wool for His blanket warm;
He wore my coat on Christmas morn.
I," said the sheep with the curly horn.

"I," said the dove, from the rafters high,
"Cooed Him to sleep, my mate and I,
We cooed Him to sleep, my mate and I;
I," said the dove, from the rafters high.

And every beast, by some good spell,
In the stable dark, was glad to tell,
Of the gift he gave Emmanuel,
The gift he gave Emmanuel.

We Wish You a Merry Christmas

Anonymous (traditional English carol)

We wish you a Merry Christmas.
We wish you a Merry Christmas.
We wish you a Merry Christmas
And a Happy New Year.

Good tidings we bring
For you and your kin.
We wish you a Merry Christmas
And a Happy New Year.

Now bring us figgy pudding.
Now bring us figgy pudding.
Now bring us figgy pudding.
Now bring some right here!

We won't go until we get it.
We won't go until we get it.
We won't go until we get it.
So bring some right here!

We wish you a Merry Christmas.
We wish you a Merry Christmas.
We wish you a Merry Christmas
And a Happy New Year.

Christmas Is A-comin'

Anonymous

Christmas is a'comin' and the geese are getting fat,
Please to put a penny in a poor man's hat;
If you haven't got a penny, a ha'penny will do,
If you haven't got a ha'penny, may God bless you.
    God bless you, gentlemen, God bless you;
    If you haven't got a ha'penny, may God bless you.

Kriss Kringle

THOMAS BAILEY ALDRICH

Just as the moon was fading
  Amid her misty rings,
And every stocking was stuffed
  With childhood's precious things,

Old Kriss Kringle looked round,
  And saw on the elm-tree bough,
High-hung an oriole's nest,
  Silent and empty now.

"Quite like a stocking," he laughed,
  "Pinned up there on the tree!
Little I thought the birds
  Expected a present from me!"

Then old Kriss Kringle, who loves
  A joke as well as the best,
Dropped a handful of flakes
  In the oriole's empty nest.

I AM INCLUDING this oddly comical poem here because of its festive, Christmas-sounding refrain. It could easily pass for a jolly Christmas carol.

Three Acres of Land

ANONYMOUS

My father left me three acres of land,
  Sing ivy, sing ivy;
My father left me three acres of land,
  Sing holly, go whistle, and ivy!

I ploughed it with a ram's horn,
  Sing ivy, sing ivy;
And sowed it all over with one peppercorn,
  Sing holly, go whistle, and ivy!

I harrowed it with a bramble bush,
  Sing ivy, sing ivy;
And reaped it with my little penknife,
  Sing holly, go whistle, and ivy!

I got the mice to carry it to the barn,
  Sing ivy, sing ivy;
And thrashed it with a goose's quill,
  Sing holly, go whistle, and ivy!

I got the cat to carry it to the mill,
  Sing ivy, sing ivy;
The miller he swore he would have her paw,
And the cat she swore she would scratch his face,
  Sing holly, go whistle, and ivy!

Christmas at Sea

ROBERT LOUIS STEVENSON

The sheets were frozen hard, and they cut the naked hand;
  The decks were like a slide, where a seaman scarce could stand;
The wind was a nor'wester, blowing squally off the sea;
  And cliffs and spouting breakers were the only things a-lee.

They heard the surf a-roaring before the break of day;
  But 'twas only with the peep of light we saw how ill we lay.
We tumbled every hand on deck instanter, with a shout,
  And we gave her the maintops'l, and stood by to go about.

All day we tacked and tacked between the South Head and the North;
  All day we hauled the frozen sheets, and got no further forth;
All day as cold as charity, in bitter pain and dread,
  For very life and nature we tacked from head to head.

We gave the South a wider berth, for there the tide-race roared;
  But every tack we made we brought the North Head close aboard:
So's we saw the cliffs and houses, and the breakers running high,
  And the coastguard in his garden, with his glass against his eye.

The frost was on the village roofs as white as ocean foam;
  The good red fires were burning bright in every 'longshore home;
The windows sparkled clear, and the chimneys volleyed out;
  And I vow we sniffed the victuals as the vessel went about.

The bells upon the church were rung with a mighty jovial cheer;
  For it's just that I should tell you how (of all days in the year)
This day of our adversity was blessed Christmas morn,
  And the house above the coastguard's was the house where I was born.

O well I saw the pleasant room, the pleasant faces there,
  My mother's silver spectacles, my father's silver hair;
And well I saw the firelight, like a flight of homely elves,
  Go dancing round the china-plates that stand upon the shelves.

And well I knew the talk they had, the talk that was of me,
  Of the shadow on the household and the son that went to sea;
And O the wicked fool I seemed, in every kind of way,
  To be here and hauling frozen ropes on blessed Christmas Day.

They lit the high sea-light, and the dark began to fall.
"All hands to loose topgallant sails," I heard the captain call.
"By the Lord, she'll never stand it," our first mate, Jackson, cried.
. . . "It's the one way or the other, Mr. Jackson," he replied.

She staggered to her bearings, but the sails were new and good,
And the ship smelt up to windward just as though she understood.
As the winter's day was ending, in the entry of the night
We cleared the weary headland, and passed below the light.

And they heaved a mighty breath, every soul on board but me,
As they saw her nose again pointing handsome out to sea;
But all that I could think of, in the darkness and the cold,
Was just that I was leaving home and my folks were growing old.

Sheets—ropes used to adjust the sails

The Tide Rises,
the Tide Falls

WE ARE CHILDREN of the earth but we were born of the salt sea and the sea is in the blood of even the most landlocked of us. The river of waters was our first home, and it still draws men with a thousand lures. The sea smiles, the sea rages. The tide rises, the tide falls. Man ventures out on the sea at his own peril, for his control, as the poet Byron once said "stops with the shore." And still man's fascination with his first home continues.

The Sea

GEORGE GORDON, LORD BYRON

And I have loved thee, Ocean! and my joy
Of youthful sports was on thy breast to be
Borne, like thy bubbles, onward. From a boy
I wantoned with thy breakers, they to me
Were a delight; and if the freshening sea
Made them a terror, 'twas a pleasing fear;
For I was as it were a child of thee,
And trusted to thy billows far and near,
And laid my hand upon thy mane,—as I do here.

They That Go Down

PSALM 107:23–33

They that go down to the sea in ships,
that do business in great waters;
these see the works of the Lord,
and his wonders in the deep.
For he commandeth, and raiseth the stormy wind,
which lifteth up the waves thereof.
They mount up to the heaven,
they go down again to the depths:
their soul is melted because of trouble.
They reel to and fro, and stagger like a drunken man,
and are at their wits' end.
Then they cry unto the Lord in their trouble,
and he bringeth them out of their distresses.
He maketh the storm a calm,
so that the waves thereof are still.
Then are they glad because they be quiet;
so he bringeth them unto their desired haven.
Oh that men would praise the Lord for his goodness,
and for his wonderful works to the children of men!

IN TENNYSON'S TIME, a sea voyage required waiting for high tide, in order that the vessel be sure to clear the sandbar that builds up at a harbor's mouth. Tennyson has taken the nautical problem of crossing the bar and endowed it with a more personal meaning.

Crossing the Bar

ALFRED, LORD TENNYSON

Sunset and evening star,
   And one clear call for me!
And may there be no moaning of the bar,
   When I put out to sea,

But such a tide as moving seems asleep,
   Too full for sound and foam,
When that which drew from out the boundless deep
   Turns again home.

Twilight and evening bell,
   And after that the dark!
And may there be no sadness of farewell,
   When I embark;

For tho' from out our bourne of Time and Place
   The flood may bear me far,
I hope to see my Pilot face to face
   When I have crost the bar.

The Noise of Waters

JAMES JOYCE

All day I hear the noise of waters
   Making moan,
Sad as the sea-bird is, when going
   Forth alone,
He hears the winds cry to the waters'
   Monotone.

The grey winds, the cold winds are blowing
   Where I go.
I hear the noise of many waters
   Far below.
All day, all night I hear them flowing
   To and fro.

The Secret of the Sea

Henry Wadsworth Longfellow

Ah! what pleasant visions haunt me
As I gaze upon the sea!
All the old romantic legends,
All my dreams, come back to me.

Sails of silk and ropes of sandal,
Such as gleam in ancient lore;
And the singing of the sailors,
And the answer from the shore.

Most of all, the Spanish ballad
Haunts me oft, and tarries long,
Of the noble Count Arnaldos
And the sailor's mystic song.

Like the long waves on a sea-beach,
Where the sand and silver shines,
With a soft, monotonous cadence,
Flow its unrhymed lyric lines;

Telling how the Count Arnaldos
With his hawk upon his hand,
Saw a fair and stately galley,
Steering onward to the land;

How he heard the ancient helmsman
Chant a song so wild and clear,
That the sailing sea-bird slowly
Poised upon the mast to hear,

Till his soul was full of longing,
And he cried with impulse strong,
"Helmsman! for the love of heaven,
Teach me, too, that wondrous song!"

"Wouldst thou"—so the helmsman answered,
"Learn the secret of the sea?
Only those who brave its dangers
Comprehend its mystery!"

In each sail that skims the horizon,
In each landward-blowing breeze,
I behold that stately galley,
Hear those mournful melodies;

Till my soul is full of longing
For the secret of the sea,
And the heart of the great ocean
Sends a thrilling pulse through me.

A Wet Sheet and a Flowing Sea

ALLAN CUNNINGHAM

A wet sheet and a flowing sea,—
  A wind that follows fast,
And fills the white and rustling sail,
  And bends the gallant mast,—
And bends the gallant mast, my boys,
  While, like the eagle free,
Away the good ship flies, and leaves
  Old England on the lee.

O for a soft and gentle wind!
  I heard a fair one cry;
But give to me the snoring breeze
  And white waves heaving high,—
And white waves heaving high, my boys,
  The good ship tight and free;
The world of waters is our home,
  And merry men are we.

There's tempest in yon horned moon,
  And lightning in yon cloud;
And hark the music, mariners!
  The wind is piping loud,—
The wind is piping loud, my boys,
  The lightning flashing free;
While the hollow oak our palace is,
  Our heritage the sea.

Sheet—rope used to adjust the sails

The Sailor's Consolation

CHARLES DIBDIN

One night came on a hurricane,
  The sea was mountains rolling.
When Barney Buntline turned his quid,
  And said to Billy Bowling:
"A strong nor-wester's blowing, Bill;
  Hark! don't ye hear it roar, now?
Lord help 'em, how I pities them
  Unhappy folks on shore now!

"Foolhardy chaps who live in towns,
  What danger they are all in,
And now lie quaking in their beds,
  For fear the roof should fall in;
Poor creatures! how they envies us,
  And wishes, I've a notion,
For our good luck, in such a storm,
  To be upon the ocean!

"And as for them who're out all day
  On business from their houses,
And late at night are coming home,
  To cheer their babes and spouses,
While you and I, Bill, on the deck
  Are comfortably lying,
My eyes! what tiles and chimney-pots
  About their heads are flying!

"And very often have we heard
  How men are killed and undone
By overturns of carriages,
  By thieves, and fires in London;
We know what risks all landsmen run,
  From noblemen to tailors;
Then, Bill, let us thank Providence
  That you and I are sailors."

Heart's Content

ANONYMOUS

"A sail! a sail! Oh, whence away,
  And whither, o'er the foam?
Good brother mariners, we pray,
  God speed you safely home!"
"Now wish us not so foul a wind,
  Until the fair be spent;
For hearth and home we leave behind:
  We sail for Heart's Content."

"For Heart's Content! And sail ye so,
  With canvas flowing free?
But, pray you, tell us, if ye know,
  Where may that harbor be?
For we that greet you, worn of time,
  Wave-racked, and tempest-rent,
By sun and star, in every clime,
  Have searched for Heart's Content.

"In every clime the world around,
  The waste of waters o'er;
An El Dorado have we found,
  That ne'er was found before.
The isles of spice, the lands of dawn,
  Where East and West are blent—
All these our eyes have looked upon,
  But where is Heart's Content?

"Oh, turn again, while yet ye may,
  And ere the hearths are cold,
And all the embers ashen-gray,
  By which ye sat of old,
And dumb in death the loving lips
  That mourned as forth ye went
To join the fleet of missing ships,
  In quest of Heart's Content;

"And seek again the harbor-lights,
  Which faithful fingers trim,
Ere yet alike the days and nights
  Unto your eyes are dim!
For woe, alas! to those that roam
  Till time and tide are spent,
And win no more the port of home—
  The only Heart's Content!"

The Sea

BARRY CORNWALL

The sea! the sea! the open sea!
The blue, the fresh, the ever free!
Without a mark, without a bound,
It runneth the earth's wide regions round;
It plays with the clouds; it mocks the skies;
Or like a cradled creature lies.

I'm on the sea! I'm on the sea!
I am where I would ever be;
With the blue above, and the blue below,
And silence wheresoe'er I go;
If a storm should come and awake the deep,
What matter? *I* shall ride and sleep.

I love, O, how I love to ride
On the fierce, foaming, bursting tide,
When every mad wave drowns the moon
Or whistles aloft his tempest tune,
And tells how goeth the world below,
And why the sou'west blasts do blow.

I never was on the dull, tame shore,
But I lov'd the great sea more and more,
And backwards flew to her billowy breast,
Like a bird that seeketh its mother's nest;
And a mother she was, and is, to me;
For I was born on the open sea!

The waves were white, and red the morn,
In the noisy hour when I was born;
And the whale it whistled, the porpoise roll'd,
And the dolphins bared their backs of gold;
And never was heard such an outcry wild
As welcom'd to life the ocean-child!

I've liv'd since then, in calm and strife,
Full fifty summers, a sailor's life,
With wealth to spend and a power to range,   45
But never have sought, nor sighed for change;
And Death, whenever he comes to me,
Shall come on the wild, unbounded sea!

Little Billee

WILLIAM MAKEPEACE THACKERAY

There were three sailors of Bristol city
Who took a boat and went to sea.
But first with beef and captain's biscuits
And pickled pork they loaded she.

There was gorging Jack and guzzling Jimmy,
And the youngest he was little Billee.
Now when they got as far as the Equator
They'd nothing left but one split pea.

Says gorging Jack to guzzling Jimmy,
"I am extremely hungaree."
To gorging Jack says guzzling Jimmy,
"We've nothing left, us must eat we."

Says gorging Jack to guzzling Jimmy,
"With one another we shouldn't agree!
There's little Bill, he's young and tender,
We're old and tough, so let's eat he."

"Oh! Billy, we're going to kill and eat you.
So undo the button of your chemie."
When Bill received this information
He used his pocket handkerchie.

"First let me say my catechism,
Which my poor mammy taught to me."
"Make haste, make haste," says guzzling Jimmy,
While Jack pulled out his snickersnee.

So Billy went up to the main-top gallant mast,
And down he fell on his bended knee.
He scarce had come to the twelfth commandmen
When up he jumps, "There's land I see:

"Jerusalem and Madagascar,
And North and South Amerikee:
There's the British flag a-riding at anchor,
With Admiral Napier, K.C.B."

So when they got aboard of the Admiral's,
He hanged fat Jack and flogged Jimmee;
But as for little Bill he made him
The Captain of a Seventy-three.

Chemie—shirt.

EVEN IN THE LAST CENTURY, some farsighted lovers of nature were concerned about the pollution that industrialization and progress were bringing about. As the second stanza of the following poem shows, Charles Kingsley was one of these. In his poem, the water that has been polluted by the smoky town becomes cleansed and purified as it moves out to sea, once again becoming inviting and healthful for mother and child to bathe in.

The Tide River

CHARLES KINGSLEY

Clear and cool, clear and cool,
By laughing shallow and dreaming pool;
Cool and clear, cool and clear,
By shining shingle and foaming weir;
Under the crags where the ouzel sings,
And the ivied wall where the church-bell rings,
Undefiled, for the undefiled;
Play by me, bathe in me, mother and child,

Dank and foul, dank and foul,
By the smoky town in its murky cowl;
Foul and dank, foul and dank,
By wharf and sewer and slimy bank;
Darker and darker the farther I go,
Baser and baser the richer I grow;
Who dare sport with the sin-defiled?
Shrink from me, turn from me, mother and child.

Strong and free, strong and free,
The flood-gates are open, away to the sea.
Free and strong, free and strong,
Cleansing my streams as I hurry along,
To the golden sands, and the leaping bar,
And the taintless tide that awaits me afar,
As I lose myself in the infinite main,
Like a soul that has sinned and is pardoned again,
Undefiled, for the undefiled;
Play by me, bathe in me, mother and child.

MERMAIDS ARE GENERALLY PICTURED in folklore and legends as beautiful sea creatures, whose seductive songs have the power to lure sailors to their doom. Tennyson's mermaid is not bent on mischief, but is content to comb her golden hair and to sing.

The Mermaid

ALFRED, LORD TENNYSON

I

Who would be   Under the sea,
A mermaid fair,   In a golden curl
Singing alone,   With a comb of pearl,
Combing her hair   On a throne?

II

I would be a mermaid fair;
I would sing to myself the whole of the day;
With a comb of pearl I would comb my hair;
And still as I combed I would sing and say,
"Who is it loves me? who loves not me?"
I would comb my hair till my ringlets would fall,
    Low adown, low adown,
And I should look like a fountain of gold
    Springing alone
    With a shrill inner sound
    Over the throne
    In the midst of the hall.

The Mermaid

ANONYMOUS

'Twas a Friday morn when we set sail,
And we were not far from the land,
When the captain spied a lovely mermaid
With a comb and a glass in her hand.

CHORUS: Oh the ocean waves may roll, may roll,
        And the stormy winds may blow,
        While we poor sailors go skipping to the tops,
        And the landlubbers lie down below, below.
        And the landlubbers lie down below.

48

Then up spoke the captain of our gallant ship,
And a well-spoken man was he,
"I have married a wife in Salem town;
And tonight she a widow will be."   CHORUS

Then up spoke the boy of our gallant ship,
And a well-spoken lad was he,
"I've a father and mother in Boston City,
And tonight they childless will be."   CHORUS

"Oh, the moon shines bright, and the stars give light;
Oh, my mother'll be looking for me;
She may look, she may weep, she may look to the deep,
She may look to the bottom of the sea."   CHORUS

Then up spoke the cook of our gallant ship,
And a red-hot cook was he,
"I care more for my kettles and pots
Than I care for the bottom of the sea."   CHORUS

Then three times round went our gallant ship,
And three times round went she;
Then three times round went our gallant ship,
And she went to the bottom of the sea.   CHORUS

The Tide Rises, the Tide Falls

HENRY WADSWORTH LONGFELLOW

The tide rises, the tide falls,
The twilight darkens, the curlew calls;
Along the sea-sands damp and brown
The traveller hastens toward the town,
　　And the tide rises, the tide falls.

The morning breaks; the steeds in their stalls
Stamp and neigh, as the hostler calls;
The day returns, but nevermore
Returns the traveller to the shore,
　　And the tide rises, the tide falls.

Darkness settles on roofs and walls,
But the sea, the sea in the darkness calls;
The little waves, with their soft, white hands,
Efface the footprints in the sands,
　　And the tide rises, the tide falls.

THE EMINENT ENGLISH poet and critic, Matthew Arnold, meditates on the ebb and flow of human life and the destiny of man. Though the element of love is touched upon, the core of the poem deals with man's loss of faith in a world torn by agonizing conflict, "where ignorant armies clash by night."

Dover Beach

MATTHEW ARNOLD

The sea is calm tonight,
The tide is full, the moon lies fair
Upon the Straits;—on the French coast, the light
Gleams, and is gone; the cliffs of England stand,
Glimmering and vast, out in the tranquil bay.
Come to the window, sweet is the night air!
Only, from the long line of spray
Where the ebb meets the moon-blanch'd sand,
Listen! you hear the grating roar
Of pebbles which the waves suck back, and fling,
At their return, up the high strand,
Begin, and cease, and then again begin,
With tremulous cadence slow, and bring
The eternal note of sadness in.

Sophocles long ago
Heard it on the Aegean, and it brought
Into his mind the turbid ebb and flow
Of human misery; we
Find also in the sound a thought,
Hearing it by this distant northern sea.
The Sea of Faith
Was once, too, at the full, and round earth's shore
Lay like the folds of a bright girdle furl'd;
But now I only hear
Its melancholy, long, withdrawing roar,
Retreating to the breath
Of the night-wind down the vast edges drear
And naked shingles of the world.

Ah love, let us be true
To one another! for the world, which seems
To lie before us like a land of dreams,
So various, so beautiful, so new,
Hath really neither joy, nor love, nor light,
Nor certitude, nor peace, nor help for pain;
And we are here as on a darkling plain
Swept with confused alarms of struggle and flight,
Where ignorant armies clash by night.

To Sea!

THOMAS LOVELL BEDDOES

To sea! to sea! the calm is o'er,
  The wanton water leaps in sport,
And rattles down the pebbly shore,
  The dolphin wheels, the sea-cows snort,
And unseen mermaid's pearly song
Comes bubbling up, the weeds among.
Fling broad the sail, dip deep the oar:
To sea! to sea! the calm is o'er.

To sea! to sea! our white-winged bark
  Shall billowing cleave its watery way,
And with its shadow, fleet and dark,
  Break the caved Triton's azure day,
Like mountain eagle soaring light
O'er antelopes on Alpine height.
The anchor heaves! The ship swings free!
Our sails swell full! To sea! to sea!

Villanelle of the Sea

A. M. SULLIVAN

Deep and dark is ocean's mystery.
There are no scars upon the tidal crest;
Land wears the wounds of time, never the sea

Which hums a requiem in a minor key
And cleans the surface like a palimpsest.
Deep and dark is ocean's mystery.

A seed may lift man's shadow in a tree,
But oceans bear no totems of his quest.
Land wears the wounds of time, never the sea

And none shall know the pain or ecstasy
When ships spin downward in the whirlpool's nest.
Deep and dark is ocean's mystery.

Though star-eyes steer beneath night's canopy,
Man's furrows fade behind him, east or west;
Land wears the wounds of time, never the sea

And no wraith points by needle and degree
The spot precise he sipped death's alkahest.
Deep and dark is ocean's mystery;
Land wears the wounds of time; never the sea.

Alkahest—liquid supposed to dissolve anything it touched

ONE OF THE MOST POPULAR sea ballads, "The Golden Vanity" has its many devoted admirers on both sides of the Atlantic. While early American versions have rewarded the boy-hero with gold and the captain's daughter, the traditional treatment of the ballad ends with the hero drowning in the lowland sea.

The Golden Vanity

ANONYMOUS

There was a lofty ship, and she put out to sea,
And she goes by the name of the Golden Vanity,
And we feared she would be taken by the Spanish enemy,
As we sailed along the lowland, lowland low,
    As we sailed along the lowland sea.

Oh, we had a little cabin boy, and boldly up spoke he,
And he said to the captain, "What will you give me,
If I'll swim alongside of the Spanish enemy,
And I sink her in the lowland, lowland low,
    If I sink her in the lowland sea?"

"Of gold and silver I will give you fee,
And my only daughter your bonny bride to be,
If you'll swim alongside of the Spanish enemy
And you sink them in the lowland, lowland low,
    If you sink them in the lowland sea."

Then the boy bared his breast and overboard sprang he,
And he swam til he came to the Spanish enemy,
Then with his auger sharp in her sides he bored holes three,
And he sank her in the lowland, lowland low,
    He sank her in the lowland sea.

Now some were playing at cards and some were playing at dice,
And some were sitting by giving very good advice,
Until the salt water it flashed into their eyes,
And it sank them in the lowland, lowland low,
    It sank them in the lowland sea.

Then the boy swam back to the cheering of the crew
But the captain would not heed him, for his promise he did rue,
And he scorned his proud entreaties, though full loudly he did sue,
And he left him in the lowland, lowland low,
    He left him in the lowland sea.

So the boy swam round til he came to the larboard side,
And to his messmates full bitterly he cried,
"Oh, messmates pick me up, for I'm drifting with the tide,
And I'm sinking in the lowland, lowland low,
    I'm sinking in the lowland sea."

Then his messmates took him up, and upon the deck he died,
And they sewed him in his hammock, which was so large and wide,
And they lowered him overboard, and he drifted with the tide,
And he sank beneath the lowland, lowland low,
    He sank beneath the lowland sea.

"How's My Boy?" is similar to William Wordsworth's "We Are Seven," in which a young girl insists that "we are seven," even though two of the family's seven have died. In the following poem, the mother faced with the loss of her son at sea is simply unable to understand what has happened—the thought of his death is beyond her grasp and is too shocking a reality for her to understand.

How's My Boy?

SYDNEY DOBELL

"Ho, sailor of the sea!
How's my boy—my boy?"
"What's your boy's name, good wife,
And in what ship sailed he?"

"My boy John—
He that went to sea—
What care I for the ship, sailor?
My boy's my boy to me.

"You come back from sea,
And not know my John?
I might as well have asked some landsman,
Yonder down in the town.
There's not an ass in all the parish
But he knows my John.

"How's my boy—my boy?
And unless you let me know,
I'll swear you are no sailor,
Blue jacket or no,
Brass buttons or no, sailor,
Anchor and crown or no!
Sure his ship was the 'Jolly Briton' "—
"Speak low, woman, speak low!"

"And why should I speak low, sailor,
About my own boy John?
If I was loud as I am proud
I'd sing him over the town!
Why should I speak low, sailor?"
"That good ship went down."

"How's my boy—my boy?
What care I for the ship, sailor?
I was never aboard her.
Be she afloat or be she aground,
Sinking or swimming, I'll be bound
Her owners can afford her!
I say, how's my John?"
"Every man on board went down,
Every man aboard her."

"How's my boy—my boy?
What care I for the men, sailor?
I'm not their mother—
How's my boy—my boy?
Tell me of him and no other!
How's my boy—my boy?"

The Tempest

JAMES THOMAS FIELDS

We were crowded in the cabin,
　　Not a soul would dare to sleep,—
It was midnight on the waters
　　And a storm was on the deep.

'Tis a fearful thing in winter
　　To be shattered by the blast,
And to hear the rattling trumpet
　　Thunder, "Cut away the mast!"

So we shuddered there in silence,—
　　For the stoutest held his breath,
While the hungry sea was roaring,
　　And the breakers talked with Death.

As thus we sat in darkness,
　　Each one busy in his prayers,
"We are lost!" the captain shouted
　　As he staggered down the stairs.

But his little daughter whispered,
　　As she took his icy hand,
"Isn't God upon the ocean
　　Just the same as on the land?"

Then we kissed the little maiden,
　　And we spoke in better cheer,
And we anchored safe in harbor
　　When the morn was shining clear.

IN THE WINTER of 1839 the New England coast was battered by one of the fiercest storms it had experienced in years. As many as twenty ships were wrecked on the reef called Norman's Woe, and a number of bodies were washed ashore, including that of a woman who was lashed to a piece of wreckage. Longfellow noted this tragic event in his diary, adding that "I must write a ballad on this." And in a further notation two weeks later we have this entry: "I sat still till twelve o'clock by the fire, smoking, when suddenly it came into my mind to write 'The Ballad of the Schooner Hesperus' which I accordingly did."

The Wreck of the Hesperus

HENRY WADSWORTH LONGFELLOW

It was the schooner Hesperus,
　　That sailed the wintry sea;
And the skipper had taken his little daughter,
　　To bear him company.

Blue were her eyes, as the fairy-flax,
　　Her cheeks like the dawn of day,
And her bosom white as the hawthorn buds,
　　That ope in the month of May.

55

The skipper he stood beside the helm,
    His pipe was in his mouth;
And he watched how the veering flaw did blow
    The smoke now West, now South.

Then up and spake an old Sailor,
    Had sailed the Spanish Main:
"I pray thee, put into yonder port,
    For I fear a hurricane.

"Last night, the moon had a golden ring.
    And tonight no moon we see!"
The skipper, he blew a whiff from his pipe,
    And a scornful laugh laughed he.

Colder and louder blew the wind,
    A gale from the North-east;
The snow fell hissing in the brine,
    And the billows frothed like yeast.

Down came the storm, and smote amain
    The vessel in its strength;
She shuddered and paused, like a frightened steed,
    Then leaped her cable's length.

"Come hither! come hither! my little daughter,
    And do not tremble so;
For I can weather the roughest gale,
    That ever wind did blow."

He wrapped her warm in the seaman's coat,
    Against the stinging blast;
He cut a rope from a broken spar
    And bound her to the mast.

"O father! I hear the church-bells ring,
    O say, what may it be?"
" 'Tis a fog-bell on a rock-bound coast!"—
    And he steered for the open sea.

"O father! I hear the sound of guns,
    O say, what may it be?"
"Some ship in distress, that cannot live
    In such an angry sea!"

"O father! I see a gleaming light,
    O say, what may it be?"
But the father answered never a word,
    A frozen corpse was he.

Lashed to the helm, all stiff and stark,
    With his face turned to the skies;
The lantern gleamed through the gleaming snow
    On his fixed and glassy eyes.

Then the maiden clasped her hands, and prayed
    That savèd she might be;
And she thought of Christ, who stilled the wave
    On the Lake of Galilee.

And fast through the midnight dark and drear,
　Through the whistling sleet and snow,
Like a sheeted ghost, the vessel swept
　Towards the reef of Norman's Woe.

And ever the fitful gusts between
　A sound came from the land;
It was the sound of the trampling surf,
　On the rocks and the hard sea sand.

The breakers were right beneath her bows,
　She drifted a weary wreck,
And a whooping billow swept the crew
　Like icicles from her deck.

She struck where the white and fleecy waves
　Looked soft as carded wool,
But the cruel rocks, they gored her side,
　Like the horns of an angry bull.

Her rattling shrouds, all sheathed in ice,
　With the masts, went by the board;
Like a vessel of glass, she stove and sank,
　Ho! ho! the breakers roared!

At daybreak, on the bleak sea-beach
　A fisherman stood aghast,
To see the form of a maiden fair,
　Lashed close to a drifting mast.

The salt sea was frozen on her breast
　The salt tears in her eyes;
And he saw her hair, like the brown sea-weed,
　On the billows fall and rise.

Such was the wreck of the Hesperus,
　In the midnight and the snow!
Christ save us all from a death like this,
　On the reef of Norman's Woe!

Flaw—gusts of wind

The Yarn of the "Nancy Bell"

W. S. GILBERT

'Twas on the shores that round our coast
　From Deal to Ramsgate span,
That I found alone on a piece of stone
　An elderly naval man.

His hair was weedy, his beard was long,
　And weedy and long was he,
And I heard this wight on the shore recite,
　In a singular minor key:

"Oh, I am a cook and a captain bold,
　And the mate of the Nancy brig,
And a bo'sun tight, and a midshipmite,
　And the crew of the captain's gig."

And he shook his fists and he tore his hair,
　Till I really felt afraid,
For I couldn't help thinking the man had been drinking,
　And so I simply said:

"Oh, elderly man, it's little I know
    Of the duties of men of the sea,
But I'll eat my hand if I understand
    How you can possibly be

"At once a cook, and a captain bold,
    And the mate of the *Nancy* brig,
And a bo'sun tight, and a midshipmite,
    And the crew of the captain's gig."

Then he gave a hitch to his trousers, which
    Is a trick all seamen larn,
And having got rid of a thumping quid,
    He spun this painful yarn:

" 'Twas in the good ship *Nancy Bell*
    That we sailed to the Indian sea,
And there on a reef we come to grief,
    Which has often occurred to me.

"And pretty nigh all o' the crew was drowned
    (There was seventy-seven o' soul),
And only ten of the *Nancy's* men
    Said 'Here!' to the muster-roll.

"There was me and the cook and the captain bold,
    And the mate of the *Nancy* brig,
And the bo'sun tight, and a midshipmite,
    And the crew of the captain's gig.

"For a month we'd neither wittles nor drink.
    Till a-hungry we did feel,
So we drawed a lot, and accordin' shot
    The captain for our meal.

"The next lot fell to the *Nancy's* mate,
    And a delicate dish he made;
Then our appetite with the midshipmite
    We seven survivors stayed.

"And then we murdered the bo'sun tight,
    And he much resembled pig;
Then we wittled free, did the cook and me,
    On the crew of the captain's gig.

"Then only the cook and me was left,
    And the delicate question, 'Which
Of us two goes to the kettle?' arose
    And we argued it out as sich.

"For I loved that cook as a brother, I did,
    And the cook he worshipped me;
But we'd both be blowed if we'd either be stowed
    In the other chap's hold, you see.

" 'I'll be eat if you dines off me,' says TOM,
    'Yes, that,' says I, 'you'll be,'—
'I'm boiled if I die, my friend,' quoth I,
    And 'Exactly so,' quoth he.

"Says he, 'Dear JAMES, to murder me
    Were a foolish thing to do,
For don't you see that you can't cook me,
    While I can—and will—cook you!'

"So he boils the water, and takes the salt
    And the pepper in portions true
(Which he never forgot), and some chopped shalot,
    And some sage and parsley too.

" 'Come here,' says he, with a proper pride,
    Which his smiling features tell,
' 'Twill soothing be if I let you see,
    How extremely nice you'll smell.'

"And he stirred it round and round and round,
    And he sniffed at the foaming froth;
When I ups with his heels, and smothers his squeals
    In the scum of the boiling broth.

"And I eat that cook in a week or less,
    And—as I eating be
The last of his chops, why, I almost drops,
    For a wessel in sight I see!

"And I never grin, and I never smile,
    And I never larf nor play,
But I sit and croak, and a single joke
    I have—which is to say:

"Oh, I am a cook and a captain bold,
    And the mate of the *Nancy* brig,
And a bo'sun tight, and a midshipmite,
    And the crew of the captain's gig!"

Wight—creature

Creatures
of the Sea and Sky

EACH CREATURE HAS ITS PLACE in the scheme of things, each has its own special aspects. The butterfly, the moth, and the bird all ride the gusty currents of the air. The fish, the dolphin, and the whale inhabit the waters of the earth. Frogs, toads, and salamanders lead double lives, spending some time on land, but living at least the early parts of their lives in water. Each creature, large and small—the minnow no less than the whale, the hummingbird no less than the eagle—each has its life to live, its part to enact even as we do.

Crickets

CONRAD AIKEN

One cricket said to another—
come, let us be ridiculous, and say love!
love love love love love
let us be absurd, woman, and say hate!
hate hate hate hate hate
and then let us be angelic and say nothing.

And the other cricket said to the first—
fool! fool! speak! speak! speak!
speak if you must, but speaking speaking speaking
what does it get us, what does it get us, what?
act act act act give
giving is love, giving is love, give!

One cricket said to another—
what is love what is love what is love
act—speak—act—speak—act—speak
give—take—give—take—give—take
more slowly as the autumn comes, but giving
and taking still,—you taking, and I giving!

And the other cricket said to the first—
yes! yes! yes! you give your word!
words words but what at the end are words
speech speech what is the use of speech
give me love give me love
love!

One cricket said to another—
in the beginning—I forget—in the beginning—
fool fool fool fool fool
too late to remember and too late to teach—
in the beginning was the word, the speech,
and in the end the word, the word, the word. . . .

But while they quarrelled, these two foolish crickets,
and bandied act with word, denying each,
weighing their actions out in terms of speech,
the frost came whitely down and furred them both,
the speech grew slower, and the action nil,
and, at the end, even the word was still;
and god began again.

There are many stories of the wisdom and learning of the great Biblical king Solomon, of how he learned the languages of men, birds, beasts, and demons. Often these stories tell of the time the king was visited by the Queen of Sheba who had heard of this great wisdom and came in order to test him. One such story, taken from that great storehouse of Jewish lore and learning, the Talmud, follows.

Solomon and the Bees

John Godfrey Saxe

When Solomon was reigning in his glory,
Into his throne the Queen of Sheba came
(So in the Talmud you may read the story),
Drawn by the magic of the monarch's fame,
To see the splendors of his court, and bring
Some fitting tribute to the mighty king.

Nor this alone; much had her Highness heard
What flowers of learning graced the royal speech;
What gems of wisdom dropped with every word;
What wholesome lessons he was wont to teach
In pleasing proverbs; and she wished, in sooth,
To know if rumor spoke the simple truth.

And straight she held before the monarch's view,
In either hand, a radiant wreath of flowers;
The one, bedecked with every charming hue,
Was newly culled from nature's choicest bowers;
The other, no less fair in every part,
Was the rare product of divinest art.

"Which is the true, and which the false?" she said.
Great Solomon was silent. All-amazed,
Each wondering courtier shook his puzzled head,
While at the garlands long the monarch gazed,
As one who sees a miracle, and fain,
For very rapture ne'er would speak again.

While thus he pondered, presently he sees,
Hard by the casement,—so the story goes—
A little band of busy, bustling bees,
Hunting for honey in a withered rose.
The monarch smiled, and raised his royal head;
"Open the window!"—that was all he said.

The window opened at the king's command;
Within the room the eager insects flew,
And sought the flowers in Sheba's dexter hand!
And so the king and all the courtiers knew
That wreath was nature's; and the baffled queen
Returned to tell the wonders she had seen.

My story teaches (every tale should bear
A fitting moral) that the wise may find,
In trifles light as atoms in the air,
Some useful lesson to enrich the mind,
Some truth designed to profit or to please—
As Israel's king learned wisdom from the bees!

Dexter—right

63

The Nightingale and Glow-Worm

WILLIAM COWPER

A nightingale, that all day long
Had cheered the village with his song,
Nor yet at eve his note suspended,
Nor yet when eventide was ended,
Began to feel—as well he might—
The keen demands of appetite;
When, looking eagerly around,
He spied, far off, upon the ground,
A something shining in the dark,
And knew the glow-worm by his spark;
So, stooping down from hawthorn top,
He thought to put him in his crop.
The worm, aware of his intent,
Harangued him thus, quite eloquent,—
"Did you admire my lamp," quoth he,
"As much as I your minstrelsy,
You would abhor to do me wrong,
As much as I to spoil your song:
For 't was the self-same Power divine
Taught you to sing, and me to shine;
That you with music, I with light,
Might beautify and cheer the night."
The songster heard his short oration,
And, warbling out his approbation,
Released him, as my story tells,
And found a supper somewhere else.

Julius Caesar and the Honey-Bee

CHARLES TENNYSON TURNER

Poring on Caesar's death with earnest eye,
I heard a fretful buzzing on the pane:
"Poor bee!" I cried, "I'll help thee by-and-by";
Then dropped mine eyes upon the page again.
Alas, I did not rise; I helped him not:
In the great voice of Roman history
I lost the pleading of the window-bee,
And all his woes and troubles were forgot.
In pity for the mighty chief, who bled
Beside his rival's statue, I delayed
To serve the little insect's present need;
And so he died for lack of human aid.
I could not change the Roman's destiny;
I might have set the honey-maker free.

On a Fly Drinking from His Cup

WILLIAM OLDYS

Busy, curious, thirsty fly!
Drink with me and drink as I:
Freely welcome to my cup,
Couldst thou sip and sip it up:
Make the most of life you may,
Life is short and wears away.

Just alike, both mine and thine,
Hasten quick to their decline:
Thine's a summer, mine no more,
Though repeated to three-score.
Three-score summers, when they're gone,
Will appear as short as one!

"CLOCK-A-CLAY" is the fanciful name given to a ladybug in
this poem by the 19th-century English poet John Clare.

Clock-a-Clay

JOHN CLARE

In the cowslip pips I lie
Hidden from the buzzing fly,
While green grass beneath me lies
Pearled wi' dew like fishes' eyes.
Here I lie, a clock-a-clay,
Waiting for the time of day.

While grassy forests quake surprise,
And the wild wind sobs and sighs,
My gold home rocks as like to fall
On its pillar green and tall;
When the pattering rain drives by
Clock-a-clay keeps warm and dry.

Day by day and night by night
All the week I hide from sight.
In the cowslip pips I lie,
In rain and dew still warm and dry.
Day and night, and night and day,
Red, black-spotted clock-a-clay.

My home it shakes in wind and showers,
Pale green pillar topped wi' flowers,
Bending at the wild wind's breath
Till I touch the grass beneath.
Here I live, lone clock-a-clay,
Watching for the time of day.

The Man and the Fish

LEIGH HUNT

You strange, astonished-looking, angle-faced,
  Dreary-mouthed, gaping wretches of the sea,
  Gulping salt-water everlastingly,
Cold-blooded, though with red your blood be graced,
And mute, though dwellers: in the roaring waste;
  And you, all shapes beside, that fishy be,—
  Some round, some flat, some long, all devilry,
Legless, unloving, infamously chaste:—

O scaly, slippery, wet, swift, staring wights,
  What is't ye do? What life lead? eh, dull goggles?
How do ye vary your vile days and nights?
  How pass your Sundays? Are ye still but joggles
In ceaseless wash? Still nought but gapes, and bites,
  And drinks, and stares, diversified with boggles?

A FISH ANSWERS

Amazing monster! that, for aught I know,
  With the first sight of thee didst make our race
  For ever stare! O flat and shocking face,
Grimly divided from the breast below!
Thou that on dry land horribly dost go
  With a split body and most ridiculous pace,
  Prong after prong, disgracer of all grace,
Long-useless-finned, haired, upright, unwet, slow!

O breather of unbreathable, sword-sharp air,
  How canst exist? How bear thyself, thou dry
And dreary sloth? What particle canst share
  Of the only blessed life, the watery?
I sometimes see of ye an actual *pair*
  Go by! linked fin by fin! most odiously.

The Frog

ANONYMOUS

What a wonderful bird the frog are—
When he stand he sit almost;
When he hop, he fly almost.
He ain't got no sense hardly;
He ain't got no tail hardly either.
When he sit, he sit on what he ain't got almost.

The Little Turtle

VACHEL LINDSAY

There was a little turtle.
    He lived in a box.
He swam in a puddle.
    He climbed on the rocks.

He snapped at a mosquito.
    He snapped at a flea.
He snapped at a minnow.
    And he snapped at me.

He caught the mosquito.
    He caught the flea.
He caught the minnow.
    But he didn't catch me.

To a Fish of the Brook

JOHN WOLCOT

Why flyest thou away with fear?
Trust me there's naught of danger near,
  I have no wicked hook,
All covered with a snaring bait,
Alas, to tempt thee to thy fate,
  And drag thee from the brook.

Enjoy thy stream, O harmless fish;
And when an angler for his dish,
  Through gluttony's vile sin,
Attempts, a wretch, to pull thee out,
God give thee strength, O gentle trout,
  To pull the rascal *in!*

Seaside Poems:
Do Fishes Go to School?

RUTH WHITMAN

After supper
before the dishes
we noticed suddenly
that fishes
were making little
leaps and swishes
under the setting sun.

Are they dolphins?
Baby whales?
Brought in by some
faroff gales?
Playing hopscotch
one by one?

Leda said, O
silly fool,
these fishes clearly
are a school . . .
Davey interrupted
yes,
but when do they have their
recess?

IN "THE HORSES OF THE SEA," Christina Rossetti is not referring to the fabled marine animal the sea horse, with the fore-
parts of a horse and the hinder parts of a fish, nor to the tiny
tropical fish named for it. She is writing about the foaming and
tossing of sea waves that appear to her like spirited horses with
their manes streaming out in the wind.

The Horses of the Sea

CHRISTINA ROSSETTI

The horses of the sea
    Rear a foaming crest,
But the horses of the land
    Serve us the best.

The horses of the land
    Munch corn and clover,
While the foaming sea-horses
    Toss and turn over.

Dame Duck's Lecture

ANONYMOUS

Close by the margin of the brook,
The old duck made her nest,
Of straw and leaves and withered grass,
And down from her own breast.

And there she sat for four long weeks,
Through rainy days and fine,
Until the ducklings all came out,
Four, five, six, seven, eight, nine.

One peeped out from beneath her wing,
One scrambled on her back.
"That's very rude," said old Dame Duck,
"Get off—quack, quack, quack."

"Too close," said Dame Duck, shoving out
The egg-shells with her bill.
Besides, it never suits young ducks
To keep them sitting still.

So, rising from her nest, she said,
"Now, children, look at me.
A well-bred duck should waddle
From side to side—d'ye see?"

"Yes," said the little ones, and then
She went on to explain:
"A well-bred duck turns in its toes,
And do try again."

"Yes," said the ducklings, waddling on.
"That's better," said the mother,
"But well-bred ducks walk in a row
Straight, one behind the other."

"Yes," said the little ducks again
All waddling in a row;
"Now to the pond," said old Dame Duck.
Splash, splash, and in they go.

The Chickens

ANONYMOUS

Said the first little chicken,
　　With a queer little squirm,
"I wish I could find
　　A fat little worm."

Said the next little chicken,
　　With an odd little shrug,
"I wish I could find
　　A fat little slug."

Said the third little chicken,
　　With a sharp little squeal,
"I wish I could find
　　Some nice yellow meal."

Said the fourth little chicken,
　　With a small sigh of grief,
"I wish I could find
　　A little green leaf."

Said the fifth little chicken,
　　With a faint little moan,
"I wish I could find
　　A wee gravel stone."

"Now, see here," said the mother,
　　From the green garden patch,
"If you want any breakfast,
　　Just come here and scratch."

The Sandpiper

CELIA THAXTER

Across the narrow beach we flit,
　　One little sandpiper and I;
And fast I gather, bit by bit,
　　The scattered driftwood bleached and dry.
The wild waves reach their hands for it,
　　The wild wind raves, the tide runs high,
As up and down the beach we flit,—
　　One little sandpiper and I.

Above our heads the sullen clouds
　　Send black and swift across the sky:
Like silent ghosts in misty shrouds
　　Stand out the white light-houses high.
Almost as far as eye can reach
　　I see the close-reefed vessels fly,
As fast we flit along the beach,—
　　One little sandpiper and I.

I watch him as he skims along,
　　Uttering his sweet and mournful cry;
He starts not at my fitful song,
　　Or flash of fluttering drapery;
He has no thought of any wrong,
　　He scans me with a fearless eye.
Stanch friends are we, well tried and strong,
　　The little sandpiper and I.

Comrade, where wilt thou be to-night
　　When the loosed storm breaks furiously?
My driftwood-fire will burn so bright!
　　To what warm shelter canst thou fly?
I do not fear for thee, though wroth
　　The tempest rushes through the sky:
For are we not God's children both,
　　Thou, little sandpiper, and I?

To a Waterfowl

William Cullen Bryant

Whither, midst falling dew,
While glow the heavens with the last steps of day,
Far, through their rosy depths, dost thou pursue
    Thy solitary way?

Vainly the fowler's eye
Might mark thy distant flight to do thee wrong,
As, darkly seen against the crimson sky,
    Thy figure floats along.

Seek'st thou the plashy brink
Of weedy lake, or marge of river wide,
Or where the rocking billows rise and sink
    On the chafed ocean-side?

There is a Power whose care
Teaches thy way along that pathless coast—
The desert and illimitable air—
    Lone wandering, but not lost.

All day thy wings have fanned,
At that far height, the cold, thin atmosphere,
Yet stoop not, weary, to the welcome land,
    Though the dark night is near.

And soon that toil shall end;
Soon shalt thou find a summer home, and rest,
And scream among thy fellows; reeds shall bend,
    Soon, o'er thy sheltered nest.

Thou'rt gone, the abyss of heaven
Hath swallowed up thy form; yet, on my heart
Deeply has sunk the lesson thou hast given,
    And shall not soon depart.

He who, from zone to zone,
Guides through the boundless sky thy certain flight,
In the long way that I must tread alone,
    Will lead my steps aright.

IN ENGLAND the cuckoo is a very special bird. It is one of the first to arrive in the spring, and its melodious call is a signal for the winter-weary to take hope—spring is here.

The Cuckoo

ANONYMOUS

The cuckoo is a pretty bird,
　She singeth as she flies;
She bringeth us good tidings,
　She telleth us no lies;
She sucketh all sweet flowers
　To keep her throttle clear,
And every time she singeth
Cuckoo-cuckoo-cuckoo!
　The summer draweth near.

The cuckoo is a giddy bird,
　No other is as she,
That flits across the meadow,
　That sings in every tree.
A nest she never buildeth,
　A vagrant she doth roam;
Her music is but tearful—
Cuckoo-cuckoo-cuckoo!
　"I nowhere have a home."

The cuckoo is a witty bird,
　Arriving with the spring.
When summer suns are waning,
　She spreadeth wide her wing.
She flies th' approaching winter,
　She hates the rain and snow;
Like her, I would be singing,
Cuckoo-cuckoo-cuckoo!
　And off with her I'd go!

To the Cuckoo

WILLIAM WORDSWORTH

O blithe new-comer! I have heard,
　I hear thee and rejoice.
O cuckoo! shall I call thee bird,
　Or but a wandering voice?

While I am lying on the grass
　Thy twofold shout I hear;
From hill to hill it seems to pass,
　At once far off and near.

Though babbling only to the vale
　Of sunshine and of flowers,
Thou bringest unto me a tale
　Of visionary hours.

Thrice welcome, darling of the spring!
　Even yet thou art to me
No bird, but an invisible thing,
　A voice, a mystery;

The same whom in my school-boy days
  I listened to; that cry
Which made me look a thousand ways,
  In bush and tree and sky.

To seek thee did I often rove
  Through woods and on the green;
And thou wert still a hope, a love;
  Still longed for, never seen.

And I can listen to thee yet;
  Can lie upon the plain
And listen, till I do beget
  That golden time again.

O blessed bird! the earth we pace
  Again appears to be
An unsubstantial, fairy place;
  That is fit home for thee!

To an Oriole

EDGAR FAWCETT

How falls it oriole, thou hast come to fly
In tropic splendor through our Northern sky?

At some glad moment was it nature's choice
To dower a scrap of sunset with a voice?

Or did some orange tulip, flaked with black,
In some forgotten garden, ages back,

Yearning toward heaven until its wish was heard,
Desire unspeakably to be a bird?

Song: The Owl

ALFRED, LORD TENNYSON

When cats run home and light is come;
  And dew is cold upon the ground,
And the far-off stream is dumb,
  And the whirring sail goes round,
  And the whirring sail goes round;
Alone and warming his five wits,
  The white owl in the belfry sits.

When merry milkmaids click the latch,
  And rarely smells the new-mown hay,
And the cock hath sung beneath the thatch
  Twice or thrice his roundelay,
  Twice or thrice his roundelay;
Alone and warming his five wits,
The white owl in the belfry sits.

73

The Owl

BARRY CORNWALL

In the hollow tree, in the old gray tower,
   The spectral owl doth dwell;
Dull, hated, despised, in the sunshine hour,
   But at dusk he's abroad and well!
Not a bird of the forest e'er mates with him;
   All mock him outright by day;
But at night, when the woods grow still and dim,
   The boldest will shrink away!
     O, when the night falls, and roosts the fowl,
     Then, then, is the reign of the hornèd owl!

And the owl hath a bride, who is fond and bold,
   And loveth the wood's deep gloom;
And, with eyes like the shine of the moonstone cold,
   She awaiteth her ghastly groom;
Not a feather she moves, not a carol she sings,
   As she waits in her tree so still;
But when her heart heareth his flapping wings,
   She hoots out her welcome shrill!
     O, when the moon shines, and dogs do howl,
     Then, then; is the joy of the hornèd owl!

Mourn not for the owl, nor his gloomy plight!
   The owl hath his share of good:
If a prisoner he be in the broad daylight,
   He is lord in the dark greenwood!
Nor lonely the bird, nor his ghastly mate,
   They are each unto each a pride;
Thrice fonder, perhaps, since a strange, dark fate
   Hath rent them from all beside!
     So, when the night falls, and dogs do howl,
     Sing, ho! for the reign of the hornèd owl!
       We know not alway
       Who are kings by day,
     But the king of the night is the bold brown owl!

What Does Little Birdie Say?

ALFRED, LORD TENNYSON

What does little birdie say
In her nest at peep of day?
Let me fly, says little birdie,
Mother, let me fly away.
Birdie, rest a little longer,
Till the little wings are stronger.
So she rests a little longer,
Then she flies away.

What does little baby say,
In her bed at peep of day?
Baby says, like little birdie,
Let me rise and fly away.
Baby sleep, a little longer,
Till the little limbs are stronger,
If she sleeps a little longer,
Baby too shall fly away.

Answer to a Child's Question

SAMUEL TAYLOR COLERIDGE

Do you ask what the birds say? The sparrow, the dove,
The linnet, and thrush say "I love, and I love!"
In the winter they're silent, the wind is so strong;
What it says I don't know, but it sings a loud song.
But green leaves, and blossoms, and sunny warm weather,
And singing and loving—all come back together.
But the lark is so brimful of gladness and love,
The green fields below him, the blue sky above,
That he sings, and he sings, and forever sings he,
"I love my Love, and my Love loves me."

Song

JOHN KEATS

I had a dove, and the sweet dove died;
  And I have thought it died of grieving:
O, what could it grieve for? its feet were tied
  With a single thread of my own hand's weaving;
Sweet little red feet, why should you die—

Why should you leave me, sweet bird, why?
You lived alone in the forest tree,
Why, pretty thing! would you not live with me?
I kiss'd you oft and gave you white peas;
Why not live sweetly, as in the green trees ?

A Bird Came Down the Walk

EMILY DICKINSON

A bird came down the walk;
He did not know I saw;
He bit an angle-worm in halves
And ate the fellow, raw.

And then he drank a dew
From a convenient grass,
And then hopped sidewise to the wall
To let a beetle pass.

He glanced with rapid eyes
That hurried all abroad,—
They looked like frightened beads, I thought
He stirred his velvet head

Like one in danger; cautious,
I offered him a crumb,
And he unrolled his feathers
And rowed him softer home

Than oars divide the ocean,
Too silver for a seam,
Or butterflies, off banks of noon,
Leap, plashless, as they swim.

The Skylark

CHRISTINA ROSSETTI

The earth was green, the sky was blue:
  I saw and heard one sunny morn
A skylark hang between the two,
  A singing speck above the corn;

A stage below, in gay accord,
  White butterflies danced on the wing,
And still the singing skylark soared,
  And silent sank, and soared to sing.

The cornfield stretched a tender green
  To right and left beside my walks;
I knew he had a nest unseen
  Somewhere among the million stalks.

And as I paused to hear his song,
  While swift the sunny moments slid,
Perhaps his mate sat listening long,
  And listened longer than I did.

The Thrush's Nest

JOHN CLARE

Within a thick and spreading hawthorn bush,
　　That overhung a molehill large and round,
I heard from morn to morn a merry thrush
　　Sing hymns to sunrise, and I drank the sound
With joy; and often, an intruding guest,
　　I watched her secret toil from day to day—
How true she warped the moss, to form a nest,
　　And modelled it within with wood and clay;
And by-and-by, like heath-bells gilt with dew,
　　There lay her shining eggs, as bright as flowers,
Ink-spotted over shells of greeny blue;
　　And there I witnessed in the sunny hours,
A brood of Nature's minstrels chirp and fly,
Glad as the sunshine and the laughing sky.

The Darkling Thrush

THOMAS HARDY

I leant upon a coppice gate
　　When Frost was spectre-gray,
And Winter's dregs made desolate
　　The weakening eye of day.
The tangled bine-stems scored the sky
　　Like strings of broken lyres,
And all mankind that haunted nigh
　　Had sought their household fires.

The land's sharp features seemed to be
　　The Century's corpse outleant,
His crypt the cloudy canopy,
　　The wind his death-lament.
The ancient pulse of germ and birth
　　Was shrunken hard and dry,
And every spirit upon earth
　　Seemed fervourless as I.

At once a voice arose among
　　The bleak twigs overhead
In a full-hearted evensong
　　Of joy illimited;
An aged thrush, frail, gaunt, and small,
　　In blast-beruffled plume,
Had chosen thus to fling his soul
　　Upon the growing gloom.

So little cause for carolings
　　Of such ecstatic sound
Was written on terrestrial things
　　Afar or nigh around,
That I could think there trembled through
　　His happy good-night air
Some blessed Hope, whereof he knew
　　And I was unaware.

77

Coppice—thicket

The Winged Worshippers

Addressed to two swallows that flew into the
Chauncy Place Church during divine service.

CHARLES SPRAGUE

Gay, guiltless pair,
What seek ye from the fields of heaven?
    Ye have no need of prayer;
Ye have no sins to be forgiven.

Why perch ye here,
Where mortals to their Maker bend?
    Can your pure spirits fear
The God ye never could offend?

Ye never knew
The crimes for which we come to weep.
    Penance is not for you,
Blessed wanderers of the *upper deep.*

To you 't is given
To wake sweet Nature's untaught lays;
    Beneath the arch of heaven
To chirp away a life of praise.

Then spread each wing
Far, far above, o'er lakes and lands,
    And join the choirs that sing
In yon blue dome not reared with hands.

Or, if ye stay,
To note the consecrated hour,
    Teach me the airy way,
And let me try your envied power.

Above the crowd
On upward wings could I but fly,
    I'd bathe in yon bright cloud,
And seek the stars that gem the sky.

'T were heaven indeed
Through fields of trackless light to soar,
    On Nature's charms to feed,
And Nature's own great God adore.

Crow

FRANCES MINTURN HOWARD

Black book clapping above a swamp,
Black rag hung on a hollow tree,
No careless singer this, but dark
Habited villainy.

Cunning, cunning, the crafty crow,
Ravisher of what treasure rare—
Thimble and button, nail and pin
Strung upon blue air.

By hill deflected, valley turned
Is man; but straight the crow flies,
Such ordered madness couches in
The burned pits of his eyes.

The Pheasant

ALEXANDER POPE

See! from the brake the whirring pheasant springs,
And mounts exulting on triumphant wings;
Short is his joy! he feels the fiery wound,
Flutters in blood, and panting beats the ground.
Ah! what avails his glossy varying dyes,
His purple crest, and scarlet-circled eyes,
The vivid green his shining plumes unfold,
His painted wings, and breast that shines with gold.

Titwillow

W. S. GILBERT

On a tree by a river a little tom-tit
    Sang "Willow, titwillow, titwillow!"
And I said to him, "Dicky-bird, why do you sit
    Singing 'Willow, titwillow, titwillow'?
"Is it a weakness of intellect, birdie?" I cried,
"Or a rather tough worm in your little inside?"
With a shake of his poor little head he replied,
    "Oh, willow, titwillow, titwillow!"

He slapped at his chest, as he sat on that bough,
    Singing "Willow, titwillow, titwillow!"
And a cold perspiration bespangled his brow,
    Oh, willow, titwillow, titwillow!
He sobbed and he sighed, and a gurgle he gave,
Then he threw himself into the billowy wave,
And an echo arose from the suicide's grave—
    "Oh, willow, titwillow, titwillow!"

Now, I feel just as sure as I'm sure that my name
    Isn't Willow, titwillow, titwillow,
That 'twas blighted affection that made him exclaim,
    "Oh, willow, titwillow, titwillow!"
And if you remain callous and obdurate, I
Shall perish as he did, and you will know why,
Though I probably shall not exclaim as I die,
    "Oh, willow, titwillow, titwillow!"

POETS HAVE LONG been fascinated by the eagle, by the sweep and grandeur of a bird whose home is in the lofty and all but inaccessible mountain peaks, whose breadth and strength of wing are the stuff of legend and fable, and whose flight seems almost miraculous as the bird hurtles downward in search of its prey or hovers nearly motionless high in the air. William Blake wrote:

> When thou seest an eagle
> Thou sees a portion of genius;
> Lift up thy head.

Judging by the following lines, Tennyson must also have been a watcher of eagles.

The Eagle

ALFRED, LORD TENNYSON

He clasps the crag with hookèd hands;
Close to the sun in lonely lands,
Ringed with the azure world, he stands.

The wrinkled sea beneath him crawls;
He watches from his mountain walls,
And like a thunderbolt he falls.

The Eagle and the Mole

ELINOR WYLIE

Avoid the reeking herd,
Shun the polluted flock,
Live like that stoic bird,
The eagle of the rock.

The huddled warmth of crowds
Begets and fosters hate;
He keeps, above the clouds,
His cliff inviolate.

When flocks are folded warm
And herds to shelter run,
He sails above the storm,
He stares into the sun.

If in the eagle's track
Your sinews cannot leap,
Avoid the lathered pack,
Turn from the steaming sheep.

If you would keep your soul
From spotted sight or sound,
Live like the velvet mole;
Go burrow underground.

And there hold intercourse
With roots of trees and stones,
With rivers at their source
And disembodied bones.

Robin Redbreast

ANONYMOUS (Traditional Welsh Song)

Welcome Robin with thy greeting,
On the threshold meekly waiting,
To the children's home now enter,
From the cold and snow of winter,
From the cold and snow of winter.

Art thou cold? or art thou hungry?
Pretty Robin, don't be angry,
All the children round thee rally,
While the snow is in the valley,
While the snow is in the valley.

Come in Robin, do not fear us,
Thy bright eye and chirping cheer us;
Thy sad notes excite our pity,
Now the frost begins to bite thee,
Now the frost begins to bite thee.

Robin come and tell thy story,
Leave outside thy care and worry;
Tell the children, Robin dearest,
Of the babies in the forest,
Of the babies in the forest.

Of the flame that burnt thy bosom,
Of thy wand'rings far and lonesome,
Of thy home among the greenwood,
Of thy happy days of childhood,
Of thy happy days of childhood.

Stay Near Me

WILLIAM WORDSWORTH

Stay near me—do not take thy flight!
A little longer stay in sight!
Much converse do I find in thee,
Historian of my infancy!
Float near me; do not yet depart!
Dead times revive in thee:
Thou bring'st, gay creature as thou art!
A solemn image to my heart,
My father's family!

Oh! pleasant, pleasant were the days,
The time, when, in our childish plays,
My sister Emmeline and I
Together chased the butterfly!
A very hunter did I rush
Upon the prey:—with leaps and springs
I followed on from brake to bush;
But she, God love her! feared to brush
The dust from off its wings.

I've Watched You Now

WILLIAM WORDSWORTH

I've watched you now a full half-hour,
Self-poised upon that yellow flower;
And, little Butterfly! indeed
I know not if you sleep or feed.
How motionless!—not frozen seas
More motionless! and then
What joy awaits you, when the breeze
Hath found you out among the trees,
And calls you forth again!

This plot of orchard-ground is ours;
My trees they are, my Sister's flowers;
Here rest your wings when they are weary;
Here lodge as in a sanctuary!
Come often to us, fear no wrong;
Sit near us on the bough!
We'll talk of sunshine and of song,
And summer days, when we were young;
Sweet childish days, that were as long
As twenty days are now.

In Search of
the Horizon

IT IS SAID of the poet John Clare that as a boy he went out
one day in search of the horizon, and Stephen Crane may
have had this story in mind when he wrote his "I Saw a Man"
which begins this section. The horizon and the far-off places
of the world have beckoned men throughout the ages. And
the same quality of mind that causes men to ask questions
about the unknown also allows them to derive answers. This
is the quality of imagination. By using his imagination, man
can go on fabulous journeys—and never even leave home.
Some of the poems in this section deal with real voyages and
real people—but most of them take place in the realm of the
imagination.

I Saw a Man Pursuing the Horizon

STEPHEN CRANE

I saw a man pursuing the horizon;
Round and round they sped.
I was disturbed at this;
I accosted the man.
"It is futile," I said,
"You can never—"
"You lie," he cried,
And ran on.

A Book

EMILY DICKINSON

There is no frigate like a book
　　To take us lands away,
Nor any coursers like a page
　　Of prancing poetry.

This traverse may the poorest take
　　Without oppress of toll;
How frugal is the chariot
　　That bears a human soul!

THE BALLADS OF SCOTLAND tell stories usually of violence and often of treachery or deceit. In "The Ballad of Sir Patrick Spens" there is violent death at sea, but as to treachery, each reader will have to decide for himself about the "ill deed" that was done to Sir Patrick. Was choosing him to put out to sea in the storm season a tribute to his seamanship? Or was it done for some darker reason? The king's mission must have been an important one to judge by the haste with which the expedition put to sea and to warrant taking the Scots nobles as passengers. However, as is true of other Scottish ballads, this one give no reasons; it simply tells its story and leaves the rest to the reader.

The Ballad of Sir Patrick Spens

ANONYMOUS

The king sits in Dumferling town,
Drinking the blood-red wine:
"O where will I get a good sailor,
To sail this ship of mine?"

Up and spoke an eldern knight,
Sat at the king's right knee:
"Sir Patrick Spens is the best sailor
That sails upon the sea."

The king has written a broad letter,
And signed it with his hand,
And sent it to Sir Patrick Spens
Was walking on the sand.

The first line that Sir Patrick read,
A loud laugh laughed he;
The next line that Sir Patrick read,
The tear blinded his eye.

"O who has done this ill deed,
This ill deed done to me,
To send me out this time of year,
To sail upon the sea?

"Make haste, make haste, my merry men all,
Our good ship sails the morn."
"O say not so my master dear,
For I fear a deadly storm.

"Late, late yester e'en I saw the new moon,
With the old moon in her arm,
And I fear, I fear, my dear master,
That we will come to harm."

O our Scots nobles were right loath
To wet their cork-heeled shoon;
But long e'er all the play was played
Their hats they swam aboon.

O long, long may their ladies sit
With their fans into their hands,
Or e'er they see Sir Patrick Spens
Come sailing to the land.

And long, long may their ladies stand
With their gold combs in their hair,
Waiting for their own dear lords,
For they'll see them no more.

Half o'er, half o'er to Aberdour,
It's fifty fathoms deep;
And there lies good Sir Patrick Spens
With the Scots lords at his feet.

A Vagabond Song

BLISS CARMAN

There is something in the autumn that is native to my blood—
Touch of manner, hint of mood;
And my heart is like a rhyme,
With the yellow and the purple and the crimson keeping time.

The scarlet of the maples can shake me like a cry
Of bugles going by.
And my lonely spirit thrills
To see the frosty asters like smoke upon the hills.

There is something in October sets the gypsy blood astir;
We must rise and follow her,
When from every hill of flame
She calls and calls each vagabond by name.

The Land of Story-Books

ROBERT LOUIS STEVENSON

At evening when the lamp is lit,
Around the fire my parents sit;
They sit at home and talk and sing,
And do not play at anything.

Now, with my little gun, I crawl
All in the dark along the wall,
And follow round the forest track
Away behind the sofa back.

There, in the night, where none can spy,
All in my hunter's camp I lie,
And play at books that I have read
Till it is time to go to bed.

These are the hills, these are the woods,
These are my starry solitudes;
And there the river by whose brink
The roaring lions come to drink.

I see the others far away
As if in firelit camp they lay,
And I, like to an Indian scout,
Around their party prowled about.

So, when my nurse comes in for me,
Home I return across the sea,
And go to bed with backward looks
At my dear land of Story-books.

My Bed Is a Boat

ROBERT LOUIS STEVENSON

My bed is like a little boat;
   Nurse helps me in when I embark;
She girds me in my sailor's coat
   And starts me in the dark.

At night, I go on board and say
   Good-night to all my friends on shore;
I shut my eyes and sail away
   And see and hear no more.

And sometimes things to bed I take,
   As prudent sailors have to do;
Perhaps a slice of wedding-cake,
   Perhaps a toy or two.

All night across the dark we steer:
   But when the day returns at last,
Safe in my room, beside the pier,
   I find my vessel fast.

CHILDREN ASK: "Why is the sky blue?" "Where does the wind go?" "Why do the stars twinkle?" In the Bible, Job is asked: "Hath the rain a father?" As long as there are questioning minds, questions will be asked, and not all can be answered.

As I Float

DAVID ROSS

What stirred the breath
To blow the wind
That moves the wave
That laps the boat
That rocks my senses
As I float?

89

By a powerful act of imagination, William Cowper has put himself in the place of Alexander Selkirk, an eighteenth-century sailor said to have quarreled with his shipmates and consequently abandoned on the island of Juan Fernandez, a desolate outpost in the Pacific Ocean. Four years later Selkirk was picked up by a ship that stopped at the island by the merest chance. Selkirk's story was also the inspiration for Daniel Defoe's classic *Robinson Crusoe*.

Verses

William Cowper

Supposed to be written by Alexander Selkirk, during his solitary abode on the island of Juan Fernandez

I am monarch of all I survey,
   My right there is none to dispute;
From the centre all round to the sea,
   I am lord of the fowl and the brute.
O Solitude! where are the charms
   That sages have seen in thy face?
Better dwell in the midst of alarms
   Then reign in this horrible place.

I am out of humanity's reach,
   I must finish my journey alone,
Never hear the sweet music of speech,
   I start at the sound of my own.
The beasts that roam over the plain
   My form with indifference see;
They are so unacquainted with man,
   Their tameness is shocking to me.

Society, friendship and love,
   Divinely bestowed upon man,
O, had I the wings of a dove,
   How soon would I taste you again!
My sorrows I then might assuage,
   In the ways of religion and truth,
Might learn from the wisdom of age,
   And be cheer'd by the sallies of youth.

Religion! what treasure untold
   Lies hid in that heavenly word!
More precious than silver or gold,
   Or all that this earth can afford.
But the sound of the church-going bell,
   These valleys and rocks never heard,
Never sigh'd at the sound of a knell,
   Or smiled when a sabbath appear'd.

Ye winds that have made me your sport,
   Convey to this desolate shore
Some cordial, endearing report
   Of a land I shall visit no more.
My friends, do they now and then send
   A wish or a thought after me?
O, tell me I yet have a friend,
   Though a friend I am never to see.

How fleet is a glance of the mind!
   Compar'd with the speed of its flight,
The tempest himself lags behind
   And the swift-winged arrows of light.
When I think of my own native land,
   In a moment I seem to be there;
But, alas! recollection at hand
   Soon hurries me back to despair.

But the sea-fowl is gone to her nest,
   The beast is laid down in his lair;
Even here is a season of rest,
   And I to my cabin repair.
There's mercy in every place,
   And mercy, encouraging thought,
Gives even affliction a grace,
   And reconciles man to his lot.

Follow the Gleam

ALFRED, LORD TENNYSON

Not of the sunlight,
Not of the moonlight,
Not of the starlight!
O young Mariner,
Down to the haven,
Call your companions,

Launch your vessel,
And crowd your canvas,
And ere it vanishes
Over the margin,
After it, follow it,
Follow The Gleam

Reveille

A. E. HOUSMAN

Wake: the silver dusk returning
   Up the beach of darkness brims,
And the ship of sunrise burning
   Strands upon the eastern rims.

Wake: the vaulted shadow shatters,
   Trampled to the floor it spanned,
And the tent of night in tatters
   Straws the sky-pavillioned land.

Up, lad, up, 'tis late for lying:
   Hear the drums of morning play;
Hark, the empty highways crying
   "Who'll beyond the hills away?"

Towns and countries woo together,
   Forelands beacon, belfries call;
Never lad that trod on leather
   Lived to feast his heart with all.

Up, lad: thews that lie and cumber
   Sunlit pallets never thrive;
Morns abed and daylight slumber
   Were not meant for man alive.

Clay lies still, but blood's a rover;
   Breath's a ware that will not keep.
Up, lad: when the journey's over
   There'll be time enough to sleep.

Eldorado

EDGAR ALLAN POE

Gayly bedight
   A gallant knight
In sunshine and in shadow,
   Had journeyed long,
   Singing a song,
In search of Eldorado.

But he grew old,
   This knight so bold,
And o'er his heart a shadow
   Fell, as he found
   No spot of ground
That looked like Eldorado.

And, as his strength
   Failed him at length,
He met a pilgrim shadow:
   "Shadow," said he
   "Where can it be,
This land of Eldorado?"

"Over the Mountains
   Of the Moon,
Down the Valley of the Shadow,
   Ride, boldly ride,"
   The shade replied,
"If you seek for Eldorado!"

Bedight—dressed.

Home Thoughts from Abroad

ROBERT BROWNING

Oh, to be in England
Now that April's there,
And whoever wakes in England
Sees, some morning, unaware,
That the lowest boughs and the brush-wood sheaf
Round the elm-tree bole are in tiny leaf,
While the chaffinch sings on the orchard bough
In England—now!

And after April, when May follows,
And the whitethroat builds, and all the swallows!
Hark, where my blossomed pear-tree in the hedge
Leans to the field and scatters on the clover
Blossoms and dewdrops—at the bent spray's edge—
That's the wise thrush; he sings each song twice over,
Lest you should think he never could recapture
The first fine careless rapture!
And though the fields look rough with hoary dew,
All will be gay when noontide wakes anew
The buttercups, the little children's dower
Far brighter than this gaudy melon-flower!

The Sea Gypsy

RICHARD HOVEY

I am fevered with the sunset,
I am fretful with the bay,
For the wander-thirst is on me
And my soul is in Cathay.

There's a schooner in the offing,
With her top-sails shot with fire,
And my heart has gone aboard her
For the Islands of Desire.

I must forth again tomorrow!
With the sunset I must be,
Hull down on the trail of rapture
In the wonder of the Sea.

The Sunset City

HENRY SYLVESTER CORNWELL

There's a city that lies in the Kingdom of Clouds,
   In the glorious country on high,
Which an azure and silvery curtain enshrouds,
   To screen it from mortal eye;

A city of temples and turrets of gold,
   That gleam by a sapphire sea,
Like jewels more splendid than earth may behold,
   Or are dreamed of by you and by me.

And about it are highlands of amber that reach
   Far away till they melt in the gloom;
And waters that hem an immaculate beach
   With fringes of luminous foam.

Aerial bridges of pearl there are,
   And belfries of marvellous shapes,
And lighthouses lit by the evening star,
   That sparkle on violet capes;

And hanging gardens that far away
   Enchantedly float aloof;
Rainbow pavilions in avenues gay,
   And banners of glorious woof!

When the Summer sunset's crimsoning fires
   Are aglow in the western sky,
The pilgrim discovers the domes and spires
   Of this wonderful city on high;

And gazing enrapt as the gathering shade
   Creeps over the twilight lea,
Sees palace and pinnacle totter and fade,
   And sink in the sapphire sea;

Till the vision loses by slow degrees
   The magical splendor it wore;
The silvery curtain is drawn, and he sees
   The beautiful city no more!

Singing through the Forests

JOHN GODFREY SAXE

Singing through the forests,
　Rattling over ridges;
Shooting under arches,
　Rumbling over bridges;
Whizzing through the mountains,
　Buzzing o'er the vale,—
Bless me! this is pleasant,
　Riding on the rail!

Men of different "stations"
　In the eye of fame,
Here are very quickly
　Coming to the same;
High and lowly people,
　Birds of every feather,
On a common level,
　Travelling together.

Gentleman in shorts,
　Looming very tall;
Gentleman at large
　Talking very small;
Gentleman in tights,
　With a loose-ish mien;
Gentleman in gray,
　Looking rather green;

Gentleman quite old,
　Asking for the news;
Gentleman in black,
　In a fit of blues;
Gentleman in claret,
　Sober as a vicar;
Gentleman in tweed,
　Dreadfully in liquor!

Stranger on the right
　Looking very sunny,
Obviously reading
　Something rather funny.
Now the smiles are thicker,—
　Wonder what they mean!
Faith, he's got the Knicker-
　Bocker Magazine!

Woman with her baby,
　Sitting vis-à-vis;
Baby keeps a-squalling,
　Woman looks at me;
Asks about the distance,
　Says it's tiresome talking,
Noises of the cars
　Are so very shocking!

95

Market-woman, careful
   Of the precious casket,
Knowing eggs are eggs,
   Tightly holds her basket;
Feeling that a smash,
   If it came, would surely
Send her eggs to pot,
   Rather prematurely.

Singing through the forests,
   Rattling over ridges;
Shooting under arches,
   Rumbling over bridges;
Whizzing through the mountains,
   Buzzing o'er the vale,—
Bless me! this is pleasant,
   Riding on the rail!

LONG BEFORE the astronauts, poets were riding their imaginations into the farthest regions of space. The following stanzas, from the long poem "Peter Bell," might almost have been written by an astronaut. As a matter of fact, it was written by the poet William Wordsworth more than a century ago.

The Crescent Boat

WILLIAM WORDSWORTH

There's something in a flying horse,
There's something in a huge balloon;
But through the clouds I'll never float
Until I have a little Boat,
Shaped like the crescent-moon.

And now I *have* a little Boat,
In shape a very crescent-moon:
Fast through the clouds my Boat can sail;
And if perchance your faith should fail,
Look up—and you shall see me soon!

The woods, my Friends, are round you roaring,
Rocking and roaring like a sea;
The noise of danger's in your ears,
And ye have all a thousand fears
Both for my little Boat and me!

Meanwhile untroubled I admire
The pointed horns of my canoe;
And, did not pity touch my breast,
To see how ye are all distrest,
Till my ribs ached, I'd laugh at you!

Away we go, my Boat and I—
Frail man ne'er sate in such another;
Whether among the winds we strive,
Or deep into the clouds we dive,
Each is contented with the other.

Away we go—and what care we
For treason, tumults, and for wars?
We are as calm in our delight
As is the crescent-moon so bright
Among the scattered stars.

Up goes my Boat among the stars
Through many a breathless field of light,
Through many a long blue field of ether,
Leaving ten thousand stars beneath her:
Up goes my little Boat so bright!

The Crab, the Scorpion, and the Bull—
We pry among them all; have shot
High o'er the red-haired race of Mars,
Covered from top to toe with scars;
Such company I like it not!

The towns in Saturn are decayed,
And melancholy Spectres throng them;—
The Pleiads, that appear to kiss
Each other in the vast abyss,
With joy I sail among them.

Swift Mercury resounds with mirth,
Great Jove is full of stately bowers;
But these, and all that they contain,
What are they to that tiny grain,
That little Earth of ours?

Then back to Earth, the dear green Earth:—
Whole ages if I here should roam,
The world for my remarks and me
Would not a whit the better be;
I've left my heart at home.

See! There she is, the matchless Earth!
There spreads the famed Pacific Ocean!
Old Andes thrusts yon craggy spear
Through the grey clouds; the Alps are here,
Like waters in commotion!

Yon tawny slip is Libya's sands;
That silver thread the river Dnieper;
And look, where clothed in brightest green
Is a sweet Isle, of isles the Queen;
Ye fairies, from all evil keep her!

And see the town where I was born!
Around those happy fields we span
In boyish gambols;—I was lost
Where I have been, but on this coast
I feel I am a man.

Never did fifty things at once
Appear so lovely, never, never;—
How tunefully the forests ring!
To hear the earth's soft murmuring
Thus could I hang forever!

97

The Children's Hour

Henry Wadsworth Longfellow

Between the dark and the daylight,
   When night is beginning to lower,
Comes a pause in the day's occupations,
   That is known as the children's hour.

I hear in the chamber above me
   The patter of little feet,
The sound of a door that is opened,
   And voices soft and sweet.

From my study I see in the lamplight,
   Descending the broad hall stair,
Grave Alice and laughing Allegra,
   And Edith with golden hair.

A whisper and then a silence,
   Yet I know by their merry eyes
They are plotting and planning together
   To take me by surprise.

A sudden rush from the stairway,
   A sudden raid from the hall,
By three doors left unguarded,
   They enter my castle wall.

They climb up into my turret,
   O'er the arms and back of my chair;
If I try to escape, they surround me:
   They seem to be everywhere.

They almost devour me with kisses,
  Their arms about me intwine,
Till I think of the Bishop of Bingen
  In his Mouse-Tower on the Rhine.

Do you think, O blue-eyed banditti,
  Because you have scaled the wall,
Such an old mustache as I am
  Is not a match for you all?

I have you fast in my fortress,
  And will not let you depart,
But put you into the dungeon
  In the round-tower of my heart.

And there will I keep you forever,
  Yes, forever and a day,
Till the walls shall crumble to ruin,
  And moulder in dust away.

One, Two, Three

HENRY CUYLER BUNNER

It was an old, old, old, old lady
  And a boy that was half-past three,
And the way that they played together
  Was beautiful to see.

She couldn't go romping and jumping,
  And the boy, no more could he;
For he was a thin little fellow,
  With a thin little twisted knee.

They sat in the yellow sunlight,
  Out under the maple tree,
And the game that they played I'll tell you,
  Just as it was told to me.

It was hide-and-go-seek they were playing,
  Though you'd never have known it to be—
With an old, old, old, old lady
  And a boy with a twisted knee.

The boy would bend his face down
  On his little sound right knee,
And he guessed where she was hiding
  In guesses One, Two, Three.

"You are in the china closet!"
  He would cry, and laugh with glee—
It wasn't the china closet,
  But he still has Two and Three.

"You are up in papa's big bedroom,
  In the chest with the queer old key,"
And she said: "You are warm and warmer;
  But you are not quite right," said she.

"It can't be the little cupboard
  Where mamma's things used to be—
So it must be in the clothes press, Gran'ma,"
  And he found her with his Three.

Then she covered her face with her fingers,
  That were wrinkled and white and wee,
And she guessed where the boy was hiding,
  With a One and a Two and a Three.

And they never had stirred from their places
  Right under the maple tree—
This old, old, old, old lady
  And the boy with the lame little knee—

This dear, dear, dear old lady
  And the boy who was half-past three.

ONE OF THE MOST strangely beautiful poems in English poetry,
is Coleridge's "Kubla Khan." An account of its composition tells
how Coleridge had taken a mild opiate while reading about the
palace of the Khan Kubla. He then lapsed into a dream state that
lasted several hours, during which time the poem took shape. On
waking he wrote down the lines that now constitute the poem as
we know it. He might have remembered more of it, where it not
for the sudden intrusion of "a person on business from Porlock."
Once the spell was broken by this caller, the remaining elements
of the poem vanished, so that what is left to us is this dream
fragment of "Kubla Khan."

Kubla Khan

SAMUEL TAYLOR COLERIDGE

In Xanadu did Kubla Khan
A stately pleasure-dome decree:
Where Alph, the sacred river, ran
Through caverns measureless to man
　　Down to a sunless sea.
So twice five miles of fertile ground
With walls and towers were girdled round:
And here were gardens bright with sinuous rills
Where blossomed many an incense-bearing tree;
And here were forests ancient as the hills,
Enfolding sunny spots of greenery.
But oh! that deep romantic chasm which slanted
Down the green hill athwart a cedarn cover!
A savage place! as holy and enchanted
As e'er beneath a waning moon was haunted
By woman wailing for her demon-lover!
And from this chasm, with ceaseless turmoil seething,
As if this earth in fast thick pants were breathing,
A mighty fountain momently was forced;
Amid whose swift half-intermitted burst
Huge fragments vaulted like rebounding hail,
Or chaffy grain beneath the thresher's flail:
And 'mid these dancing rocks at once and ever
It flung up momently the sacred river.
Five miles meandering with a mazy motion

Through wood and dale the sacred river ran,
Then reached the caverns measureless to man,
And sank in tumult to a lifeless ocean:
And 'mid this tumult Kubla heard from far
Ancestral voices prophesying war!

The shadow of the dome of pleasure
Floated midway on the waves;
Where was heard the mingled measure
From the fountain and the caves.
It was a miracle of rare device,
A sunny pleasure-dome with caves of ice!

A damsel with a dulcimer
In a vision once I saw:
It was an Abyssinian maid,
And on her dulcimer she played,
Singing of Mount Abora.
Could I revive within me
Her symphony and song,
To such a deep delight 'twould win me,
That with music loud and long,
I would build that dome in air,
That sunny dome! those caves of ice!
And all who heard should see them there,
And all should cry, Beware! Beware!
His flashing eyes, his floating hair!
Weave a circle round him thrice,
And close your eyes with holy dread,
For he on honey-dew hath fed,
And drunk the milk of Paradise.

Requiem

ROBERT LOUIS STEVENSON

Under the wide and starry sky,
Dig the grave and let me lie.
Glad did I live and gladly die,
    And I laid me down with a will.

This be the verse you grave for me:
Here he lies where he longed to be;
Home is the sailor, home from sea,
    And the hunter home from the hill.

Spells and Enchantments

MEN HAVE EVER been enthralled with the supernatural, with events and occurrences that have no natural explanation, whether caused by the hand of God or by some other agency. This section includes poems that show how various poets have handled this theme.

THE OLD TESTAMENT story of Daniel is a dramatic one. Belshazzar, the king of the Babylonians, holds the Jews captive, and he and his courtiers, or satraps, have profaned the sacred Judean vessels by using them as drinking goblets at their banquets. At one such banquet, a disembodied hand suddenly appears and writes a mysterious message on the wall. None can read it until Daniel is brought out. The inscription foretells doom for Belshazzar. Here is Lord Byron's retelling of the story.

Vision of Belshazzar

GEORGE GORDON, LORD BYRON

The King was on his throne,
  The Satraps thronged the hall;
A thousand bright lamps shone
  O'er that high festival.
A thousand cups of gold,
  In Judah deemed divine—
Jehovah's vessels hold
  The godless heathen's wine!

In that same hour and hall,
  The fingers of a hand
Came forth against the wall,
  And wrote as if on sand:
The fingers of a man;—
  A solitary hand
Along the letters ran,
  And traced them like a wand.

The monarch saw, and shook,
　And bade no more rejoice;
All bloodless waxed his look,
　And tremulous his voice.
"Let the men of lore appear,
　The wisest of the earth,
And expound the words of fear,
　Which mar our royal mirth."

Chaldea's seers are good,
　But here they have no skill;
And the unknown letters stood,
　Untold and awful still.
And Babel's men of age
　Are wise and deep in lore;
But now they were not sage,
　They saw—but knew no more.

A captive in the land,
　A stranger and a youth,
He heard the King's command,
　He saw that writing's truth.
The lamps around were bright,
　The prophecy in view;
He read it on that night—
　The morrow proved it true.

"Belshazzar's grave is made,
　His kingdom passed away,
He, in the balance weighed,
　Is light and worthless clay:
The shroud, his robe of state,
　His canopy, the stone:
The Mede is at his gate!
　The Persian on his throne!"

WILLIAM BUTLER YEATS (1865–1939) is one of the towering poets of our time. He helped to establish the celebrated Abbey Theatre of Dublin, and won the Nobel Prize for literature in 1923. Here is one of his early poems, a legend of a silver trout that by some fairy magic was changed into a "glimmering girl with apple blossom in her hair."

The Song of Wandering Aengus

WILLIAM BUTLER YEATS

I went out to the hazel wood,
Because a fire was in my head,
And cut and peeled a hazel wand,
And hooked a berry to a thread;
And when white moths were on the wing,
And moth-like stars were flickering out,
I dropped the berry in a stream
And caught a little silver trout.

When I had laid it on the floor
I went to blow the fire aflame,
But something rustled on the floor,
And some one called me by my name:
It had become a glimmering girl
With apple blossom in her hair
Who called me by my name and ran
And faded through the brightening air.

Though I am old with wandering
Through hollow lands and hilly lands,
I will find out where she has gone,
And kiss her lips and take her hands;
And walk among long dappled grass,
And pluck till time and times are done
The silver apples of the moon,
The golden apples of the sun.

La belle Dame sans Merci

JOHN KEATS

O, what can ail thee, knight at arms,
  Alone and palely loitering;
The sedge has withered from the lake,
  And no birds sing.

O, what can ail thee, knight at arms,
  So haggard and so woe-begone?
The squirrel's granary is full,
  And the harvest's done.

I see a lily on thy brow
  With anguish moist and fever-dew,
And on thy cheeks a fading rose
  Fast withereth too.

I met a lady in the meads,
  Full beautiful—a faery's child,
Her hair was long, her foot was light,
  And her eyes were wild.

I made a garland for her head,
  And bracelets too, and fragrant zone,
She looked at me as she did love,
  And made sweet moan.

I set her on my pacing steed
  And nothing else saw all day long;
For sideways would she lean, and sing
  A faery's song.

She found me roots of relish sweet,
  And honey wild and manna dew;
And sure in language strange she said—
  I love thee true.

She took me to her elfin grot,
  And there she gazed and sighed full sore:
And there I shut her wild wild eyes
  With kisses four.

And there she lullèd me asleep,
  And there I dreamed, ah woe betide,
The latest dream I ever dreamed
  On the cold hill side.

I saw pale kings and princes too,
  Pale warriors, death-pale were they all:
They cry'd—"La belle Dame sans Merci
  Hath thee in thrall!"

I saw their starved lips in the gloam
  With horrid warning gapèd wide,
And I awoke, and found me here
  On the cold hill side.

And this is why I sojourn here
  Alone and palely loitering,
Though the sedge is withered from the lake,
  And no birds sing.

The Ballad of the Harp-Weaver

EDNA ST. VINCENT MILLAY

"Son," said my mother,
    When I was knee-high,
"You've need of clothes to cover you,
    And not a rag have I.

"There's nothing in the house
    To make a boy breeches,
Nor shears to cut a cloth with
    Nor thread to take stitches.

"There's nothing in the house
    But a loaf-end of rye,
And a harp with a woman's head
    Nobody will buy,"
    And she began to cry.

That was in the early fall.
    When came the late fall,
"Son," she said, "the sight of you
    Makes your mother's blood crawl,—

"Little skinny shoulder-blades
    Sticking through your clothes!
And where you'll get a jacket from
    God above knows.

"It's lucky for me, lad,
    Your daddy's in the ground,
And can't see the way I let
    His son go around!"
    And she made a queer sound.

That was in the late fall.
    When the winter came,
I'd not a pair of breeches
    Nor a shirt to my name.

I couldn't go to school,
    Or out of doors to play.
And all the other little boys
    Passed our way.

"Son," said my mother,
    "Come, climb into my lap,
And I'll chafe your little bones
    While you take a nap."

And, oh, but we were silly
    For half an hour or more,
Me with my long legs
    Dragging on the floor.

A-rock-rock-rocking
    To a mother goose rhyme!
Oh, but we were happy
    For half an hour's time!

But there was I, a great boy,
    And what would folks say,
To hear my mother singing me
    To sleep all day,
    In such a daft way?

Men say the winter
    Was bad that year;
Fuel was scarce,
    And food was dear.

A wind with a wolf's head
    Howled about our door,
And we burned up the chairs
    And sat upon the floor.

All that was left us
    Was a chair we couldn't break,
And the harp with a woman's head
    Nobody would take,
    For song or pity's sake.

The night before Christmas
    I cried with the cold,
I cried myself to sleep
    Like a two-year-old.

And in the deep night
    I felt my mother rise,
And stare down upon me
    With love in her eyes.

I saw my mother sitting
    On the one good chair,
A light falling on her
    From I couldn't tell where,

Looking nineteen,
    And not a day older,
And the harp with a woman's head
    Leaned against her shoulder.

Her thin fingers, moving
    In the thin, tall strings,
Were weav-weav-weaving
    Wonderful things.

Many bright threads,
    From where I couldn't see,
Were running through the harp-strings
    Rapidly.

And gold threads whistling
    Through my mother's hand.
I saw the web grow,
    And the pattern expand.

She wove a child's jacket,
    And when it was done
She laid it on the floor
    And wove another one.

She wove a red cloak
    So regal to see,
"She's made it for a king's son,"
    I said, "and not for me."
    But I knew it was for me.

She wove a pair of breeches
    Quicker than that!
She wove a pair of boots
    And a little cocked hat.

She wove a pair of mittens,
    She wove a little blouse,
She wove all night
    In the still, cold house.

She sang as she worked,
    And the harp-strings spoke;
Her voice never faltered,
    And the thread never broke.
    And when I awoke,—

There sat my mother
    With the harp against her shoulder,
Looking nineteen
    And not a day older,

A smile about her lips,
    And a light about her head,
And her hands in the harp-strings
    Frozen dead.

And piled up beside her
    And toppling to the skies,
Were the clothes of a king's son.
    Just my size.

Little Orphant Annie

JAMES WHITCOMB RILEY

Little Orphant Annie's come to our house to stay,
An' wash the cups an' saucers up, an' brush the crumbs away,
An' shoo the chickens off the porch, an' dust the hearth, an' sweep,
An' make the fire, an' bake the bread, an' earn her board-an'-keep;
An' all us other children, when the supper-things is done,
We set around the kitchen fire an' has the mostest fun
A-list'nin' to the witch-tales 'at Annie tells about,
An' the Gobble-uns 'at gits you
    Ef you
        Don't
            Watch
                Out!

Wunst they wuz a little boy wouldn't say his prayers,—
An' when he went to bed at night, away up-stairs,
His Mammy heered him holler, an' his Daddy heered him bawl,
An' when they turn't the kivvers down, he wuzn't there at all!
An' they seeked him in the rafter-room, an' cubby-hole, an' press,
An' seeked him up the chimbly-flue, an' ever'-wheres, I guess;
But all they ever found wuz thist his pants an' roundabout:—
An' the Gobble-uns 'll git you
    Ef you
        Don't
            Watch
                Out!

An' one time a little girl 'ud allus laugh an' grin,
An' make fun of ever' one, an' all her blood-an'-kin;
An' wunst, when they was "company," an' ole folks was there,
She mocked 'em an' shocked 'em, an' said she didn't care!
An' thist as she kicked her heels, an' turn't to run an' hide,
They was two great Black Things a-standin' by her side,
An' they snatched her through the ceilin' 'fore she knowed what she's about!
An' the Gobble-uns 'll git you
    Ef you
        Don't
            Watch
                Out!

An' little Orphant Annie says, when the blaze is blue,
An' the lamp-wick sputters, an' the wind goes woo-oo!
An' you hear the crickets quit, an' the moon is gray,
An' the lightnin'-bugs in dew is all squenched away,—
You better mind yer parunts, an' yer teachers fond an' dear,
An' churish them 'at loves you, an' dry the orphant's tear,
An' he'p the pore an' needy ones 'at clusters all about,
Er the Gobble-uns 'll git you
    Ef you
        Don't
            Watch
                Out!

The Witch's House

LAURA BENÉT

Its wicked little windows leer
  Beneath a mouldy thatch,
And village children come and peer
  Before they lift the latch.

A one-eyed crow hops to the door,
  Fat spiders crowd the pane,
And dark herbs scattered on the floor
  Waft fragrance down the lane.

It sits so low, the little hutch,
  So secret, shy and squat,
As if in its mysterious clutch
  It nursed one knew not what.

That beggars passing by the ditch
  Are haunted with desire
To force the door, and see the witch
  Vanish in flames of fire.

111

In the New York *Evening Mirror* of January 29, 1845 there appeared a poem signed "Quarles." Those who moved in the literary circles of the day knew it was an assumed name, but were unable to identify its owner. Not until later that year did Edgar Allan Poe acknowledge himself to be the author of the poem by including it in his new volume of verse. The poem has become famous, and has afforded delight to readers and reciters for more than a hundred years.

The Raven

Edgar Allan Poe

Once upon a midnight dreary, while I pondered, weak and weary,
Over many a quaint and curious volume of forgotten lore,—
While I nodded, nearly napping, suddenly there came a tapping,
As of some one gently rapping, rapping at my chamber door.
" 'Tis some visitor," I muttered, "tapping at my chamber door:
    Only this and nothing more."

Ah, distinctly I remember it was in the bleak December,
And each separate dying ember wrought its ghost upon the floor.
Eagerly I wished the morrow;—vainly I had sought to borrow
From my books surcease of sorrow—sorrow for the lost Lenore,
For the rare and radiant maiden whom the angels name Lenore:
    Nameless here for evermore.

And the silken sad uncertain rustling of each purple curtain
Thrilled me—filled me with fantastic terrors never felt before;
So that now, to still the beating of my heart, I stood repeating
" 'Tis some visitor entreating entrance at my chamber door,
Some late visitor entreating entrance at my chamber door:
    This it is and nothing more."

Presently my soul grew stronger; hesitating then no longer,
"Sir," said I, "or Madam, truly your forgiveness I implore;
But the fact is I was napping, and so gently you came rapping,
And so faintly you came tapping, tapping at my chamber door,
That I scarce was sure I heard you"—here I opened wide the door:—
    Darkness there and nothing more.

Deep into that darkness peering, long I stood there wondering, fearing,
Doubting, dreaming dreams no mortal ever dared to dream before;
But the silence was unbroken, and the stillness gave no token,
And the only word there spoken was the whispered word, "Lenore?"
This I whispered, and an echo murmured back the word, "Lenore:"
    Merely this and nothing more.

Back into the chamber turning, all my soul within me burning,
Soon again I heard a tapping somewhat louder than before.
"Surely," said I, "surely that is something at my window lattice;
Let me see, then, what thereat is, and this mystery explore;
Let my heart be still a moment and this mystery explore:
    'Tis the wind and nothing more."

Open here I flung the shutter, when, with many a flirt and flutter,
In there stepped a stately Raven of the saintly days of yore.
Not the least obeisance made he; not a minute stopped or stayed he;
But, with mien of lord or lady, perched above my chamber door,
Perched upon a bust of Pallas just above my chamber door:
    Perched, and sat, and nothing more.

Then this ebony bird beguiling my sad fancy into smiling
By the grave and stern decorum of the countenance it wore,—
"Though thy crest be shorn and shaven, thou," I said, "art sure no craven,
Ghastly grim and ancient Raven wandering from the Nightly shore:
Tell me what thy lordly name is on the Night's Plutonian shore!"
    Quoth the Raven, "Nevermore."

Much I marvelled this ungainly fowl to hear discourse so plainly,
Though its answer little meaning—little relevancy bore;
For we cannot help agreeing that no living human being
Ever yet was blessed with seeing bird above his chamber door,
Bird or beast upon the sculptured bust above his chamber door,
    With such name as "Nevermore."

But the Raven, sitting lonely on the placid bust, spoke only
That one word, as if his soul in that one word he did outpour.
Nothing further then he uttered, not a feather then he fluttered,
Till I scarcely more than muttered,—"Other friends have flown before;
On the morrow *he* will leave me, as my Hopes have flown before."
    Then the bird said, "Nevermore."

Startled at the stillness broken by reply so aptly spoken,
"Doubtless," said I, "what it utters is its only stock and store,
Caught from some unhappy master whom unmerciful Disaster
Followed fast and followed faster till his songs one burden bore:
Till the dirges of his Hope that melancholy burden bore
    Of 'Never—nevermore.' "

But the Raven still beguiling my sad fancy into smiling,
Straight I wheeled a cushioned seat in front of bird and bust and door;
Then, upon the velvet sinking, I betook myself to linking
Fancy unto fancy, thinking what this ominous bird of yore,
What this grim, ungainly, ghastly, gaunt, and ominous bird of yore
    Meant in croaking "Nevermore."

This I sat engaged in guessing, but no syllable expressing
To the fowl whose fiery eyes now burned into my bosom's core;
This and more I sat divining, with my head at ease reclining
On the cushion's velvet-lining that the lamp-light gloated o'er,
But whose velvet violet lining the lamp-light gloating o'er
    She shall press, ah, nevermore!

Then, methought, the air grew denser, perfumed from an unseen censer
Swung by seraphim whose foot-falls tinkled on the tufted floor.
"Wretch," I cried, "thy God hath lent thee—by these angels he hath sent thee
Respite—respite and nepenthe from thy memories of Lenore!
Quaff, oh quaff this kind nepenthe, and forget this lost Lenore!"
    Quoth the Raven, "Nevermore."

"Prophet!" said I, "thing of evil! prophet still, if bird or devil!
Whether Tempter sent, or whether tempest tossed thee here ashore,
Desolate yet all undaunted, on this desert land enchanted—
On this home by Horror haunted—tell me truly, I implore:
Is there—*is* there balm in Gilead?—tell me—tell me, I implore!"
    Quoth the Raven, "Nevermore."

"Prophet!" said I, "thing of evil—prophet still, if bird or devil!
By that Heaven that bends above us, by that God we both adore,
Tell this soul with sorrow laden if, within the distant Aidenn,
It shall clasp a sainted maiden whom the angels name Lenore:
Clasp a rare and radiant maiden whom the angels name Lenore!"
    Quoth the Raven, "Nevermore."

"Be that word our sign of parting, bird or fiend!" I shrieked, upstarting:
"Get thee back into the tempest and the Night's Plutonian shore!
Leave no black plume as a token of that lie thy soul hath spoken!
Leave my loneliness unbroken! quit the bust above my door!
Take thy beak from out my heart, and take thy form from off my door!"
    Quoth the Raven, "Nevermore."

And the Raven, never flitting, still is sitting, still is sitting
On the pallid bust of Pallas just above my chamber door;
And his eyes have all the seeming of a demon's that is dreaming,
And the lamp-light o'er him streaming throws his shadow on the floor:
And my soul from out that shadow that lies floating on the floor
      Shall be lifted—nevermore!

THE FOLLOWING POEM is a spell, an enchantment of a different
order, drawing its magic around the reader and giving enjoyment
whether its meaning is clearly understood or not.

To Morfydd

LIONEL JOHNSON

A voice on the winds,
A voice on the waters,
    Wanders and cries:
Oh! what are the winds?
And what are the waters?
    Mine are your eyes!

Western the winds are,
And western the waters,
    Where the light lies:
Oh! what are the winds?
And what are the waters?
    Mine are your eyes!

Cold, cold, grow the winds,
And wild grow the waters,
    Where the sun dies:
Oh! what are the winds?
And what are the waters?
    Mine are your eyes!

And down the night winds,
And down the night waters,
    The music flies:
Oh! what are the winds?
And what are the waters?
Cold be the winds,
And wild be the waters,
    So mine be your eyes!

Miracles

CONSIDER THE EGG AND THE SEED, from which spring all the creatures and beings of earth and air and water. Consider the insubstantial wind, made of nothing, and yet capable of propelling sailing ships and felling great trees. Consider the sun, moon, and stars. Certainly all things of creation are miracles and marvels.

Miracles

WALT WHITMAN

Why, who makes much of a miracle?
As to me I know of nothing else but miracles,
Whether I walk the streets of Manhattan,
Or dart my sight over the roofs of houses toward the sky,
Or wade with naked feet along the beach just in the edge
     of the water,
Or stand under trees in the woods,

.   .   .   .

Or watch honey-bees busy around the hive of a summer
     forenoon,
Or animals feeding in the fields,
Or birds, or the wonderfulness of insects in the air,
Or the wonderfulness of the sundown, or of the stars
     shining so quiet and bright,
Or the exquisite delicate thin curve of the new
     moon in spring;
These with the rest, one and all, are to me miracles,
The whole referring, yet each distinct and in its place.

To me every hour of the light and dark is a miracle,
Every cubic inch of space is a miracle,
Every square yard of the surface of the earth is spread
     with the same,
Every foot of the interior swarms with the same.

To me the sea is a continual miracle,
The fishes that swim—the rocks—the motion of the waves
     —the ships with men in them,
What stranger miracles are there?

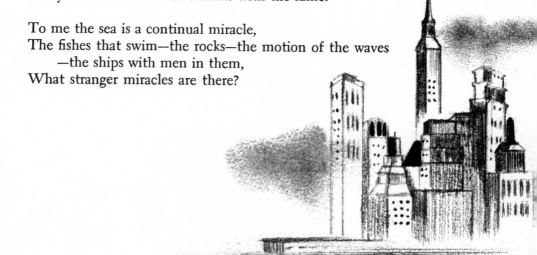

The Light Is Sweet

ECCLESIASTES 11:7

Truly the light is sweet,
And a pleasant thing it is
For the eyes to behold the sun.

Morning

EMILY DICKINSON

Will there really be a morning?
Is there such a thing as day?
Could I see it from the mountains
If I were as tall as they?

Has it feet like water-lilies?
Has it feathers like a bird?
Is it brought from famous countries
Of which I have never heard?

Oh, some scholar! Oh, some sailor!
Oh! some wise man from the skies!
Please to tell a little pilgrim
Where the place called morning lies!

I See the Moon

ANONYMOUS

I see the moon,
And the moon sees me;
God bless the moon,
And God bless me.

Washed in Silver

JAMES STEPHENS

Gleaming in silver are the hills!
Blazing in silver is the sea!

And a silvery radiance spills
Where the moon drives royally!

Clad in silver tissue, I
March magnificently by!

The Man in the Moon

ANONYMOUS

The Man in the Moon as he sails the sky
Is a very remarkable skipper,
But he made a mistake when he tried to take
A drink of milk from the Dipper.
He dipped right out of the Milky Way,
And slowly and carefully filled it,
The Big Bear growled, and the Little Bear howled
And frightened him so that he spilled it!

The Moon

ANONYMOUS

The Moon has a face like the clock in the hall;
She shines on thieves on the garden wall,
On streets and fields and harbour quays,
And birdies asleep in the forks of the trees.

The squalling cat and the squeaking mouse,
The howling dog by the door of the house,
The bat that lies in bed at noon,
All love to be out by the light of the moon.

But all of the things that belong to the day
Cuddle to sleep to be out of her way;
And flowers and children close their eyes
Till up in the morning the sun shall arise.

Escape at Bedtime

ROBERT LOUIS STEVENSON

The lights from the parlor and kitchen shone out
    Through the blinds and the windows and bars;
And high overhead and all moving about,
    There were thousands of millions of stars.
There ne'er were such thousands of leaves on a tree,
    Nor of people in church or the Park,
As the crowds of the stars that looked down upon me,
    And that glittered and winked in the dark.
The Dog, and the Plow, and the Hunter, and all,
    And the star of the sailor, and Mars,
These shone in the sky, and the pail by the wall
    Would be half full of water and stars.
They saw me at last, and they chased me with cries,
    And they soon had me packed into bed;
But the glory kept shining and bright in my eyes,
    And the stars going round in my head.

121

It's hard to imagine Walt Whitman sitting quietly in a lecture hall listening to someone—however learned—talk about the stars. Whitman tried it, and described the experience in the following poem.

When I Heard the Learn'd Astronomer

WALT WHITMAN

When I heard the learn'd astronomer,
When the proofs, the figures, were ranged in columns
    before me,
When I was shown the charts and diagrams, to add,
    divide, and measure them,
When I sitting heard the astronomer where he lectured
    with much applause in the lecture-room,
How soon unaccountable I became tired and sick,
Till rising and gliding out I wander'd off by myself,
In the mystical moist night-air, and from time to time,
Look'd up in perfect silence at the stars.

Who Has Seen the Wind?

CHRISTINA ROSSETTI

Who has seen the wind?
Neither I nor you;
But when the leaves hang trembling
The wind is passing thro'.

Who has seen the wind?
Neither you nor I;
But when the trees bow down their heads
The wind is passing by.

The West Wind

JOHN MASEFIELD

It's a warm wind, the west wind, full of birds' cries;
I never hear the west wind but tears are in my eyes.
For it comes from the west lands, the old brown hills,
And April's in the west wind, and daffodils.

It's a fine land, the west land, for hearts as tired as mine,
Apple orchards blossom there, and the air's like wine.
There is cool green grass there, where men may lie at rest,
And the thrushes are in song there, fluting from the nest.

"Will you not come home, brother? you have been long away,
It's April, and blossom time, and white is the spray;
And bright is the sun, brother, and warm is the rain,—
Will you not come home, brother, home to us again?

"The young corn is green, brother, where the rabbits run,
It's blue sky, and white clouds, and warm rain and sun.
It's song to a man's soul, brother, fire to a man's brain,
To hear the wild bees and see the merry spring again.

"Larks are singing in the west, brother, above the green wheat,
So will ye not come home, brother, and rest your tired feet?
I've a balm for bruised hearts, brother, sleep for aching eyes,"
Says the warm wind, the west wind, full of birds' cries.

It's the white road westwards is the road I must tread
To the green grass, the cool grass, and rest for heart and head,
To the violets and the brown brooks and the thrushes' song,
In the fine land, the west land, the land where I belong.

The Wind

ROBERT LOUIS STEVENSON

I saw you toss the kites on high
And blow the birds about the sky;
And all around I heard you pass,
Like ladies' skirts across the grass—
    O wind, a-blowing all day long,
    O wind, that sings so loud a song!

I saw the different things you did,
But always you yourself you hid.
I felt you push, I heard you call,
I could not see yourself at all—
    O wind, a-blowing all day long,
    O wind, that sings so loud a song!

O you that are so strong and cold,
O blower, are you young or old?
Are you a beast of field and tree,
Or just a stronger child than me?
    O wind, a-blowing all day long,
    O wind, that sings so loud a song!

Clouds

CHRISTINA ROSSETTI

White sheep, white sheep,
On a blue hill,
When the wind stops
You all stand still
When the wind blows
You walk away slow.
White sheep, white sheep,
Where do you go?

Laughing Song

WILLIAM BLAKE

When the green woods laugh with the voice of joy,
And the dimpling stream runs laughing by;
When the air does laugh with our merry wit,
And the green hill laughs with the noise of it;

When the meadows laugh with lively green,
And the grasshopper laughs in the merry scene,
When Mary and Susan and Emily
With their sweet round mouth sing "Ha, Ha, He!"

When the painted birds laugh in the shade,
Where our table with cherries and nuts is spread,
Come live and be merry, and join with me,
To sing the sweet chorus of "Ha, Ha, He!"

The Rhodora

(*On being asked whence is the flower*)

RALPH WALDO EMERSON

In May, when sea-winds pierced our solitudes,
I found the fresh Rhodora in the woods,
Spreading its leafless blooms in a damp nook,
To please the desert and the sluggish brook.
The purple petals, fallen in the pool,
Made the black water with their beauty gay;
Here might the red-bird come his plumes to cool,
And court the flower that cheapens his array.
Rhodora! if the sages ask thee why
This charm is wasted on the earth and sky,
Tell them, dear, that if eyes were made for seeing,
Then Beauty is its own excuse for being.
Why thou wert there, O rival of the rose!
I never thought to ask, I never knew:
But, in my simple ignorance, suppose
The self-same Power that brought me there brought you.

What Is the Grass?

WALT WHITMAN

A child said *What is the grass?* fetching it to me
    with full hands;
How could I answer the child? I do not know what it is
    any more than he.

I guess it must be the flag of my disposition, out of
    hopeful green stuff woven.
Or I guess it is the handkerchief of the Lord,
A scented gift and remembrancer designedly dropt,
Bearing the owner's name some way in the corners, that
    we may see and remark, and say *Whose?* . . .
I believe a leaf of grass is no less than the journey-work
    of the stars,
And the pismire is equally perfect, and a grain of sand,
    and the egg of the wren,
And the tree-toad is a chef-d'œuvre for the highest,
And the running blackberry would adorn the
    parlors of heaven,
And the narrowest hinge in my hand puts to
    scorn all machinery,
And the cow crunching with depress'd head
    surpasses any statue,
And a mouse is miracle enough to stagger
    sextillions of infidels.

Pismire—ant.

The Year

COVENTRY PATMORE

The crocus, while the days are dark,
    Unfolds its saffron sheen;
At April's touch, the crudest bark
    Discovers gems of green.

Then sleep the seasons, full of might;
    While slowly swells the pod
And rounds the peach, and in the night
    The mushroom bursts the sod.

The winter comes: the frozen rut
    Is bound with silver bars;
The snow-drift heaps against the hut;
    And night is pierced with stars.

ALTHOUGH THE FOLLOWING POEM is a song that reflects a yearning for something not of this world, it nonetheless reflects a recognition of the mystery and wonder of creation.

To Jane

PERCY BYSSHE SHELLEY

I

The keen stars were twinkling,
And the fair moon was rising among them,
    Dear Jane!
The guitar was twinkling,
But the notes were not sweet till you sung them
    Again.

As the moon's soft splendour
O'er the faint cold starlight of Heaven
   Is thrown,
  So your voice most tender
To the strings without soul had then given
   Its own.

III

The stars will awaken,
Though the moon sleep a full hour later,
   To-night;
  No leaf will be shaken
Whilst the dews of your melody scatter
   Delight.

Though the sound overpowers,
Sing again, with your dear voice revealing
   A tone
Of some world far from ours,
Where music and moonlight and feeling
   Are one.

The First Dandelion

WALT WHITMAN

Simple and fresh and fair from winter's close emerging
As if no artifice of fashion, business, politics, had ever been,
Forth from its sunny nook of shelter'd grass—innocent, golden,
    calm as the dawn,
The spring's first dandelion shows its trustful face.

Single Majesty

MARK VAN DOREN

Behold him, that great solitary
Tree in the forgotten field.
Fences, falling, left him long ago
To lord it, and does,
That archer,
That great reacher oak,
That master of this meadow, bent
By nothing but strong wind.
No fellow crowds him,
Nothing but the sun on all sides
Shapes him—oh, so full
That crown, as if no other lord
Lived anywhere, no grass
But waited for his shadow,
No birds were
But his.
Behold him and forget him if you can,
That king
Of this lost meadow.

My Heart Leaps Up

WILLIAM WORDSWORTH

My heart leaps up when I behold
    A rainbow in the sky;
So was it when my life began,
So is it now I am a man,
So be it when I shall grow old,
    Or let me die!
The Child is father of the Man;
And I could wish my days to be
Bound each to each by natural piety.

Baby Seeds

ANONYMOUS

In a milkweed cradle,
Snug and warm,
Baby seeds are hiding,
Safe from harm.
Open wide the cradle,
Hold it high!
Come Mr. Wind,
Help them fly.

129

Leisure

W. H. DAVIES

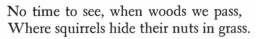

What is this life if, full of care,
We have no time to stand and stare?

No time to stand beneath the boughs
And stare as long as sheep or cows.

No time to see, when woods we pass,
Where squirrels hide their nuts in grass.

No time to see, in broad daylight,
Streams full of stars, like skies at night.

No time to turn at Beauty's glance,
And watch her feet, how they can dance.

No time to wait till her mouth can
Enrich that smile her eyes began.

A poor life this if, full of care,
We have no time to stand and stare.

Pied Beauty

GERARD MANLEY HOPKINS

Glory be to God for dappled things—
    For skies of couple-colour as a brinded cow;
        For rose-moles all in stipple upon trout that swim;
Fresh-firecoal chestnut-falls; finches' wings;
    Landscape plotted and pieced—fold, fallow, and plough;
        And áll trádes, their gear and tackle and trim.

All things counter, original, spare, strange;
    Whatever is fickle, freckled (who knows how?)
        With swift, slow; sweet, sour; adazzle, dim;
He fathers-forth whose beauty is past change:
                Praise him.

IN HIS FREELY CADENCED POEM "Moment of Visitation," the contemporary poet Gustav Davidson laments the passing of the "thousand things of marvel and delight" that called to him in his youth. He also speaks of the wonder that may seize you upon the instant, and warns that to be unaware of its presence at "the moment of visitation" is to lose its wonder forever.

Moment of Visitation

GUSTAV DAVIDSON

There are sounds within this sound
too delicate for apprehending,
voices I shall never hear
though others hear them.

Many things of the thousand things
of marvel and delight
that called to the senses when
as a youth
I rode down the morning of the world—
these
are now forever denied me.

To walk a road
and not to name the trees
branching over me,
nor the oriole on the wing,
nor
the fish flashing in the stream;

or
to enter a house
and be unarmed with sight
and compassion.

Oh that I had had
wisdom
at the beginning,
since there is no going back.

Wonder
is an instantaneous thing,
like love,
which suddenly seizes you,
or like conversion.

To be late,
to stand unaware
at the moment of visitation,
that
is to be forever lost.

Give Me the Splendid Silent Sun

WALT WHITMAN

Give me the splendid silent sun with all its beams full-dazzling,
Give me juicy autumnal fruit ripe and red from the orchard,
Give me a field where the unmowed grass grows,
Give me an arbor, give me the trellised grape,
Give me fresh corn and wheat, give me serene-moving animals
    teaching content.
Give me nights perfectly quiet as on high plateaus west of the
    Mississippi, and I am looking up at the stars,
Give me odorous at sunrise a garden of beautiful flowers where I
    can walk undisturbed.

Meditation

THOMAS TRAHERNE

Certainly Adam in Paradise had not more sweet
and curious apprehensions of the world than I
    when I was a child.
Heaven and earth did sing my Creator's praises,
and could not make more melody to Adam
    than to me.
The green trees when I saw them first through
one of the gates transported and ravished me.
Boys and girls tumbling in the street were
    moving jewels.

132

A Thing of Beauty

JOHN KEATS

A thing of beauty is a joy forever:
Its loveliness increases; it will never
Pass into nothingness; but still will keep
A bower quiet for us, and a sleep
Full of sweet dreams, and health, and quiet breathing.
Therefore, on every morrow, are we wreathing
A flowery band to bind us to the earth,
Spite of despondence, of the inhuman dearth
Of noble natures, of the gloomy days,
Of all the unhealthy and o'er-darkened ways
Made for our searching: yes, in spite of all,
Some shape of beauty moves away the pall
From our dark spirits. Such the sun, the moon,
Trees old, and young, sprouting a shady boon
For simple sheep; and such are daffodils
With the green world they live in; and clear rills
That for themselves a cooling covert make
'Gainst the hot season; the mid forest brake,
Rich with a sprinkling of fair musk-rose blooms:
And such too is the grandeur of the dooms
We have imagined for the mighty dead;
All lovely tales that we have heard or read:
An endless fountain of immortal drink,
Pour unto us from the heaven's brink.

Nor do we merely feel these essences
For one short hour; no, even as the trees
That whisper round a temple become soon
Dear as the temple's self, so does the moon,
The passion poesy, glories infinite,
Haunt us till they become a cheering light
Unto our souls, and bound to us so fast,
That, whether there be shine, or gloom o'ercast,
They always must be with us, or we die.

Miniatures

"I THINK NO VIRTUE GOES WITH SIZE," said Ralph Waldo Emerson, observing the little titmouse. Ben Jonson was not taken in by size either. In one poem he says that man is not any more worthy for growing in bulk like a tree. Hugeness for the sake of hugeness is not necessarily a virtue, and may be a defect:

> In small proportions we just beauties see;
> And in short measures, life may perfect be.

135

The Chair

THEODORE ROETHKE

A funny thing about a Chair:
You hardly ever think it's *there*.
To know a Chair is really it,
You sometimes have to go and sit.

A Centipede Was Happy Quite

ANONYMOUS

A centipede was happy quite,
    Until a frog in fun
Said, "Pray, which leg comes after which?"
This raised her mind to such a pitch,
She lay distracted in the ditch
    Considering how to run.

The Rain

ANONYMOUS

The rain it raineth every day,
  Upon the just and unjust fella,
But more upon the just, because
  The unjust hath the just's umbrella.

If

ANONYMOUS

If all the land were apple-pie,
And all the sea were ink;
And all the trees were bread and cheese,
What should we do for drink?

Epigram

ENGRAVED ON THE COLLAR OF A DOG
WHICH I GAVE TO HIS ROYAL HIGHNESS

ALEXANDER POPE

I am his Highness' dog at Kew;
Pray tell me, sir, whose dog are you?

Epitaph

ANONYMOUS

This is the grave of Mike O'Day
Who died maintaining his right of way.
His right was clear, his will was strong,
But he's just as dead as if he'd been wrong.

Suffolk Epitaph

ANONYMOUS

Stranger pass by and waste no time
On bad biography and careless rhyme.
For what I am, this humble dust encloses;
For what I was is no affair of yourses.

Epigram

ALEXANDER POPE

Sir, I admit your general rule,
That every poet is a fool,
But you yourself may serve to show it,
That every fool is not a poet.

You Fancy Wit

ALEXANDER POPE

You beat your pate, and fancy wit will come.
Knock as you please,—there's nobody at home.

Epitaph Intended for Sir Isaac Newton

ALEXANDER POPE

Nature and Nature's laws lay hid in night:
God said, Let Newton be! and all was light.

Riddle

ANONYMOUS

What shoemaker makes shoes without leather,
With all the four elements put together?
Fire and water, earth and air;
Ev'ry customer has two pair.

Answer: ɹǝoɥs-ǝsɹoɥ ∀

Riddle

ANONYMOUS

In marble halls as white as milk,
Lined with a skin as soft as silk,
Within a fountain crystal-clear,
A golden apple doth appear.
No doors there are to this stronghold,
Yet thieves break in and steal the gold.

Answer: ᵷᵷǝ u∀

An Epitaph and a Reply

ANONYMOUS

Remember man that passeth by,
As thou art now so once was I;
And as I so must thou be;
Prepare thyself to follow me.
　　On a grave, Linton, England, 1825.

Under this inscription someone wrote:

To follow you is not my intent,
Unless I know which way you went.

What Can't Be Cured

ANONYMOUS

What can't be cured
Must be endured.

In the Dumps

ANONYMOUS

We're all in the dumps,
For diamonds are trumps;
The kittens are gone to St. Paul's!
The babies are bit,
The moon's in a fit,
And the houses are built without walls.

A Man in the Wilderness

ANONYMOUS

A man in the wilderness asked me,
How many strawberries grow in the sea?
I answered him, as I thought good,
As many as red herrings grow in the wood.

The Giant Fisherman

W. KING

His angle-rod made of a sturdy oak;
His line a cable which in storms ne'er broke;
His hook he baited with a dragon's tail,
And sat upon a rock, and bobbed for whale.

The Hands of Toil

JAMES RUSSELL LOWELL

No man is born into the world whose work
Is not born with him; there is always work,
And tools to work withal, for those who will;
And blessed are the horny hands of toil.

Man Is a Fool

ANONYMOUS

As a rule, man is a fool,
When it's hot, he wants it cool;
When it's cool, he wants it hot,
Always wanting what is not.

For Want of a Nail

ANONYMOUS

For want of a nail, the shoe was lost,
For want of a shoe, the horse was lost,
For want of a horse, the rider was lost,
For want of a rider, the battle was lost,
For want of a battle, the kingdom was lost.
And all for the want of a horseshoe nail.

Work Is Love

ANONYMOUS

Work is love made visible.
And if you cannot work with love
But only with distaste, it is better
That you should leave your work and
Sit at the gate of the temple and take
Alms from those who work with joy.

Jolly Red Nose

FRANCIS BEAUMONT AND JOHN FLETCHER

Nose, nose, jolly red nose,
And who gave thee this jolly red nose?
Nutmegs and ginger, cinnamon and cloves,
And they gave me this jolly red nose.

The Human Heart

WILLIAM WORDSWORTH

Thanks to the human heart by which we live,
Thanks to its tenderness, its joys, and fears,
To me the meanest flower that blows can giv
Thoughts that do often lie too deep for tears.

After Many a Summer

ALFRED, LORD TENNYSON

The woods decay, the woods decay and fall,
The vapours weep their burden to the ground;
Man comes and tills the field and lies beneath,
And after many a summer dies the swan.

The Man of Thessaly

ANONYMOUS

There was a Man of Thessaly,
  And he was wondrous wise:
He jumped into a brier hedge
  And scratched out both his eyes.
But when he saw his eyes were out,
  With all his might and main
He jumped into another hedge
  And scratched them in again.

I Met a Man

ANONYMOUS

As I was going up the stair
I met a man who wasn't there.
He wasn't there again today—
Oh! how I wish he'd go away!

Music

THE POWER THAT LIES IN MUSIC has long been recognized, perhaps most strongly by the ancient Greeks, who had tales and legends of the bard Orpheus. Orpheus, accompanying himself on a lyre, could sing so sweetly that he charmed not only men and beasts but also stones and trees— and on one occasion he charmed a river right out of its course. The Greeks also had the god Pan, who set men to dancing with the wisps of song he blew through his reed pipe. In the Old Testament, the power of song is recognized in the person of King David, who was extraordinarily gifted on the harp. Whatever the instrument, man has always made music to express his joy or to lessen some grief of his heart.

An ENTRY IN ONE of the journals of the American philosopher Henry David Thoreau, dated June 27, 1847, speaks of the "clink of the smith's hammer . . . the farmer is ploughing, the craftsmen are busy in their shops, the trader stands up in the counter, and all works go steadily forward." Walt Whitman, in the following excerpt, not only depicts a nation busily at work, but sets that nation to music.

I Hear America Singing

WALT WHITMAN

I hear America singing, the varied carols I hear;
Those of mechanics—each one singing his, as it should be,
    blithe and strong;
The carpenter singing his, as he measures his plank or beam,
The mason singing his, as he makes ready for work, or
    leaves off work;
The boatman singing what belongs to him in his boat—the deck-
    hand singing on the steamboat deck;
The shoemaker singing as he sits on his bench—the hatter singing
    as he stands;
The wood-cutter's song—the ploughboy's, on his way in the morning,
    or at the noon intermission, or at sundown;
The delicious singing of the mother—or of the young wife at
    work—or of the girl sewing or washing;
Each singing what belongs to him or her, and to none else;
The day what belongs to the day—at night, the party of young
    fellows, robust, friendly.
Singing, with open mouths, their strong melodious songs.

The Crow Doth Sing

WILLIAM SHAKESPEARE

The crow doth sing as sweetly as the lark
When neither is attended, and I think
The nightingale, if she should sing by day,
When every goose is cackling, would be thought
No better a musician than the wren.
How many things by season season'd are
To their right praise and true perfection!

Music

WILLIAM SHAKESPEARE

Orpheus with his lute made trees
   And the mountain-tops that freeze
Bow themselves when he did sing.
   To his music plants and flowers
Ever sprung: as sun and showers
   There had made a lasting spring.

Everything that heard him play,
   Even the billows of the sea,
Hung their heads, and then lay by.
   In sweet music is such art,
Killing care and grief of heart
   Fall asleep, or, hearing, die.

Ode

ARTHUR O'SHAUGHNESSY

We are the music-makers
   And we are the dreamers of dreams,
Wandering by lone sea-breakers,
   And sitting by desolate streams;—
World-losers and world-forsakers,
   On whom the pale moon gleams:
Yet we are the movers and shakers
   Of the world for ever, it seems.

With wonderful deathless ditties
   We build up the world's great cities,
And out of a fabulous story
   We fashion an empire's glory:
One man with a dream, at pleasure,
   Shall go forth and conquer a crown;
And three with a new song's measure
   Can trample an empire down.

We, in the ages lying
   In the buried past of the earth,
Built Nineveh with our sighing,
   And Babel itself with our mirth;
And o'erthrew them with prophesying,
   To the old of the new world's worth;
For each age is a dream that is dying,
   Or one that is coming to birth.

A Song of Enchantment

WALTER DE LA MARE

A song of Enchantment I sang me there,
In a green-green wood, by waters fair,
Just as the words came up to me
I sang it under the wild wood tree.

Widdershins turned I, singing it low,
Watching the wild birds come and go;
No cloud in the deep dark blue to be seen
Under the thick-thatched branches green.

Twilight came: silence came:
The planet of Evening's silver flame;
By darkening paths I wandered through
Thickets trembling with drops of dew.

But the music is lost and the words are gone
Of the song I sang as I sat alone,
Ages and ages have fallen on me—
On the wood and the pool and the elder tree.

Widdershins—in a counterclockwise direction.

146

Song's Eternity

JOHN CLARE

What is song's eternity?
  Come and see.
Can it noise and bustle be?
  Come and see.
Praises sung or praises said
  Can it be?
Wait awhile and these are dead—
  Sigh—sigh;
Be they high or lowly bred
  They die.

What is song's eternity?
  Come and see.
Melodies of earth and sky,
  Here they be.
Song once sung to Adam's ears
  Can it be?
Ballads of six thousand years
  Thrive, thrive;
Songs awaken with the spheres
  Alive.

Mighty songs that miss decay,
  What are they?
Crowds and cities pass away
  Like a day.
Books are out and books are read;
  What are they?
Years will lay them with the dead—
  Sigh, sigh;
Trifles unto nothing wed,
  They die.

Dreamers, mark the honey bee;
  Mark the tree
Where the blue cap 'tootle tee'
  Sings a glee
Sung to Adam and to Eve—
  Here they be.
When floods covered every bough,
  Noah's ark
Heard that ballad singing now;
  Hark, hark,

'Tootle tootle tootle tee'—
  Can it be
Pride and fame must shadows be?
  Come and see—
Every season own her own;
  Bird and bee
Sing creation's music on;
  Nature's glee
Is in every mood and tone
  Eternity.

IT IS DIFFICULT TO EXPLAIN why certain words when placed in a particular order have the power to affect us as they do. Some words delight us, some move us to tears, some make us laugh, and others hold us as in a trance. Consider the line: "The horns of Elfland faintly blowing." There is the music of the melodious letter "l" several times repeated. In "Bugle Song," Tennyson communicates a sense of splendor and glory by the kinds of words he chooses and the order in which they march and sing across the page.

Bugle Song

ALFRED, LORD TENNYSON

The splendor falls on castle walls
   And snowy summits old in story;
The long light shakes across the lakes,
   And the wild cataract leaps in glory.
Blow, bugle, blow, set the wild echoes flying,
Blow, bugle; answer, echoes, dying, dying, dying.

O, hark, O, hear! how thin and clear,
   And thinner, clearer, farther going!
O, sweet and far from cliff and scar
   The horns of Elfland faintly blowing!
Blow, let us hear the purple glens replying;
Blow, bugle; answer, echoes, dying, dying, dying.

O love, they die in yon rich sky,
   They faint on hill or field or river;
Our echoes roll from soul to soul,
   And grow for ever and for ever.
Blow, bugle, blow, set the wild echoes flying,
And answer, echoes, answer, dying, dying, dying.

CHARLES ANGOFF, novelist and poet, has distinguished himself in a number of other fields: as teacher, critic, editor, essayist, and biographer. From *The Bell of Time* (one of his several books of verse) here is his "Song For Boys and Girls," in which the mood is joyous and wistful by turns, even as the dance of life alternates between grave and gay.

Song for Boys and Girls

CHARLES ANGOFF

Gather round
And look around.
Time is gay
Night and day.

Whirl and sigh,
Madly, softly.
There is yet time
To learn
To cry.

What is sealed
And broken
Can never
be healed.

Make your vows
Gently,
Give your kisses
Slowly.

Space is for love
Here and everywhere.
Sorrow is
Far away.

Whirl round
And round.
This yearning
Has no ending.

The Rivals

JAMES STEPHENS

I heard a bird at dawn
Singing sweetly on a tree,
That the dew was on the lawn,
And the wind was on the lea;
But I didn't listen to him,
For he didn't sing to me!

I didn't listen to him,
For he didn't sing to me
That the dew was on the lawn,
And the wind was on the lea!
I was singing at the time,
Just as prettily as he!

I was singing all the time,
Just as prettily as he,
About the dew upon the lawn,
And the wind upon the lea!
So I didn't listen to him,
As he sang upon a tree!

A Swing Song

WILLIAM ALLINGHAM

Swing, swing,
Sing, sing
Here's my throne, and I am a King!
Swing, sing,
Swing, sing,
Farewell earth, for I'm on the wing!

Low, high,
Here I fly,
Like a bird through sunny sky;
Free, free
Over the lea,
Over the mountain, over the sea!

Up, down,
Up and down,
Which is the way to London Town?
Where, where?
Up in the air,
Close your eyes, and now you are there!

Soon, soon,
Afternoon,
Over the sunset, over the moon;
Far, far
Over all bar,
Sweeping on from star to star!

No, no,
Low, low,
Sweeping daisies with my toe.
Slow, slow,
To and fro,
Slow——
　　slow——
　　　　slow——
　　　　　　slow.

Look at Six Eggs

CARL SANDBURG

Look at six eggs
In a mockingbird's nest.

Listen to six mockingbirds
Flinging follies of O-be-joyful
Over the marshes and uplands.

Look at songs
Hidden in eggs.

THE POETIC CHARACTER, wrote John Keats in a letter, "lives in gusto, be it foul or fair, high or low, rich or poor, mean or elevated." In other words, the poetic imagination finds delight everywhere. Emerson, too, finds that not only in beautiful things such as birds, roses, or rainbows is there music, but even "in the darkest, meanest things."

Music

RALPH WALDO EMERSON

Let me go where'er I will,
I hear a sky-born music still:
It sounds from all things old,
It sounds from all things young,
From all that's fair, from all that's foul,
Peals out a cheerful song.

It is not only in the rose,
It is not only in the bird,
Not only where the rainbow glows,
Nor in the song of woman heard,
But in the darkest, meanest things
There alway, alway something sings.

'T is not in the high stars alone,
Nor in the cup of budding flowers,
Nor in the redbreast's mellow tone,
Nor in the bow that smiles in showers,
But in the mud and scum of things
There alway, alway something sings.

There's Music in a Hammer

ANONYMOUS

There's music in a hammer,
There's music in a nail,
There's music in a pussy cat,
When you step upon her tail.

Song in the Songless

GEORGE MEREDITH

They have no song, the sedges dry,
   And still they sing.
It is within my breast they sing,
   As I pass by.
Within my breast they touch a string,
   They wake a sigh.
There is but sound of sedges dry;
   In me they sing.

151

The Song of Hiawatha

HENRY WADSWORTH LONGFELLOW

Should you ask me, whence these stories?
Whence these legends and traditions,
With the odors of the forest,
With the dew and damp of meadows,
With the curling smoke of wigwams,
With the rushing of great rivers,
With their frequent repetitions,
And their wild reverberations,
As of thunder in the mountains?
I should answer, I should tell you,

"From the forests and the prairies,
From the great lakes of the Northland,
From the land of the Ojibways,
From the land of the Dacotahs,
From the mountains, moors, and fen-lands
Where the heron, the Shuh-shuh-gah,
Feeds among the reeds and rushes.
I repeat them as I heard them
From the lips of Nawadaha,
The musician, the sweet singer."
    Should you ask where Nawadaha
Found these songs so wild and wayward,
Found these legends and traditions,
I should answer, I should tell you,
"In the bird's-nests of the forest,

In the lodges of the beaver,
In the hoof-prints of the bison,
In the eyry of the eagle!
    "All the wild-fowl sang them to him,
In the moorlands and the fen-lands,
In the melancholy marshes;
Chetowaik, the plover, sang them,
Mahng, the loon, the wild-goose, Wawa,
The blue heron, the Shuh-shuh-gah,
And the grouse, the Mushkodasa!"
    If still further you should ask me,
Saying, "Who was Nawadaha?
Tell us of this Nawadaha,"
I should answer your inquiries
Straightway in such words as follow.

    "In the vale of Tawasentha,
In the green and silent valley,
By the pleasant water-courses,
Dwelt the singer Nawadaha.
Round about the Indian village
Spread the meadows and the cornfields,
And beyond them stood the forest,
Stood the groves of singing pinetrees,
Green in Summer, white in Winter,
Ever sighing, ever singing.
    "And the pleasant water-courses,

You could trace them through the valley,
By the rushing in the Spring-time,
By the alders in the Summer,
By the white fog in the Autumn,
By the black line in the Winter;
And beside them dwelt the singer,
In the vale of Tawasentha,
In the green and silent valley.
　　"There he sang of Hiawatha,
Sang the Song of Hiawatha,
Sang his wondrous birth and being,
How he prayed and how he fasted,
How he lived, and toiled, and suffered,
That the tribes of men might prosper,
That he might advance his people!"
　　Ye who love the haunts of Nature,
Love the sunshine of the meadow,
Love the shadow of the forest,

Love the wind among the branches,
And the rain-shower and the snowstorm,
And the rushing of great rivers
Through their palisades of pinetrees,
And the thunder in the mountains,
Whose innumerable echoes
Flap like eagles in their eyries;—
Listen to these wild traditions,
To this Song of Hiawatha!
　　Ye who love a nation's legends,
Love the ballads of a people,
That like voices from afar off
Call to us to pause and listen,
Speak in tones so plain and childlike,
Scarcely can the ear distinguish
Whether they are sung or spoken;—
Listen to this Indian Legend,
To this Song of Hiawatha!

Lean Out of the Window

JAMES JOYCE

Lean out of the window,
　　Goldenhair,
I heard you singing
　　A merry air.

My book was closed;
　　I read no more,
Watching the fire dance
　　On the floor.

I have left my book,
　　I have left my room,
For I heard you singing
　　Through the gloom.

Singing and singing
　　A merry air,
Lean out of the window,
　　Goldenhair.

A Time for Singing

GUSTAV DAVIDSON

It matters not what star I follow
Or what high purposes I plead;
Here is a flashing, notch-tailed swallow,
And a thrush to heed.

Spring is enough for any fellow
With senses tuned and heart upspringing;
Here's April, gay in green and yellow,
And a time for singing

IN SHAKESPEARE's *The Merchant of Venice*, there appear these lines:

The man that hath no music in himself
Nor is not moved with concord of sweet sounds
Is fit for treasons, stratagems, and spoils. . . .

Whether the songs he used in his plays were of sorrow or joy, Shakespeare was aware of the effect that music had upon his audiences. As a result, his plays were as graced with songs as a summer meadow is with flowers. These songs upon the bare page, and without benefit of the composer's score, still carry the lilt and lift of their own music.

Ariel's Song

WILLIAM SHAKESPEARE

Come unto these yellow sands,
  And then take hands:
Curtsied when you have, and kiss'd—
  The wild waves whist;
Foot it featly here and there;
And, sweet sprites, the burthen bear.
  Hark, hark!
        Bow-wow.
  The watch-dogs bark:
        Bow-wow.
Hark, hark! I hear
The strain of strutting chanticleer
Cry, Cock-a-diddle-dow.

Song

WILLIAM SHAKESPEARE

Tell me where is fancy bred,
Or in the heart or in the head?
How begot, how nourished?
    Reply, reply.
  It is engendered in the eyes,
  With gazing fed; and fancy dies
In the cradle where it lies.
    Let us all ring fancy's knell:
    I'll begin it,—Ding, dong, bell.

Under the Greenwood Tree

WILLIAM SHAKESPEARE

Under the greenwood tree
Who loves to lie with me,
And turn his merry note
Unto the sweet bird's throat,
Come hither, come hither, come hither:
    Here shall he see
    No enemy
But winter and rough weather.

155

Merry Are the Bells

ANONYMOUS

Merry are the bells, and merry would they ring,
  Merry was myself, and merry would I sing;
With a merry ding-dong, happy, gay and free,
  And a merry sing-song, happy let us be.

Waddle goes your gait, and hollow are your hose;
  Noddle goes your pate, and purple is your nose;
Merry is your sing-song, happy, gay and free;
  With a merry ding-dong, happy let us be.

Merry have we met, and merry have we been;
  Merry let us part, and merry meet again;
With a merry sing-song, happy, gay and free;
  With a merry ding-dong, happy let us be.

Song

JOHN FLETCHER

Do not fear to put thy feet
Naked in the river sweet;
Think not leech, or newt, or toad.
Will bite thy foot, when thou hast trod:
Nor let the water rising high,
As thou wad'st in, make thee cry
And sob; but ever live with me,
And not a wave shall trouble thee!

Choric Song

ALFRED, LORD TENNYSON

There is sweet music here that softer falls
Than petals from blown roses on the grass,
Or night-dews on still waters between walls
Of shadowy granite, in a gleaming pass;
Music that gentlier on the spirit lies,
Than tired eyelids upon tired eyes;
Music that brings sweet sleep down from the blissful skies.
Here are cool mosses deep,
And thro' the moss the ivies creep,
And in the stream the long-leaved flowers weep,
And from the craggy ledge the poppy hangs in sleep.

Afton Water

ROBERT BURNS

Flow gently, sweet Afton, among thy green braes,
Flow gently, I'll sing thee a song in thy praise;
My Mary's asleep by thy murmuring stream,
Flow gently, sweet Afton, disturb not her dream.

Thou stock-dove whose echo resounds thro' the glen,
Ye wild whistling blackbirds in yon thorny den,
Thou green-crested lapwing, thy screaming forbear,
I charge you disturb not my slumbering fair.

How lofty, sweet Afton, thy neighboring hills,
Far mark'd with the courses of clear, winding rills;
There daily I wander as noon rises high,
My flocks and my Mary's sweet cot in my eye.

How pleasant thy banks and green valleys below,
Where wild in the woodlands the primroses blow;
There oft as mild ev'ning weeps over the lea,
The sweet-scented birk shades my Mary and me.

Thy crystal stream, Afton, how lovely it glides,
And winds by the cot where my Mary resides;
How wanton thy waters her snowy feet lave,
As gathering sweet flow'ret she stems thy clear wave.

Flow gently, sweet Afton, among thy green braes,
Flow gently, sweet river, the theme of my lays;
My Mary's asleep by thy murmuring stream,
Flow gently, sweet Afton, disturb not her dream.

Cot—cottage. Birk—birch. Lave—wash.

It is told that when King Saul was troubled by moods of melancholy, David played for him on the harp and comforted him with song. Such is the power of sweet sounds that one famous English poet, Robert Herrick, called upon music to melt his pain and help him over an illness.

To Music to Becalm His Fever

ROBERT HERRICK

Charm me asleep, and melt me so
  With thy delicious numbers,
That being ravished, hence I go
  Away in easy slumbers.
    Ease my sick head,
    And make my bed,
Thou power that canst sever
    From me this ill,
    And quickly still,
    Though thou not kill
      My fever.

Fall on me like a silent dew,
  Or like those maiden showers
Which, by peep of day, do strew
  A baptism o'er the flowers.
    Melt, melt my pains
    With thy soft strains,
That, having ease me given,
    With full delight
    I leave this light,
    And take my flight
      For Heaven.

KING DAVID, the enraptured psalmist and poet, would praise the Lord not only with poems but also with musical instruments, and with dancing.

Psalm 150

THE BIBLE

Praise ye the Lord.

Praise God in his sanctuary,
Praise him in the firmament of his power.

Praise him for his mighty acts,
Praise him according to his excellent greatness.

Praise him with the sound of the trumpet,
Praise him with the psaltery and harp.

Praise him with the timbrel and dance,
Praise him with stringed instruments and organs

Praise him upon the loud cymbals,
Praise him upon the high sounding cymbals.

Let every thing that hath breath praise the Lord
Praise ye the Lord.

The Flowers That Bloom in the Spring

W. S. GILBERT

The flowers that bloom in the spring,
      Tra la
Breathe promise of merry sunshine—
As we merrily dance and we sing,
      Tra la,
We welcome the hope that they bring,
      Tra la,
Of a summer of roses and wine.
    And that's what we mean when we say that a thing
    Is welcome as flowers that bloom in the spring.

THERE IS MUSIC in the sound of the human voice, as Longfellow points out in this poem, which helps underline the pleasure that can come from reading poetry out loud. Even when read to oneself, this poem retains a mysterious musical lilt.

The Day Is Done

HENRY WADSWORTH LONGFELLOW

The day is done, and the darkness
  Falls from the wings of Night,
As a feather is wafted downward
  From an eagle in his flight.

I see the lights of the village
  Gleam through the rain and the mist,
And a feeling of sadness comes o'er me
  That my soul cannot resist:

A feeling of sadness and longing,
  That is not akin to pain,
And resembles sorrow only
  As the mist resembles rain.

Come, read to me some poem,
  Some simple and heartfelt lay,
That shall soothe this restless feeling,
  And banish the thoughts of day.

Not from the grand old masters,
  Not from the bards sublime,
Whose distant footsteps echo
  Through the corridors of Time.

For, like strains of martial music,
  Their mighty thoughts suggest
Life's endless toil and endeavor;
  And tonight I long for rest.

Read from some humbler poet,
  Whose songs gushed from his heart,
As showers from the clouds of summer,
  Or tears from the eyelids start;

Who, through long days of labor,
  And nights devoid of ease,
Still heard in his soul the music
  Of wonderful melodies.

Such songs have power to quiet
  The restless pulse of care,
And come like the benediction
  That follows after prayer.

Then read from the treasured volume
  The poem of thy choice,
And lend to the rhyme of the poet
  The beauty of thy voice.

And the night shall be filled with music,
  And the cares, that infest the day,
Shall fold their tents, like the Arabs,
  And as silently steal away.

Neither Spirit nor Bird

MARY AUSTIN

Neither spirit nor bird;
That was my flute you heard
Last night by the river.
When you came with your wicker jar
Where the river drags the willows,
That was my flute you heard,
Wacoba, Wacoba,
Calling, Come to the willows!

Neither the wind nor a bird
Rustled the lupine blooms.
That was my blood you heard
Answer your garment's hem
Whispering through the grasses;
That was my blood you heard
By the wild rose under the willows.

That was no beast that stirred,
That was my heart you heard,
Pacing to and fro
In the ambush of my desire,
To the music my flute let fall.
Wacoba, Wacoba,
That was my heart you heard
Leaping under the willows.

I, Too

LANGSTON HUGHES

I, too, sing America.

I am the darker brother.
They send me to eat in the kitchen
When company comes,
But I laugh,
And eat well,
And grow strong.

Tomorrow,
I'll sit at the table
When company comes.
Nobody'll dare
Say to me,
"Eat in the kitchen,"
Then.

Besides,
They'll see how beautiful I am
And be ashamed—

I, too, am America.

161

Nonsense!

I N NONSENSE VERSE, either preposterous words are used in logical ways, or perfectly sensible words are used in preposterous ways. Occasionally the two are combined. One of the great masters of nonsense was Lewis Carroll, whose "Jabberwocky" tells its adventurous tale in meaningless words, and whose "Ways and Means" uses perfectly standard words put together in a highly original way. Carroll stands with W. S. Gilbert and Edward Lear as the three kings of nonsense. This section closes with a selection of that special verse form, the limerick. Not all of these limericks are nonsensical, but most are at least pretty far-fetched.

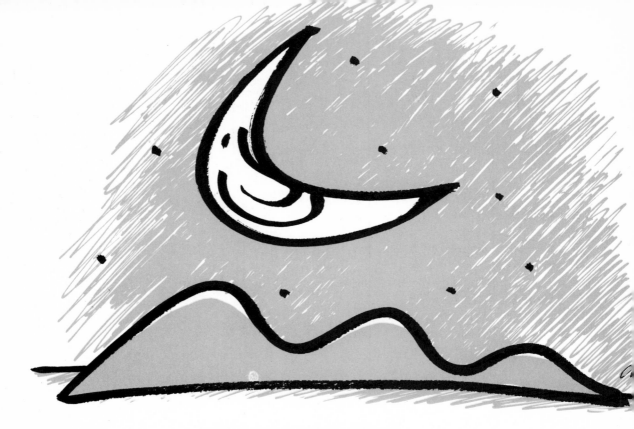

The Moon Is Up

ANONYMOUS

The moon is up, the moon is up!
    The larks begin to fly,
    And, like a drowsy buttercup,
    Dark Phœbus skims the sky,
The elephant, with cheerful voice,
    Sings blithely on the spray;
The bats and beetles all rejoice,
    Then let me, too, be gay.

I would I were a porcupine,
    And wore a peacock's tail;
To-morrow, if the moon but shine,
    Perchance I'll be a whale.
Then let me, like the cauliflower,
    Be merry while I may,
And, ere there comes a sunny hour
    To cloud my heart, be gay!

WITH NO PUNCTUATION, this poem makes wonderful nonsense.
A little punctuation, however, reduces it to sense.

I Saw a Peacock

ANONYMOUS

I saw a peacock with a fiery tail
I saw a blazing comet drop down hail
I saw a cloud wrapped with ivy round
I saw an oak creep on along the ground
I saw a pismire swallow up a whale
I saw the sea brim full of ale
I saw a Venice glass full fathom deep
I saw a well full of men's tears that weep
I saw red eyes all of a flaming fire
I saw a house bigger than the moon and higher
I saw the sun at twelve o'clock at night
I saw the man that saw this wondrous sight.

Pismire—ant

"THE GREAT PANJANDRUM" was written by the 18th-century
English dramatist Samuel Foote in order to test the memory of
an actor who boasted that he could repeat any given lines by
hearing them once.

The Great Panjandrum

SAMUEL FOOTE

So she went into the garden
to cut a cabbage-leaf
to make an apple-pie;
and at the same time
a great she-bear, coming down the street,
pops its head into the shop.
What! no soap?
So he died,
and she very imprudently
married the Barber:
and there were present
the Picninnies,
and the Joblillies,
and the Garyulies,
and the great Panjandrum himself,
with the little round button at top;
and they all fell to playing the game
of catch-as-catch-can,
till the gunpowder ran out
at the heels of their boots.

165

Rhyme for a Simpleton

ANONYMOUS

I said, "This horse, sir, will you shoe?"
  And soon the horse was shod.
I said, "This deed, sir, will you do?"
  And soon the deed was dod!

I said, "This stick, sir, will you break?"
  At once the stick he broke.
I said, "This coat, sir, will you make?"
  And soon the coat he moke!

Counting-Out Rhymes

ANONYMOUS

I

Hinty, minty, cuty, corn,
Apple seed, and apple thorn,
Wire, briar, limber lock,
Three geese in a flock.
One flew east, and one flew west,
One flew over the cuckoo's nest.
    Up on yonder hill,
That is where my father dwells;
He has jewels, he has rings,
He has many pretty things.
He has a hammer with two nails,
He has a cat with twenty tails.
Strike Jack, lick Tom!
    Blow the bellows, old man!

II

Rosy apple, lemon or pear,
Bunch of roses shall she wear;
Gold and silver by her side,
I know who will be the bride;
Take her by her lily-white hand,
Lead her to the altar;
Give her kisses,—one, two, three,—
Mother's runaway daughter.

The Walloping Window-Blind

CHARLES E. CARRYL

A capital ship for an ocean trip
   Was the "Walloping Window-blind"—
No gale that blew dismayed her crew
   Or troubled the captain's mind.
The man at the wheel was taught to feel
   Contempt for the wildest blow,
And it often appeared, when the weather had cleared,
   That he'd been in his bunk below.

The boatswain's mate was very sedate,
   Yet fond of amusement, too;
And he played hop-scotch with the starboard watch,
   While the captain tickled the crew.
And the gunner we had was apparently mad,
   For he sat on the after rail,
And fired salutes with the captain's boots,
   In the teeth of the booming gale.

The captain sat in a commodore's hat
   And dined in a royal way
On toasted pigs and pickles and figs
   And gummery bread each day.
But the cook was Dutch and behaved as such:
   For the food that he gave the crew
Was a number of tons of hot-cross buns
   Chopped up with sugar and glue.

And we all felt ill as mariners will,
   On a diet that's cheap and rude;
And we shivered and shook as we dipped the cook
   In a tub of his gluesome food.
Then nautical pride we laid aside,
   And we cast the vessel ashore
On the Gilliby Isles, where the Poohpooh smiles,
   And the Anagazanders roar.

Composed of sand was that favored land,
    And trimmed with cinnamon straws;
And pink and blue was the pleasing hue
    Of the Tickletoeteaser's claws.
And we sat on the edge of a sandy ledge
    And shot at the whistling bee;
And the Binnacle-bats wore water-proof hats
    As they danced in the sounding sea.

On rubagub bark, from dawn to dark,
    We fed, till we all had grown
Uncommonly shrunk,—when a Chinese junk
    Came by from the torriby zone.
She was stubby and square, but we didn't much care,
    And we cheerily put to sea;
And we left the crew of the junk to chew
    The bark of the rubagub tree.

The Jumblies

Edward Lear

They went to sea in a Sieve, they did,
    In a Sieve they went to sea:
In spite of all their friends could say,
On a winter's morn, on a stormy day,
    In a Sieve they went to sea!
And when the Sieve turned round and round,
And every one cried, "You'll all be drowned!"
They called aloud, "Our Sieve ain't big,
But we don't care a button! we don't care a fig!
    In a Sieve we'll go to sea!"
        Far and few, far and few,
            Are the lands where the Jumblies live;
            Their heads are green, and their hands are blue,
                And they want to sea in a Sieve.

They sailed away in a Sieve, they did,
  In a Sieve they sailed so fast,
With only a beautiful pea-green veil
Tied with a riband by way of a sail,
  To a small tobacco-pipe mast;
And every one said, who saw them go,
"O won't they be soon upset, you know!
For the sky is dark, and the voyage is long,
And happen what may, it's extremely wrong
  In a Sieve to sail so fast!"
    Far and few, far and few,
      Are the lands where the Jumblies live;
      Their heads are green, and their hands are blue,
      And they went to sea in a Sieve.

The water it soon came in, it did,
  The water it soon came in;
So to keep them dry, they wrapped their feet
In a pinky paper all folded neat,
  And they fastened it down with a pin.
And they passed the night in a crockery-jar,
And each of them said, "How wise we are!
Though the sky be dark, and the voyage be long,
Yet we never can think we were rash or wrong,
  While round in our Sieve we spin!"
    Far and few, far and few,
      Are the lands where the Jumblies live;
      Their heads are green, and their hands are blue,
      And they went to sea in a Sieve.

And all night long they sailed away;
  And when the sun went down,
They whistled and warbled a moony song
To the echoing sound of a coppery gong,
  In the shade of the mountains brown.
"O Timballoo! How happy we are,
When we live in a Sieve and a crockery-jar,
And all night long in the moonlight pale,
We sail away with a pea-green sail,
  In the shade of the mountains brown!"
    Far and few, far and few,
      Are the lands where the Jumblies live;
      Their heads are green, and their hands are blue,
      And they went to sea in a Sieve.

They sailed to the Western Sea, they did,
   To a land all covered with trees,
And they bought an Owl, and a useful Cart,
And a pound of Rice, and a Cranberry Tart,
   And a hive of silvery Bees.
And they bought a Pig, and some green Jack-daws,
And a lovely Monkey with lollipop paws,
And forty bottles of Ring-Bo-Ree,
   And no end of Stilton Cheese.
     Far and few, far and few,
       Are the lands where the Jumblies live;
      Their heads are green, and their hands are blue,
       And they went to sea in a Sieve.

And in twenty years they all came back,
   In twenty years or more,
And every one said, "How tall they've grown!
For they've been to the Lakes, and the Torrible Zone,
   And the hills of the Chankly Bore";
And they drank their health, and gave them a feast
Of dumplings made of beautiful yeast;
And every one said, "If we only live,
We too will go to sea in a Sieve,—
   To the hills of the Chankly Bore!"
     Far and few, far and few,
       Are the lands where the Jumblies live;
      Their heads are green, and their hands are blue,
       And they went to sea in a Sieve.

It took the rather severe-looking, no-nonsense-minded Oxford don, Lewis Carroll, a mathematician and scholar, to give us the deliciously wacky "Jabberwocky," and thus add a new and zany dimension to our language. If the poem is read aloud with the proper emphasis as indicated by the sound of the words, it presents a brief drama of the marvelously absurd.

Jabberwocky

Lewis Carroll

'Twas brillig, and the slithy toves
   Did gyre and gimble in the wabe:
All mimsy were the borogoves,
   And the mome raths outgrabe.

"Beware the Jabberwock, my son!
   The jaws that bite, the claws that catch!
Beware the Jubjub bird, and shun
   The frumious Bandersnatch!"

He took his vorpal sword in hand;
   Long time the manxome foe he sought—
So rested he by the Tumtum tree,
   And stood awhile in thought.

And, as in uffish thought he stood,
   The Jabberwock, with eyes of flame,
Came whiffling through the tulgey wood,
   And burbled as it came!

One, two! One, two! And through and through
   The vorpal blade went snicker-snack!
He left it dead, and with its head
   He went galumphing back.

"And hast thou slain the Jabberwock?
   Come to my arms, my beamish boy!
O frabjous day! Callooh, Callay!"
   He chortled in his joy.

'Twas brillig, and the slithy toves
   Did gyre and gimble in the wabe:
All mimsy were the borogoves,
   And the mome raths outgrabe.

The Voice of the Lobster

LEWIS CARROLL

" 'Tis the voice of the Lobster; I heard him declare,
'You have baked me too brown, I must sugar my hair.'
As a duck with its eyelids, so he with his nose
Trims his belt and his buttons, and turns out his toes.
When the sands are all dry, he is gay as a lark,
And will talk in contemptuous tones of the Shark:
But, when the tide rises and sharks are around,
His voice has a timid and tremulous sound.

"I passed by his garden, and marked, with one eye,
How the Owl and the Panther were sharing a pie:
The Panther took pie-crust, and gravy, and meat,
While the Owl had the dish as its share of the treat.
When the pie was all finished, the Owl, as a boon,
Was kindly permitted to pocket the spoon:
While the Panther received knife and fork with a growl,
And concluded the banquet by—"

The Dinkey-Bird

EUGENE FIELD

In an ocean, 'way out yonder
   (As all sapient people know),
Is the land of Wonder-Wander,
   Whither children love to go;
It's their playing, romping, swinging,
   That give great joy to me
While the Dinkey-Bird goes singing
   In the amfalula tree!

There the gum-drops grow like cherries
   And taffy's thick as peas—
Caramels you pick like berries
   When, and where, and how you please;
Big red sugar-plums are clinging
   To the cliffs beside that sea
Where the Dinkey-Bird is singing
   In the amfalula tree.

So when children shout and scamper
   And make merry all the day,
When there's naught to put a damper
   To the ardor of their play;
When I hear their laughter ringing
   Then I'm sure as sure can be
That the Dinkey-Bird is singing
   In the amfalula tree.

For the Dinkey-Bird's bravuras
   And staccatos are so sweet—
His roulades, apoggiaturas,
   And robustos so complete,
That the youth of every nation—
   Be they near or far away—
Have especial delectation
   In that gladsome roundelay.

Their eyes grow bright and brighter
  Their lungs begin to crow,
Their hearts get light and lighter,
  And their cheeks are all aglow;
For an echo cometh bringing
  The news to all and me,
That the Dinkey-Bird is singing
  In the amfalula tree.

I'm sure you like to go there
  To see your feathered friend—
And so many goodies grow there
  You would like to comprehend!
Speed, little dreams, your winging
  To that land across the sea
Where the Dinkey-Bird is singing
  In the amfalula tree!

Incidents in the Life of My Uncle Arly

Edward Lear

I

Oh! my aged Uncle Arly,
Sitting on a heap of barley
  Through the silent hours of night,
Close beside a leafy thicket;
On his nose there was a cricket,
In his hat a Railway-Ticket,
  (But his shoes were far too tight.)

II

Long ago, in youth, he squander'd
All his goods away, and wander'd
  To the Timskoop-hills afar.
There on golden sunsets glazing
Every evening found him gazing,
Singing, "Orb! you're quite amazing!
  How I wonder what you are!"

III

Like the ancient Medes and Persians,
Always by his own exertions
  He subsisted on those hills;
Whiles, by teaching children spelling,
Or at times by merely yelling,
Or at intervals by selling
  "Propter's Nicodemus Pills."

173

IV

Later, in his morning rambles,
He perceived the moving brambles
    Something square and white disclose:—
'T was a First-class Railway-Ticket;
But on stooping down to pick it
Off the ground, a pea-green cricket
    Settled on my uncle's nose.

V

Never, nevermore, oh! never
Did that cricket leave him ever,—
    Dawn or evening, day or night;
Clinging as a constant treasure,
Chirping with a cheerious measure,
Wholly to my uncle's pleasure,
    (Though his shoes were far too tight.)

VI

So for three and forty winters,
Till his shoes were worn to splinters
    All those hills he wander'd o'er,—
Sometimes silent, sometimes yelling;
Till he came to Borley-Melling,
Near his old ancestral dwelling,
    (But his shoes were far too tight.)

VII

On a little heap of barley
Died my aged Uncle Arly,
    And they buried him one night
Close beside the leafy thicket;
There, his hat and Railway-Ticket;
There, his ever faithful cricket;
    (But his shoes were far too tight.)

Ways and Means

Lewis Carroll

I'll tell thee everything I can:
  There's little to relate.
I saw an aged aged man,
  A-sitting on a gate.
"Who are you, aged man?" I said.
  "And how is it you live?"
And his answer trickled through my head,
  Like water through a sieve.

He said "I look for butterflies
  That sleep among the wheat:
I make them into mutton-pies,
  And sell them in the street.
I sell them unto men," he said,
  "Who sail on stormy seas;
And that's the way I get my bread—
  A trifle, if you please."

But I was thinking of a plan
  To dye one's whiskers green,
And always use so large a fan
  That they could not be seen.
So, having no reply to give
  To what the old man said,
I cried "Come, tell me how you live!"
  And thumped him on the head.

His accents mild took up the tale:
  He said "I go my ways,
And when I find a mountain-rill,
  I set it in a blaze;
And thence they make a stuff they call
  Rowland's Macassar-Oil—
Yet twopence-halfpenny is all
  They give me for my toil."

But I was thinking of a way
  To feed oneself on batter,
And so go on from day to day
  Getting a little fatter.
I shook him well from side to side,
  Until his face was blue:
"Come, tell me how you live," I cried,
  "And what it is you do!"

He said "I hunt for haddocks' eyes
  Among the heather bright,
And work them into waistcoat-buttons
  In the silent night.
And these I do not sell for gold
  Or coin of silvery shine,
But for a copper halfpenny,
  And that will purchase nine.

I sometimes dig for buttered rolls,
  Or set limed twigs for crabs:
I sometimes search the grassy knolls
  For wheels of Hansom-cabs.
And that's the way" (he gave a wink)
  "By which I get my wealth—
And very gladly will I drink
  Your Honour's noble health."

I heard him then, for I had just
  Completed my design
To keep the Menai bridge from rust
  By boiling it in wine.
I thanked him much for telling me
  The way he got his wealth,
But chiefly for his wish that he
  Might drink my noble health.

And now, if e'er by chance I put
    My fingers into glue,
Or madly squeeze a right-hand foot
    Into a left-hand shoe,
Or if I drop upon my toe
    A very heavy weight,
I weep for it reminds me so
'Of that old man I used to know—
Whose look was mild, whose speech was slow,
Whose hair was whiter than the snow,
Whose face was very like a crow,
With eyes, like cinders, all aglow,
Who seemed distracted with his woe,
Who rocked his body to and fro,
And muttered mumblingly and low,
As if his mouth were full of dough,
Who snorted like a buffalo—
That summer evening long ago,
    A-sitting on a gate.

FATHER WILLIAM has appeared in the work of several poets.
He first saw life in a preachy and forgettable poem by Robert
Southey and, changed beyond recognition, was then described in
a poem in *Alice in Wonderland* by Lewis Carroll. The author of
the lines that follow is unknown.

Father William

ANONYMOUS

"You are old, Father William," the young man said,
    "And your nose has a look of surprise;
Your eyes have turned round to the back of your head,
    And you live upon cucumber pies."
"I know it, I know it," that old man replied,
    "And it comes from employing a quack,
Who said if I laughed when the crocodile died
    I should never have pains in my back."

"You are old, Father William," the young man said,
    "And your legs always get in your way;
You use too much mortar in mixing your bread,
    And you try to drink timothy hay."
"Very true, very true," said the wretched old man,
    "Every word that you tell me is true;
And it's caused by my having my kerosene can
    Painted red where it ought to be blue."

"You are old, Father William," the young man said,
    "And your teeth are beginning to freeze,
Your favorite daughter has wheels in her head,
    And the chickens are eating your knees."
"You are right," said the old man, "I cannot deny,
    That my troubles are many and great,
But I'll butter my ears on the Fourth of July,
    And then I'll be able to skate."

A Chronicle

ANONYMOUS

Once—but no matter when—
    There lived—no matter where—
A man, whose name—but then
    I need not that declare.

He—well, he had been born,
    And so he was alive;
His age—I details scorn—
    Was somethingty and five.

He lived—how many years
    I truly can't decide;
But this one fact appears:
    He lived—until he died.

"He died," I have averred,
    But cannot prove 'twas so,
But that he was interred,
    At any rate, I know.

I fancy he'd a son,
    I hear he had a wife:
Perhaps he'd more than one,
    I know not, on my life!

But whether he was rich,
    Or whether he was poor,
Or neither—both—or which,
    I cannot say, I'm sure.

I can't recall his name,
    Or what he used to do:
But then—well, such is fame!
    'Twill so serve me and you.

And that is why I thus
    About this unknown man
Would fain create a fuss,
    To rescue, if I can

177

From dark oblivion's blow,
  Some record of his lot:
But, ah! I do not know
  Who—where—when—
    why—or what.

MORAL

In this brief pedigree
  A moral we should find—
But what it ought to be
  Has quite escaped my mind!

The Twins

HENRY S. LEIGH

In form and feature, face and limb,
  I grew so like my brother,
That folks got taking me for him,
  And each for one another.
It puzzled all our kith and kin,
  It reached an awful pitch;
For one of us was born a twin,
  Yet not a soul knew which.

One day (to make the matter worse),
  Before our names were fixed,
As we were being washed by nurse
  We got completely mixed;
And thus, you see, by Fate's decree,
  (Or rather nurse's whim),
My brother John got christened *me*,
  And I got christened *him*.

This fatal likeness even dogg'd
  My footsteps when at school,
And I was always getting flogg'd,
  For John turned out a fool.
I put this question hopelessly
  To everyone I knew—
What *would* you do, if you were me,
  To prove that you were *you*?

Our close resemblance turned the tide
  Of my domestic life;
For somehow my intended bride
  Became my brother's wife.
In short, year after year the same
  Absurd mistake went on;
And when I died—the neighbors came
  And buried brother John!

LIMERICKS

THE ORIGIN OF THE LIMERICK is the concern of the literary historian, not of ours. What concerns us here is that this literary five-liner be witty, impudent, and playful. Included among the examples of this sly verse form is one that, as it doesn't rhyme, is not a true limerick. It is nonetheless both fitting and funny.

There was an old man who said, "Do
Tell me *how* I should add two and two?
    I think more and more
    That it makes about four—
But I fear that is almost too few."

ANONYMOUS

The Reverend Henry Ward Beecher
Called a hen a most elegant creature;
    The hen, pleased with that,
    Laid an egg in his hat,
And thus did the hen reward Beecher.

OLIVER WENDELL HOLMES

A fly and a flea in a flue
Were imprisoned, so what could they do?
    Said the fly, "Let us flee!"
    "Let us fly!" said the flea.
So they flew through a flaw in the flue.

ANONYMOUS

A Briton who swore at his king,
Was doomed on the gallows to swing;
    When the rope was made fast,
    He cried out "At last
I'm getting the hang of the thing."

DAVID ROSS

That bottle of perfume that Willie sent
Was highly displeasing to Millicent.
    Her thanks were so cold
    They quarreled, I'm told,
Through that silly scent Willie sent Millicent.

ANONYMOUS

An indolent vicar of Bray
Let his lovely red roses decay;
    His wife, more alert,
    Bought a powerful squirt,
And said to her spouse, "Let us spray."

ANONYMOUS

A yak who was new to the zoo
Made a friend of an old looking gnu;
   Said the gnu to the yak
   "If you'll please scratch my back,
I'll do the same favor for you."

DAVID ROSS

There was a young lady of Niger
Who smiled as she rode on a tiger:
   They came back from the ride
   With the lady inside
And the smile on the face of the tiger.

ANONYMOUS

An epicure, dining at Crewe,
Found quite a large mouse in his stew.
   Said the waiter, "Don't shout
   And wave it about,
Or the rest will be wanting one too!"

ANONYMOUS

There was a faith-healer of Deal,
Who said, "Although pain isn't real,
   If I sit on a pin,
   And it punctures my skin,
I dislike what I fancy I feel."

ANONYMOUS

There was an old lady of Steen,
Whose musical sense was not keen;
   She said, "Well, it's odd,
   But I cannot tell 'God
Save the Weasel' from 'Pop Goes the Queen.'

ANONYMOUS

There was an old man from Peru
Who dreamed he was eating his shoe.
   He woke in a fright
   In the middle of the night
And found it was perfectly true.

ANONYMOUS

There was a young woman named Bright,
Whose speed was much faster than light.
   She set out one day
   In a relative way,
And returned on the previous night.

ANONYMOUS

There was an Old Man with a beard,
Who said, "It is just as I feared!—
   Two Owls and a Hen,
   Four Larks and a Wren
Have all built their nests in my beard."

EDWARD LEAR

There once was a young man named Hall
Who fell in the spring in the fall.
    'Twould have been a sad thing
    Had he died in the spring,
But he didn't—he died in the fall.

ANONYMOUS

A maiden at college, named Breeze,
Weighted down by B.A.'s and M.D.'s
    Collapsed from the strain.
    Said her doctor, "It's plain
You are killing yourself by degrees!"

ANONYMOUS

There was a young lady of Crete,
Who was so exceedingly neat,
    When she got out of bed
    She stood on her head,
To make sure of not soiling her feet.

ANONYMOUS

There was an old Looney of Rhyme
Whose candor was simply sublime:
    When they asked, "Are you there?"
    He said, "Yes, but take care,
For I'm never 'all there' at a-time!"

ANONYMOUS

A clergyman told from his text
How Samson was scissored and vexed;
    Then a barber arose
    From his sweet Sunday doze,
Got rattled, and shouted, "Who's next?"

ANONYMOUS

There was an old man in a tree
Who was horribly bored by a bee,
    When they said, "Does it buzz?"
    He replied, "Yes it does,
It's a regular brute of a bee."

EDWARD LEAR

There was an old man of St. Bees,
Who was stung in the arm by a wasp;
    When they asked, "Does it hurt?"
    He replied, "No, it doesn't,
But I thought all the while 'twas a hornet!"

W. S. GILBERT

Present Mirth

"PRESENT MIRTH," William Shakespeare tells us, brings "present laughter," and laughing together with friends and loved ones is one of the radiant joys of living. The Old Testament tells us that "a merry heart doeth good like a medicine," and an Italian proverb informs us that "laughter makes good blood." In the weight of all this evidence, we can only agree with the philosopher who said that the merry of heart have achieved wisdom, and prepare to be amused.

Abdul Abulbul Amir

ANONYMOUS

The sons of the Prophet are valiant and bold,
   And quite unaccustomed to fear;
And the bravest of all was a man, so I'm told,
   Called Abdul Abulbul Amir.

When they wanted a man to encourage the van,
   Or harass the foe from the rear,
Storm fort or redoubt, they were sure to call out
   For Abdul Abulbul Amir.

There are heroes in plenty, and well known to fame,
   In the legions that fight for the Czar;
But none of such fame as the man by the name
   Of Ivan Petrofsky Skovar.

He could imitate Irving, tell fortunes by cards,
   And play on the Spanish guitar;
In fact, quite the cream of the Muscovite guards
   Was Ivan Petrofsky Skovar.

One day this bold Muscovite shouldered his gun,
   Put on his most cynical sneer,
And was walking downtown when he happened to run
   Into Abdul Abulbul Amir.

"Young man," said Abulbul, "is existence so dull
   That you're anxious to end your career?
Then, infidel, know you have trod on the toe
   Of Abdul Abulbul Amir.

"So take your last look at the sea, sky and brook,
   Make your latest report on the war;
For I mean to imply you are going to die,
   O, Ivan Petrofsky Skovar."

So this fierce man he took his trusty chibouk,
   And murmuring, "Allah Akbar!"
With murder intent he most savagely went
   For Ivan Petrofsky Skovar.

The Sultan rose up, the disturbance to quell,
   Likewise, give the victor a cheer.
He arrived just in time to bid hasty farewell
   To Abdul Abulbul Amir.

A loud-sounding splash from the Danube was heard
   Resounding o'er meadows afar;
It came from the sack fitting close to the back
   Of Ivan Petrofsky Skovar.

There lieth a stone where the Danube doth roll,
   And on it in characters queer
Are: "Stranger, when passing by, pray for the soul
   Of Abdul Abulbul Amir."

A Muscovite maiden her vigil doth keep
   By the light of the pale northern star,
And the name she repeats every night in her sleep
   Is Ivan Petrofsky Skovar.

Irving—Sir Henry Irving (1838–1905), noted English actor.
Chibouk—Turkish pipe, often five feet long.

In the history of England four kings bore the name of George between 1714 and 1830. History has not been particularly kind to these Georges, but some who lived under one or more of them have been even less so. The poet Landor, for example, certainly lived up to his middle name in the following lines.

The Georges

Walter Savage Landor

George the First was always reckoned
Vile, but viler George the Second;
And what mortal ever heard
Any good of George the Third?
When from earth the Fourth descended
God be praised, the Georges ended!

The maidens who are sung about in old riddle-ballads win their husbands either through comeliness or wit, or a combination of both. Here, a knight in quest of a bride has three riddles for three young sisters. Traditionally, only the youngest and prettiest sister can answer him, and she becomes his bride. We can picture him lifting her into his saddle, and galloping off with her into the lovely English countryside.

The Riddling Knight

Anonymous

There were three sisters fair and bright,
Jennifer, Gentle, and Rosemary,
And they three loved one valiant knight—
As the dew flies over the mulberry-tree.

The eldest sister let him in,
Jennifer, Gentle, and Rosemary,
And barr'd the door with a silver pin,
As the dew flies over the mulberry-tree.

The second sister made his bed,
Jennifer, Gentle, and Rosemary,
And placed soft pillows under his head,
As the dew flies over the mulberry-tree.

The youngest sister that same night,
Jennifer, Gentle, and Rosemary,
Was resolved for to wed wi' this valiant knight,
As the dew flies over the mulberry-tree.

"And if you can answer questions three,
Jennifer, Gentle, and Rosemary,
O then, fair maid, I'll marry wi' thee,
As the dew flies over the mulberry-tree.

"O what is louder nor a horn,
Jennifer, Gentle, and Rosemary,
O what is sharper nor a thorn?
As the dew flies over the mulberry-tree

"Or what is heavier nor the lead,
Jennifer, Gentle, and Rosemary,
Or what is better nor the bread?
As the dew flies over the mulberry-tree.

"Or what is longer nor the way,
Jennifer, Gentle, and Rosemary,
Or what is deeper nor the sea?—"
As the dew flies over the mulberry-tree.

"O shame is louder nor a horn,
Jennifer, Gentle, and Rosemary,
And hunger is sharper nor a thorn,
As the dew flies over the mulberry-tree.

"O sin is heavier nor the lead,
Jennifer, Gentle, and Rosemary,
The blessing's better nor the bread,
As the dew flies over the mulberry-tree.

"O the wind is longer nor the way,
Jennifer, Gentle, and Rosemary,
And love is deeper nor the sea."
As the dew flies over the mulberry-tree.

"You've answere'd my questions three.
Jennifer, Gentle, and Rosemary,
And now, fair maid, I'll marry wi' thee,"
As the dew flies over the mulberry-tree.

A Riddle

'T was in heaven pronounced, and 't was muttered in hell,
And echo caught faintly the sound as it fell;
On the confines of earth 't was permitted to rest,
And the depths of the ocean its presence confessed;
'T will be found in the sphere when 't is riven asunder,
Be seen in the lightning and heard in the thunder.
'T was allotted to man with his earliest breath,
Attends him at birth, and awaits him in death,
Presides o'er his happiness, honor, and health,
Is the prop of his house, and the end of his wealth.
In the heaps of the miser 't is hoarded with care,
But is sure to be lost on his prodigal heir.
It begins every hope, every wish it must bound,
With the husbandman toils, and with monarchs is crowned.
Without it the soldier, the seaman may roam,
But woe to the wretch who expels it from home!
In the whispers of conscience its voice will be found,
Nor e'en in the whirlwind of passion be drowned.
'T will not soften the heart; but though deaf be the ear,
It will make it acutely and instantly hear.
Yet in shade let it rest, like a delicate flower,
Ah,—breathe on it softly,—it dies in an hour.

The letter H

A Riddle

ANONYMOUS

The beginning of eternity,
The end of time and space,
The beginning of every end,
The end of every place.

The letter E

Lines to a Young Lady

EDWARD LEAR

How pleasant to know Mr. Lear!
　Who has written such volumes of stuff!
Some think him ill-tempered and queer,
　But a few think him pleasant enough.

His mind is concrete and fastidious,
　His nose is remarkably big;
His visage is more or less hideous,
　His beard it resembles a wig.

He has ears, and two eyes, and ten fingers,
　Leastways, if you reckon two thumbs;
Long ago he was one of the singers,
　But now he is one of the dumbs.

He sits in a beautiful parlor,
　With hundreds of books on the wall;
He drinks a great deal of Marsala,
　But never gets tipsy at all.

He has many friends, laymen and clerical;
　Old Foss is the name of his cat;
His body is perfectly spherical,
　He weareth a runcible hat.

When he walks in a waterproof white,
　The children run after him so!
Calling out, "He's come out in his night-
　Gown, that crazy old Englishman, oh!"

He weeps by the side of the ocean,
　He weeps on the top of the hill;
He purchases pancakes and lotion,
　And chocolate shrimps from the mill.

He reads but he cannot speak Spanish,
　He cannot abide ginger-beer:
Ere the days of his pilgrimage vanish,
　How pleasant to know Mr. Lear!

Lord Chancellor's Song

W. S. GILBERT

When you're lying awake with a dismal headache and repose is tabooed
　　by anxiety,
I conceive you may use any language you choose to indulge in without
　　impropriety;
For your brain is on fire—the bed-clothes conspire of your usual slumber
　　to plunder you:
First your counterpane goes, and uncovers your toes, and your sheet slips
　　demurely from under you;
Then the blanketing tickles—you feel like mixed pickles—so terribly sharp
　　is the pricking,
And you're hot and you're cross, and you tumble and toss till there's nothing
　　'twixt you and the ticking.
Then the bedclothes all creep to the ground in a heap, and you pick 'em
　　all up in a tangle;

Next your pillow resigns and politely declines to remain at its usual angle!

Well, you get some repose in the form of a doze, with hot eye-balls and head ever aching,

But your slumbering teems with such horrible dreams that you'd very much better be waking:

For you dream you are crossing the Channel, and tossing about in a steamer from Harwich—

Which is something between a large bathing-machine and a very small second-class carriage—

And you're giving a treat (penny ice and cold meat) to a party of friends and relations—

They're a ravenous horde—and they all came on board at Sloane Square and South Kensington Stations.

And bound on that journey you find your attorney (who started that morning from Devon);

He's a bit undersized, and you don't feel surprise when he tells you he's only eleven.

Well, you're driving like mad with that singular lad (by the by, the ship's now a four-wheeler),

And you're playing round games, and he calls you bad names when you tell him that "ties pay the dealer";

But this you can't stand, so you throw up your hand and you find you're as cold as an icicle,

In your shirt and your socks (the black silk with gold clocks), crossing Salisbury Plain on a bicycle:

And he and the crew are on bicycles too—which they've somehow or other invested in—

And he's telling the tars all the particulars of a company he's interested in—

It's a scheme of devices to get at low prices all goods from cough mixtures to cables

(Which tickled the sailors), by treating retailers as though they were all vegetables—

You get a good spadesman to plant a small tradesman (first take off his boots with a boot-tree),

And his legs will take root, and his fingers will shoot, and they'll blossom
    and bud like a fruit-tree—
From the greengrocer tree you get grapes and green pea, cauliflower, pine-
    apple, and cranberries,
While the pastrycook plant, cherry brandy will grant, apple-puffs, and three-
    corners, and Banburys—
The shares are a penny, and ever so many are taken by Rothschild and
    Baring,
And just as a few are allotted to you, you awake with a shudder despairing—

You're a regular wreck with a crick in your neck, and no wonder you snore,
    for your head's on the floor, and you've needles and pins from your soles
    to your shins, and your flesh is a-creep, for your left leg's asleep, and
    you've cramp in your toes, and a fly in your nose, and some fluff in
    your lung, and a feverish tongue, and a thirst that's intense, and a
    general sense that you haven't been sleeping in clover;
But the darkness has past, and it's daylight at last, and the night has been
    long—ditto ditto my song—and thank goodness they're both of them
    over!

It Chanced to Be Our Washing Day

OLIVER WENDELL HOLMES

It chanced to be our washing day,
    And all our things were drying;
The storm came roaring through the lines,
    And set them all a-flying;
I saw the shirts and petticoats
    Go riding off like witches;
I lost, ah! bitterly I wept—
    I lost my Sunday breeches!

I saw them straddling through the air,
    Alas! too late to win them;
I saw them chase the clouds, as if
    The devil had been in them;
They were my darlings and my pride,
    My boyhood's only riches—
"Farewell, farewell," I faintly cried—
    "My breeches! O my breeches!"

That night I saw them in my dreams,
    How changed from what I knew them!
The dews had steeped their faded threads,
    The winds had whistled through them!
I saw the wide and ghastly rents
    Where demon claws had torn them;
A hole was in their amplest part,
    As if an imp had worn them.

I have had many happy years,
    And tailors kind and clever,
But those young pantaloons have gone
    Forever and forever!
And not till fate has cut the last
    Of all my earthly stitches,
This aching heart shall cease to mourn
    My loved! my long-lost breeches!

When Father Carves the Duck

E. V. WRIGHT

We all look on with anxious eyes
    When father carves the duck,
And mother almost always sighs
    When father carves the duck;
Then all of us prepare to rise,
And hold our bibs before our eyes,
And be prepared for some surprise,
    When father carves the duck.

He braces up and grabs a fork
    Whene'er he carves a duck,
And won't allow a soul to talk
    Until he's carved the duck.
The fork is jabbed into the sides,
Across the breast the knife he slides,
While every careful person hides
    From flying chips of duck.

The platter's always sure to slip
    When father carves a duck,
And how it makes the dishes skip!
    Potatoes fly amuck!
The squash and cabbage leap in space,
We get some gravy in our face,
And father mutters Hindoo grace
    Whene'er he carves a duck.

We then have learned to walk around
    The dining room and pluck
From off the window sills and walls
    Our share of father's duck.
While father growls and blows and jaws
And swears the knife was full of flaws,
And mother laughs at him because
    He couldn't carve a duck.

Methuselah

ANONYMOUS

Methuselah ate what he found on his plate,
    And never, as people do now,
Did he note the amount of the caloric count;
    He ate it because it was chow.

He wasn't disturbed, as at dinner he sat,
    Destroying a roast or a pie,
To think it was lacking in lime or in fat,
    Or a couple of vitamins shy.

He cheerfully chewed every species of food,
    Untroubled by worries or fears,
Lest his health might be hurt by some fancy desert—
    And he lived over nine hundred years!

The Deacon's Masterpiece or,
The Wonderful "One-Hoss Shay"

A Logical Story

OLIVER WENDELL HOLMES

Have you heard of the wonderful one-hoss shay,
That was built in such a logical way
It ran a hundred years to a day,
And then, of a sudden, it—ah, but stay,
I'll tell you what happened without delay,
Scaring the parson into fits,
Frightening people out of their wits,—
Have you ever heard of that, I say?

Seventeen hundred and fifty-five.
Georgius Secundus was then alive,—
Snuffy old drone from the German hive.
That was the year when Lisbon-town
Saw the earth open and gulp her down,
And Braddock's army was done so brown,
Left without a scalp to its crown.
It was on the terrible Earthquake-day
That the Deacon finished the one-hoss shay.

Now in building of chaises, I tell you what,
There is always *somewhere* a weakest spot,—
In hub, tire, felloe, in spring or thill,
In panel, or crossbar, or floor, or sill,
In screw, bolt, thoroughbrace,—lurking still,
Find it somewhere you must and will,—
Above or below, or within or without,—
And that's the reason, beyond a doubt,
That a chaise *breaks down*, but doesn't *wear out*.

But the Deacon swore (as Deacons do,
With an "I dew vum," or an "I tell yeou")
He would build one shay to beat the taown
'n' the keounty 'n' all the kentry raoun';
It should be so built that it *couldn'* break daown:
"Fur," said the Deacon, " 't 's mighty plain
Thut the weakes' place mus' stan' the strain;
'n' the way t' fix it, uz I maintain, Is only jest
T' make that place uz strong uz the rest."

So the Deacon inquired of the village folk
Where he could find the strongest oak,
That couldn't be split nor bent nor broke,—
That was for spokes and floor and sills;
He sent for lancewood to make the thills;
The crossbars were ash, from the straightest trees,
The panels of white-wood, that cuts like cheese,
But lasts like iron for things like these;
The hubs of logs from the "Settler's ellum,"—
Last of its timber,—they couldn't sell 'em,
Never an axe had seen their chips,
And the wedges flew from between their lips,
Their blunt ends frizzled like celery-tips;
Step and prop-iron, bolt and screw,
Spring, tire, axle, and linchpin too,
Steel of the finest, bright and blue;
Thoroughbrace bison-skin, thick and wide;
Boot, top, dasher, from tough old hide
Found in the pit when the tanner died.
That was the way he "put her through."
"There!" said the Deacon, "naow she'll dew!"

Do! I tell you, I rather guess
She was a wonder, and nothing less!
Colts grew horses, beards turned gray,
Deacon and deaconess dropped away,
Children and grandchildren—where were they?
But there stood the stout old one-hoss shay
As fresh as on Lisbon-earthquake-day!

EIGHTEEN HUNDRED;—it came and found
The Deacon's masterpiece strong and sound.
Eighteen hundred increased by ten;—
"Hahnsum kerridge" they called it then.
Eighteen hundred and twenty came;—
Running as usual—much the same.
Thirty and forty at last arrive,
And then come fifty, and FIFTY-FIVE.

Little of all we value here
Wakes on the morn of its hundreth year
Without both feeling and looking queer.
In fact, there's nothing that keeps its youth,
So far as I know, but a tree and truth.
(This is a moral that runs at large;
Take it.—You're welcome.—No extra charge.)

FIRST OF NOVEMBER,—the Earthquake-day,
There are traces of age in the one-hoss shay,
A general flavor of mild decay,
But nothing local, as one may say.
There couldn't be,—for the Deacon's art
Had made it so like in every part
That there wasn't a chance for one to start.
For the wheels were just as strong as the thills,
And the floor was just as strong as the sills,
And the panels just as strong as the floor,
And the whipple-tree neither less nor more,
And the back-crossbar as strong as the fore,
And spring and axle and hub *encore*.
And yet, *as a whole*, it is past a doubt
In another hour it will be *worn out*!

First of November, fifty-five!
This morning the parson takes a drive.
Now, small boys, get out of the way!
Here comes the wonderful one-hoss shay,
Drawn by a rat-tailed, ewe-necked bay.
"Huddup!" said the parson.—Off went they.
The parson was working his Sunday's text,—
Had got to *fifthly*, and stopped perplexed
At what the—Moses—was coming next.
All at once the horse stood still,
Close by the meet'n'-house on the hill.
First a shiver, and then a thrill,
Then something decidedly like a spill,—
And the parson was sitting upon a rock,
At half past nine by the meet'n'-house clock,—
Just the hour of the Earthquake shock!
What do you think the parson found,
When he got up and stared around?
The poor old chaise in a heap or mound,
As if it had been to the mill and ground!
You see, of course, if you're not a dunce,
How it went to pieces all at once,—
All at once, and nothing first,—
Just as bubbles do when they burst.

End of the wonderful one-hoss shay.
Logic is logic. That's all I say.

The Ploughboy in Luck

ANONYMOUS

My daddy is dead, but I can't tell you how;
He left me six horses to follow the plough;
    With my whim wham waddle ho!
    Strim stram straddle ho!
    Bubble ho! pretty boy over the brow.

I sold my six horses to buy me a cow;
And wasn't that a pretty thing to follow the plough?
    With my whim wham waddle ho!
    Strim stram straddle ho!
    Bubble ho! pretty boy over the brow.

I sold my cow to buy me a calf,
For I never made a bargain but I lost the best half.
    With my whim wham waddle ho!
    Strim stram straddle ho!
    Bubble ho! pretty boy over the brow.

I sold my calf to buy me a cat,
To sit down before the fire to warm her pretty back,
    With my whim wham waddle ho!
    Strim stram straddle ho!
    Bubble ho! pretty boy over the brow.

I sold my cat to buy me a mouse,
But she took fire in her tail and so burnt up my house,
    With my whim wham waddle ho!
    Strim stram straddle ho!
    Bubble ho! pretty boy over the brow.

An Expostulation

ISAAC BICKERSTAFF

When late I attempted your pity to move,
    What made you so deaf to my prayers?
Perhaps it was right to dissemble your love,
    But—why did you kick me down stairs?

Morning

CHARLES STUART CALVERLEY

Tis the hour when white-horsed Day
Chases Night her mares away,
When the Gates of Dawn (they say)
   Phoebus opes:
And I gather that the Queen
May be uniformly seen,
Should the weather be serene,
   On the slopes.

When the ploughman, as he goes
Leathern-gaitered o'er the snows,
From his hat and from his nose
   Knocks the ice;
And the panes are frosted o'er
And the lawn is crisp and hoar,
As has been observed before
   Once or twice.

When arrayed in breastplate red
Sings the robin, for his bread,
On the elmtree that hath shed
   Every leaf;
While, within, the frost benumbs
The still sleepy schoolboy's thumbs,
And in consequence his sums
   Come to grief.

But when breakfast–time hath come,
And he's crunching crust and crumb,
He'll no longer look a glum
   Little dunce;
But be as brisk as bees that settle
On a summer rose's petal:
Wherefore, Polly, put the kettle
   On at once.

The Nose and the Eyes

WILLIAM COWPER

Between Nose and Eyes a strange contest arose;
   The spectacles set them, unhappily, wrong;
The point in dispute was, as all the world knows,
   To whom the said spectacles ought to belong.

So Tongue was the lawyer, and argued the cause,
   With a great deal of skill, and a wig full of learning,
While chief baron Ear sat to balance the laws,—
   So famed for his talent in nicely discerning.

"In behalf of the Nose, it will quickly appear
   (And your lordship," he said, "will undoubtedly find)
That the Nose has the spectacles always to wear,
   Which amounts to possession, time out of mind."

Then, holding the spectacles up to the court,
   "Your lordship observes, they are made with a straddle,
As wide as the ridge of the Nose is; in short,
   Designed to sit close to it, just like a saddle.

"Again, would your lordship a moment suppose
　　('T is a case that has happened, and may happen again)
That the visage or countenance had *not* a Nose,
　　Pray, who *would*, or who *could*, wear spectacles then?

"On the whole, it appears, and my argument shows,
　　With a reasoning the court will never condemn,
That the spectacles, plainly, were made for the Nose,
　　And the Nose was, as plainly, intended for them."

Then shifting his side (as a lawyer knows how),
　　He pleaded again in behalf of the Eyes:
But what were his arguments, few people know,
　　For the court did not think them equally wise.

So his lordship decreed, with a grave, solemn tone,
　　Decisive and clear, without one *if* or *but*,
That whenever the Nose put his spectacles on,
　　By daylight or candlelight,—Eyes should be *shut*.

Mr. Nobody

ANONYMOUS

I know a funny little man,
　　As quiet as a mouse,
Who does the mischief that is done
　　In everybody's house!
There's no one ever sees his face,
　　And yet we all agree
That every plate we break was cracked
　　By Mr. Nobody.

'Tis he who always tears our books,
　　Who leaves the door ajar,
He pulls the buttons from our shirts,
　　And scatters pins afar;
That squeaking door will always squeak
　　For, prithee, don't you see,
We leave the oiling to be done
　　By Mr. Nobody.

He puts damp wood upon the fire,
　　That kettles cannot boil;
His are the feet that bring in mud,
　　And all the carpets soil.
The papers always are mislaid,
　　Who had them last but he?
There's no one tosses them about
　　But Mr. Nobody.

The finger-marks upon the door
　　By none of us are made;
We never leave the blinds unclosed,
　　To let the curtains fade.
The ink we never spill, the boots
　　That lying round you see
Are not our boots; they all belong
　　To Mr. Nobody.

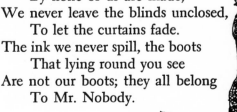

Robinson Crusoe's Island

CHARLES E. CARRYL

The night was thick and hazy
When the "Piccadilly Daisy"
Carried down the crew and captain in the sea;
And I think the water drowned 'em;
For they never, never found 'em,
And I know they didn't come ashore with me.

Oh! 'twas very sad and lonely
When I found myself the only
Population on this cultivated shore;
But I've made a little tavern
In a rocky little cavern,
And I sit and watch for people at the door.

I spent no time in looking
For a girl to do my cooking,
As I'm quite a clever hand at making stews;
But I had that fellow Friday,
Just to keep the tavern tidy,
And to put a Sunday polish on my shoes.

I have a little garden
That I'm cultivating lard in,
As the things I eat are rather tough and dry;
For I live on toasted lizards,
Prickly pears, and parrot gizzards,
And I'm really very fond of beetle-pie.

The clothes I had were furry,
And it made me fret and worry
When I found the moths were eating off the hair;
And I had to scrape and sand 'em,
And I boiled 'em and I tanned 'em,
Till I got the fine morocco suit I wear.

I sometimes seek diversion
In a family excursion
With the few domestic animals you see;
And we take along a carrot
As refreshment for the parrot,
And a little can of jungleberry tea.

Then we gather, as we travel,
Bits of moss and dirty gravel,
And we chip off little specimens of stone;
And we carry home as prizes
Funny bugs, of handy sizes,
Just to give the day a scientific tone.

If the roads are wet and muddy,
We remain at home and study,—
For the Goat is very clever at a sum,—
And the Dog, instead of fighting,
Studies ornamental writing,
While the Cat is taking lessons on the drum.

We retire at eleven,
And we rise again at seven;
And I wish to call attention, as I close,
To the fact that all the scholars
Are correct about their collars,
And particular in turning out their toes.

Changed

CHARLES STUART CALVERLEY

I know not why my soul is rack'd:
　　Why I ne'er smile as was my wont:
I only know that, as a fact,
　　　　I don't.
I used to roam o'er glen and glade
　　Buoyant and blithe as other folk:
And not unfrequently I made
　　　　A joke.

A minstrel's fire within me burn'd.
　　I'd sing, as one whose heart must break,
Lay upon lay: I nearly learn'd
　　　　To shake.
All day I sang; of love, of fame,
　　Of fights our fathers fought of yore,
Until the thing almost became
　　　　A bore.

I cannot sing the old songs now!
　　It is not that I deem them low;
'Tis that I can't remember how
　　　　They go.
I could not range the hills till high
　　Above me stood the summer moon:
And as to dancing, I could fly
　　　　As soon.

The sports, to which with boyish glee
　　I sprang erewhile, attract no more;
Although I am but sixty-three
　　　　Or four.
Nay, worse than that, I've seem'd of late
　　To shrink from happy boyhood—boys
Have grown so noisy, and I hate
　　　　A noise

They fright me, when the beech is green,
　　By swarming up its stem for eggs:
They drive their horrid hoops between
　　　　My legs—
It's idle to repine, I know;
　　I'll tell you what I'll do instead:
I'll drink my arrowroot, and go
　　　　To bed.

The Confession

RICHARD HARRIS BARHAM

There's somewhat on my breast, father,
　　There's somewhat on my breast!
The livelong day I sigh, father,
　　And at night I cannot rest.
I cannot take my rest, father,
　　Though I would fain do so;
A weary weight oppresseth me—
　　This weary weight of woe!

'Tis not the lack of gold, father,
  Nor want of worldly gear;
My lands are broad, and fair to see,
  My friends are kind and dear.
My kin are leal and true, father,
  They mourn to see my grief;
But, oh! 'tis not a kinsman's hand
  Can give my heart relief!

'Tis not that Janet's false, father,
  'Tis not that she's unkind;
Though busy flatterers swarm around,
  I know her constant mind.
'Tis not *her* coldness, father,
  That chills my laboring breast;
It's that confounded cucumber
  I ate, and can't digest.

Leal—loyal.

A Farmer's Boy

ANONYMOUS

They strolled down the lane together,
The sky was studded with stars.
They reached the gate in silence,
And he lifted down the bars.
She neither smiled nor thanked him
Because she knew not how;
For he was just a farmer's boy
And she a Jersey cow!

There Was a Little Girl

HENRY WADSWORTH LONGFELLOW

There was a little girl,
And she had a little curl
  Right in the middle of her forehead.
When she was good
She was very, very good,
  And when she was bad she was horrid.

One day she went upstairs,
When her parents, unawares,
  In the kitchen were occupied with meals
And she stood upon her head
In her little trundle-bed,
  And then began hooraying with her heels.

Her mother heard the noise,
And she thought it was the boys
  A-playing at a combat in the attic;
But when she climbed the stair,
And found Jemima there,
  She took and she did spank her most emphatic.

The Naughty Boy

[From a Letter to Fanny Keats, July 3, 1818]

JOHN KEATS

There was a naughty Boy,
  A naughty boy was he,
He would not stop at home,
  He could not quiet be—
    He took
    In his Knapsack
    A Book
    Full of vowels
    And a shirt
    With some towels—
    A slight cap
    For night cap—
    A hair brush,

    Comb ditto,
    New Stockings
    For old ones
    Would split O!
    This Knapsack
    Tight at's back
    He rivetted close
    And followed his Nose
    To the North,
    To the North,
    And follow'd his nose
    To the North.

GEORGE CANNING, born in London in 1770, achieved prominence as a statesman of his time, and was also esteemed for his witty rhymes. In "The Elderly Gentleman," the idea, although slight, is nevertheless manipulated with consummate skill.

The Elderly Gentleman

GEORGE CANNING

By the side of a murmuring stream
  an elderly gentleman sat.
On the top of his head was a wig,
  and a-top of his wig was his hat.

The wind it blew high and blew strong,
  as the elderly gentleman sat;
And bore from his head in a trice,
  and plunged in the river his hat.

The gentleman then took his cane
  which lay by his side as he sat;
And he dropped in the river his wig,
  in attempting to get out his hat.

His breast it grew cold with despair,
  and full in his eye madness sat;
So he flung in the river his cane
  to swim with his wig, and his hat.

Cool reflection at last came across
  while this elderly gentleman sat;
So he thought he would follow the stream
  and look for his cane, wig, and hat.

His head being thicker than common,
  o'er-balanced the rest of his fat;
And in plumped this son of a woman
  to follow his wig, cane, and hat.

The Height of the Ridiculous

OLIVER WENDELL HOLMES

I wrote some lines once on a time
  In wondrous merry mood,
And thought, as usual, men would say
  They were exceeding good.

They were so queer, so very queer,
  I laughed as I would die;
Albeit, in the general way,
  A sober man am I.

I called my servant, and he came;
  How kind it was of him,
To mind a slender man like me,
  He of the mighty limb!

"These to the printer," I exclaimed,
  And, in my humorous way,
I added (as a trifling jest),
  "There'll be the devil to pay."

He took the paper, and I watched,
  And saw him peep within;
At the first line he read, his face
  Was all upon the grin.

He read the next; the grin grew broad,
  And shot from ear to ear;
He read the third; a chuckling noise
  I now began to hear.

The fourth; he broke into a roar;
  The fifth; his waistband split;
The sixth; he burst five buttons off,
  And tumbled in a fit.

Ten days and nights, with sleepless eye,
  I watched that wretched man,
And since, I never dare to write
  As funny as I can.

The Milkmaid

JEFFREYS TAYLOR

A milkmaid, who poised a full pail on her head,
Thus mused on her prospects in life, it is said:
"Let me see,—I should think that this milk will procure
　　One hundred good eggs, or fourscore, to be sure.

"Well then,—stop a bit,—it must not be forgotten,
Some of these may be broken, and some may be rotten;
But if twenty for accident should be detached,
　　It will leave me just sixty sound eggs to be hatched.

"Well, sixty sound eggs,—no, sound chickens, I mean:
Of these some may die,—we'll suppose seventeen,
Seventeen! not so many,—say ten at the most,
　　Which will leave fifty chickens to boil or to roast.

"But then there's their barley: how much will they need?
Why, they take but one grain at a time when they feed,—
So that's a mere trifle; now then, let us see,
　　At a fair market price how much money there'll be.

"Six shillings a pair—five—four—three-and-six,
To prevent all mistakes, that low price I will fix;
Now what will that make? fifty chickens, I said,—
　　Fifty times three-and-sixpence—*I'll ask Brother Ned.*

"O, but stop,—three-and-sixpence a *pair* I must sell 'em;
Well, a pair is a couple,—now then let us tell 'em;
A couple in fifty will go (my poor brain!)
　　Why, just a score times, and five pair will remain.

"Twenty-five pair of fowls—now how tiresome it is
That I can't reckon up so much money as this!
Well, there's no use in trying, so let's give a guess,—
　　I'll say twenty pounds, *and it can't be no less.*

"Twenty pounds, I am certain, will buy me a cow,
Thirty geese, and two turkeys,—eight pigs and a sow;
Now if these turn out well, at the end of the year,
　　I shall fill both my pockets with guineas, 't is clear."

Forgetting her burden, when this she had said,
The maid superciliously tossed up her head;
When, alas for her prospects! her milk-pail descended.
　　And so all her schemes for the future were ended.

This moral, I think, may be safely attached,—
"Reckon not on your chickens before they are hatched."

The Rum Tum Tugger

T. S. ELIOT

The Rum Tum Tugger is a Curious Cat:
If you offer him pheasant he would rather have grouse.
If you put him in a house he would much prefer a flat,
If you put him in a flat then he'd rather have a house.
If you set him on a mouse then he only wants a rat,
If you set him on a rat then he'd rather chase a mouse.
Yes the Rum Tum Tugger is a Curious Cat—
   And there isn't any call for me to shout it:
      For he will do
      As he do do
         And there's no doing anything about it!

The Rum Tum Tugger is a terrible bore:
When you let him in, then he wants to be out;
He's always on the wrong side of every door,
As soon as he's at home, then he'd like to get about.
He likes to lie in the bureau drawer,
But he makes such a fuss if he can't get out.
Yes the Rum Tum Tugger is a Curious Cat—
   And it isn't any use for you to doubt it:
      For he will do
      As he do do
         And there's no doing anything about it!

The Rum Tum Tugger is a curious beast:
His disobliging ways are a matter of habit.
If you offer him fish then he always wants a feast;
When there isn't any fish then he won't eat rabbit.
If you offer him cream then he sniffs and sneers,
For he only likes what he finds for himself;
So you'll catch him in it right up to the ears,
If you put it away on the larder shelf.
The Rum Tum Tugger is artful and knowing,
The Rum Tum Tugger doesn't care for a cuddle;
But he'll leap on your lap in the middle of your sewing,
For there's nothing he enjoys like a horrible muddle.
Yes the Rum Tum Tugger is a Curious Cat—
   And there isn't any need for me to spout it:
      For he will do
      As he do do
         And there's no doing anything about it!

THE BATTLE OF THE SEXES takes many an ingenious twist and turn, with sometimes the wife coming out ahead, sometimes the husband. The following two poems give battle reports on various skirmishes in that long-standing struggle.

The Old Man
Who Lived in the Woods

ANONYMOUS

There was an old man who lived in the woods,
  As you can plainly see,
Who said he could do more work in a day,
  Than his wife could do in three.

"With all my heart," the old woman said,
  "But then you must allow,
That you must do my work for a day,
  And I'll go follow the plow.

"You must milk the tiny cow,
  Lest she should go quite dry,
And you must feed the little pigs
  That live in yonder sty.

"You must watch the speckled hen,
  For fear she lays astray,
And not forget the spool of yarn
  That I spin every day."

The old woman took the staff in her hand,
  And went to follow the plow;
And the old man took the pail on his head
  And went to milk the cow.

But Tiny she winked and Tiny she blinked,
  And Tiny she tossed her nose,
And Tiny she gave him a kick on the shins
  Till the blood ran down to his toes.

Then "Whoa, Tiny!" and "So, Tiny!
  My pretty little cow, stand still!
If ever I milk you again," he said,
  "It will be against my will."

And then he went to feed the pigs
  That lived within the sty;
The old sow ran against his legs
  And threw him in the mire.

And then he watched the speckled hen
  Lest she might lay astray;
But he quite forgot the spool of yarn
  That his wife spun every day.

Then the old man swore by the sun and the moon
  And the green leaves on the trees,
That his wife could do more work in a day
  Than he could do in three.

And when he saw how well she plowed,
  And ran the furrows even,
He swore she could do more work in a day
  Than he could do in seven.

Sweet William, His Wife,
and the Sheepskin

ANONYMOUS

Sweet William, he married a wife,
Gentle Jenny called Rosemary,
To be the sweet comfort of his life,
As the dew flies over the mulberry tree.

But Jenny would not in the kitchen go,
For fear of soiling her pretty white shoe.

She would not weave, and she would not spin,
For fear of hurting her gay gold ring.

One day sweet William came in from the plow,
Saying, "Dear wife, is dinner ready now?"

"There's a little cornbread that's left on the shelf,
If you want any more you can bake it yourself."

Sweet William went out to his sheep pen,
And stripped an old wether of its sheep skin.

He laid the skin around his wife's back,
And with a stout stick went whickety-whack!

"I'll tell my father and all my kin
How you hit me hard with a hickory limb."

"You can tell your father and all your kin,
I was only tanning my own sheep skin."

Next day when William came in from the plow
He said, "Dear wife, is dinner ready now?"

She covered the table and spread the board,
And, "Yes, my dear husband," was her every word.

Now they live free from all sorrow and strife,
And they say she makes William a very good wife.

Creatures on Land

ON THE SIXTH DAY of creation, as told in the Book of Genesis, "God made the beast of the earth after his kind, and the cattle after their kind, and every thing that creepeth upon the earth after his kind." At one time or another, poets have written something about virtually each beast, all cattle, and everything that creepeth. A random selection of poems on these subjects follows.

209

I Think I Could Turn and Live with Animals

W ALT W HITMAN

I think I could turn and live with animals, they are so
    placid and self-contained;
I stand and look at them long and long.
They do not sweat and whine about their condition;
They do not lie awake in the dark and weep for their sins;
They do not make me sick discussing their duty to God;
Not one is dissatisfied—not one is demented with the
    mania of owning things;
Not one kneels to another, nor to his kind that lived
    thousands of years ago;
Not one is respectable or industrious over the whole earth.

Variation on a Sentence

There are few or no bluish animals. . . .
Thoreau's Journals, F EB . 21, 1855

L OUISE B OGAN

Of white and tawny, black as ink,
Yellow, and undefined, and pink,
And piebald, there are droves, I think.

(Buff kine in herd, gray whales in pod,
Brown woodchucks, colored like the sod,
All creatures from the hand of God.)

And many of a hellish hue;
But, for some reason hard to view,
Earth's bluish animals are few.

For all that he is so tiny—or maybe because of it—the mouse has earned an honorable place in literature. Here is a story of yet another mouse, who is a budding and stage-struck actor. The contemporary poet and critic Charles Wagner presents the theatre mouse who treads the boards at night, after the audience has gone, unmindful of his severest critic, the cat.

Theatre Mouse

Charles A. Wagner

At night, when all the feet have fled,
he pokes his small, dramatic head
out of the wings and struts about
as though some invisible talent scout
were sitting front to watch his bit,
noting his pantomime and wit.

The silent house of huddled chairs
in blank amazement stares and stares;
the midnight traffic of the street
is music to his nimble feet;
no juvenile or leading man
takes half the freedom this mouse can:

his only witness is a cat,
crouching where two-legged critics sat!

The City Mouse

CHRISTINA ROSSETTI

The city mouse lives in a house;—
    The garden mouse lives in a bower,
He's friendly with the frogs and toads,
    And sees the pretty plants in flower.

The city mouse eats bread and cheese;—
    The garden mouse eats what he can;
We will not grudge him seeds and stalks.
    Poor little timid furry man.

Three Wishes

ANONYMOUS

I wish I had a yellow cat
    To sit before the fire.
If only I could have just that
    'Twould be my heart's desire.

I wish I had an open fire
    To warm my yellow cat.
'Twould gratify my soul's desire
    If only I had that.

I wish I had a little home
    To hold my cat and fire,
And then I'm sure that I would have
    My very heart's desire.

The Kitten and the Falling Leaves

WILLIAM WORDSWORTH

See the Kitten on the wall,
Sporting with the leaves that fall,
Withered leaves—one, two and three—
From the lofty elder-tree!
Through the calm and frosty air
Of this morning bright and fair,
Eddying round and round they sink
Softly, slowly: one might think,
From the motions that are made,
Every little leaf conveyed
Sylph or Faery hither tending,
To this lower world descending,
Each invisible and mute,
In his wavering parachute.

—But the Kitten, how she starts,
Crouches, stretches paws, and darts!
First at one, and then its fellow
Just as light and just as yellow.
There are many now—now one—
Now they stop and there are none:

What intenseness of desire
In her upward eye of fire!
With a tiger-leap half way
Now she meets the coming prey,
Lets it go as fast, and then
Has it in her power again:

Now she works with three or four,
Like an Indian conjurer;
Quick as he in feats of art,
Far beyond in joy of heart.
Were her antics played in the eye
Of a thousand standers-by,
Clapping hands with shout and stare,
What would little Tabby care
For the plaudits of the crowd?

CHRISTOPHER SMART (1722–1771) was a joyful eccentric in his early years, but toward the end of his life his eccentricities deepened into abberations and he was committed to an institution. It was while there that he wrote a number of remarkable poems, including these lines inspired by Jeoffry, his cat.

My Cat Jeoffry

CHRISTOPHER SMART

For I will consider my cat Jeoffry.
For he is the servant of the Living God, duly and daily serving him.
For first he looks upon his fore-paws to see if they are clean.
For secondly he kicks up behind to clear away there.
For thirdly he works it upon stretch with the fore-paws extended.
For fourthly he sharpens his paws by wood.
For fifthly he washes himself.
For sixthly he rolls upon wash.
For seventhly he fleas himself, that he may not be interrupted upon the beat.
For eighthly he rubs himself against a post.
For ninthly he looks up for his instructions.
For tenthly he goes in quest of food.
For having consider'd God and himself he will consider his neighbor.
For he meets another cat he will kiss her in kindness.
For when he takes his prey he plays with it to give it chance.
For one mouse in seven escapes by his dallying.
For when his day's work is done his business more properly begins.
For he is the quickest to his mark of any creature.
For he is tenacious of his point.
For he is a mixture of gravity and waggery.
For there is nothing sweeter than his peace when at rest.
For there is nothing brisker than his life when in motion.
For his tongue is exceeding pure so that it has in purity what it wants in
    musick.
For he is docile and can learn certain things.
For he can spraggle upon waggle at the word of command.
For he can catch the cork and toss it again.
For he camels his back to bear the first notion of business.
For by stroking of him I have found out electricity.
For he purrs in thankfulness when God tells him he's a good cat.

That Cat

BEN KING

The cat that comes to my window sill
When the moon looks cold and the night is still—
He comes in a frenzied state alone
With a tail that stands like a pine tree cone,
And says: "I have finished my evening lark,
And I think I can hear a hound dog bark.
My whiskers are froze 'nd stuck to my chin.
I do wish you'd git up and let me in."
    That cat gits in.

But if in the solitude of the night
He doesn't appear to be feeling right,
And rises and stretches and seeks the floor,
And some remote corner he would explore,
And doesn't feel satisfied just because
There's no good spot for to sharpen his claws,
And meows and canters uneasy about
Beyond the least shadow of any doubt
    That cat gits out.

Cure for a Pussy Cat

ANONYMOUS

Who's that ringing at my door bell?
    A little pussy cat that isn't very well.
Rub its little nose with a little mutton fat,
    For that's the best cure for a little pussy cat.

The Cats of Kilkenny

ANONYMOUS

There were once two cats of Kilkenny,
Each thought there was one cat too many;
So they fought and they fit,
And they scratched and they bit,
Till, excepting their nails
And the tips of their tails,
Instead of two cats, there weren't any.

WILLIAM COWPER loved the English countryside and animals in equal measure and delighted in writing about both. In the following two animal poems, Cowper first chides his spaniel, Beau, for killing a bird, then turns around and allows Beau to reply in self-defense.

On a Spaniel Called Beau
Killing a Young Bird

WILLIAM COWPER

A Spaniel, Beau, that fares like you,
  Well-fed, and at his ease,
Should wiser be, than to pursue
  Each trifle that he sees.

But you have kill'd a tiny bird,
  Which flew not till to-day,
Against my orders, whom you heard
  Forbidding you the prey.

Nor did you kill, that you might eat,
  And ease a doggish pain,
For him, though chas'd with furious heat,
  You left where he was slain.

Nor was he of the thievish sort,
  Or one whom blood allures,
But innocent was all his sport,
  Whom you have torn for yours.

My dog! what remedy remains,
  Since, teach you all I can,
I see you, after all my pains,
  So much resemble man!

Beau's Reply

WILLIAM COWPER

Sir! when I flew to seize the bird,
  In spite of your command,
A louder voice than yours I heard
  And harder to withstand:

You cried—Forbear!—but in my breast
  A mightier cried—Proceed!
'Twas nature, Sir, whose strong behest
  Impell'd me to the deed.

Yet much as nature I respect,
  I ventur'd once to break
(As you perhaps may recollect)
  Her precept, for your sake;

And when your linnet, on a day,
  Passing his prison-door,
Had flutter'd all his strength away,
  And panting press'd the floor,

Well knowing him a sacred thing,
  Not destin'd to my tooth,
I only kiss'd his ruffled wing,
  And lick'd the feathers smooth.

Let my obedience then excuse
  My disobedience now,
Nor some reproof yourself refuse
  From your aggriev'd Bow-wow!

If killing birds be such a crime,
  (Which I can hardly see)
What think you, Sir, of killing Time
  With verse address'd to me?

Epitaph to a Newfoundland Dog

George Gordon, Lord Byron

Near this spot
Are deposited the Remains of one
Who possessed Beauty without Vanity,
Strength without Insolence,
Courage without Ferocity,
And all the Virtues of Man, without his Vices.
This Praise, which would be unmeaning Flattery
If inscribed over human ashes,
Is but a just Tribute to the Memory of
BOATSWAIN, a Dog,
Who was born at Newfoundland, May, 1803,
And died at Newstead Abbey, Nov. 18, 1808.

Elegy on the Death of a Mad Dog

OLIVER GOLDSMITH

Good people all, of every sort,
　Give ear unto my song;
And if you find it wondrous short,
　It cannot hold you long.

In Islington there was a man,
　Of whom the world might say,
That still a godly race he ran,
　Whene'er he went to pray.

A kind and gentle heart he had,
　To comfort friends and foes;
The naked every day he clad,
　When he put on his clothes.

And in that town a dog was found,
　As many dogs there be,
Both mongrel, puppy, whelp, and hound,
　And curs of low degree.

This dog and man at first were friends;
　But when a pique began,
The dog, to gain some private ends,
　Went mad and bit the man.

Around from all the neighbouring streets
　The wondering neighbours ran,
And swore the dog had lost his wits,
　To bite so good a man.

The wound it seem'd both sore and sad
　To every Christian eye;
And while they swore the dog was mad,
　They swore the man would die.

But soon a wonder came to light,
　That show'd the rogues they lied:
The man recover'd of the bite,
　The dog it was that died.

Dapple Gray

ANONYMOUS

I had a little pony,
　His name was Dapple Gray;
I lent him to a lady
　To ride a mile away.

She whipped him, and she slashed him,
　She rode him through the mire;
I would not lend my pony now,
　For all the lady's hire.

For thousands of years man and horse have toiled and even died together. Horse and rider have gone through fire and flood and battle. The horse described in the following selection from the Book of Job is a majestic, awe-inspiring creature groomed for battle.

The Horse

Job 39:19–25

Hast thou given the horse strength?
Hast thou clothed his neck with thunder?
Canst thou make him afraid as a grasshopper?
The glory of his nostrils is terrible.
He paweth in the valley and rejoiceth in his strength:
He goeth to meet the armed men;
He mocketh at fear and is not affrighted,
Neither turneth he back from the sword.
The quiver rattleth against him,
The glittering spear and the shield—
He swalloweth the ground with fierceness and rage,
Neither believeth he that it is the sound of the trumpet;
He saith among the trumpets, "Ha! ha!"
And he smelleth the battle afar off,
The thunder of the captains and the shouting.

The Horse

William Shakespeare

I will not change my horse with any that treads . . .
When I bestride him, I soar, I am a hawk.
He trots the air; the earth sings when he touches it.
The basest horn of his hoof is more musical
Than the pipe of Hermes . . .
He's of the color of the nutmeg and of the heat of the ginger . . .
He is pure air and fire, and the dull elements
Of earth and water never appear in him,
But only in patient stillness while his rider mounts him . . .
It is the prince of palfreys. His neigh is like
The bidding of a monarch, and his countenance
Enforces homage.

Donkeys

EDWARD FIELD

They are not silent like workhorses
Who are happy or indifferent about the plow and wagon;
Donkeys don't submit like that
For they are sensitive
And cry continually under their burdens;
Yes, they are animals of sensibility
Even if they aren't intelligent enough
To count money or discuss religion.

Laugh if you will when they heehaw
But know that they are crying
When they make that noise that sounds like something
Between a squawking water pump and a foghorn.

And when I hear them sobbing
I suddenly notice their sweet eyes and ridiculous ears
And their naive bodies that look as though they never grew up
But stayed children, as in fact they are;
And being misunderstood as children are
They are forced to walk up mountains
With men and bundles on their backs.

Somehow I am glad that they do not submit without a protest
But as their masters are of the deafest
The wails are never heard.

I am sure that donkeys know what life should be
But, alas, they do not own their bodies;
And if they had their own way, I am sure
That they would sit in a field of flowers
Kissing each other, and maybe
They would even invite us to join them.

For they never let us forget that they know
(As everyone knows who stays as sweet as children)
That there is a far better way to spend time; ·
You can be sure of that when they stop in their tracks
And honk and honk and honk.

And if I tried to explain to them
Why work is not only necessary but good,
I am afraid that they would never understand
And kick me with their back legs
As commentary on my wisdom.

So they remain unhappy and sob
And their masters who are equally convinced of being right
Beat them and hear nothing.

The Cow

ROBERT LOUIS STEVENSON

The friendly cow, all red and white,
　　I love with all my heart:
She gives me cream with all her might,
　　To eat with apple-tart.

She wanders lowing here and there,
　　And yet she cannot stray,
All in the pleasant open air,
　　The pleasant light of day;

And blown by all the winds that pass
And wet with all the showers,
She walks among the meadow grass
And eats the meadow flowers.

The Lamb

WILLIAM BLAKE

Little Lamb, who made thee?
Dost thou know who made thee,
Gave thee life and bade thee feed
By the stream and o'er the mead;
Gave thee clothing of delight,
Softest clothing, woolly, bright;
Gave thee such a tender voice,
Making all the vales rejoice?
　　Little lamb, who made thee?
　　Dost thou know who made thee?

Little lamb, I'll tell thee;
Little lamb, I'll tell thee.
He is callèd by thy name,
For He calls Himself a Lamb;
He is meek and He is mild,
He became a little child.
I a child and thou a lamb,
We are callèd by His name.
　　Little lamb, God bless thee!
　　Little lamb, God bless thee!

221

The Ram

ANONYMOUS

As I was going to Derby,
  Upon a market day,
I met the finest ram, sir,
  That ever was fed on hay.

This ram was fat behind, sir,
  This ram was fat before,
This ram was ten yards high, sir,
  Indeed he was no more.

The wool upon his back, sir,
  Reached up unto the sky,
The eagles built their nests there,
  For I heard the young ones cry.

The space between the horns, sir,
  Was as far as man could reach,
And there they built a pulpit,
  But no one in it preached.

This ram had four legs to walk upon,
  This ram had four legs to stand,
And every leg he had, sir,
  Stood on an acre of land.

Now the man that fed the ram, sir,
  He fed him twice a day,
And each time that he fed him, sir,
  He ate a rick of hay.

The man that killed this ram, sir,
  Was up to his knees in blood,
And the boy that held the pail, sir,
  Was carried away in the flood.

Indeed, sir, it's the truth, sir,
  For I never was taught to lie,
And if you go to Derby, sir,
  You may eat a bit of the pie.

The God of Sheep

JOHN FLETCHER

All ye woods, and trees, and bowers,
All ye virtues and ye powers
That inhabit in the lakes,
In the pleasant springs or brakes,
  Move your feet
  To our sound,
  Whilst we greet
  All this ground
With his honour and his name
That defends our flocks from blame.

He is great, and he is just,
He is ever good, and must
Thus be honoured, Daffadillies,
Roses, pinks and lovèd lilies
  Let us fling,
  Whilst we sing,
  Ever holy,
  Ever holy,
Ever honoured, ever young!
Thus great Pan is ever sung.

The Goat

ANONYMOUS

There was a man, now please take note,
There was a man, who had a goat.
He lov'd that goat, indeed he did,
He lov'd that goat, just like a kid.

One day that goat felt frisk and fine,
Ate three red shirts from off the line.
The man he grabbed him by the back,
And tied him to a railroad track.

But when the train hove into sight,
That goat grew pale and green with fright.
He heaved a sigh, as if in pain,
Coughed up those shirts and flagged the train.

The Goat Paths

JAMES STEPHENS

I

The crooked paths
Go every way
Upon the hill
—They wind about
Through the heather,
In and out
Of a quiet
Sunniness.

And the goats
Day after day
Stray
In sunny quietness;
Cropping here,
And cropping there
—As they pause,
And turn,
And pass—
Now a bit
Of heather spray
Now a mouthful
Of the grass.

II

In the deeper
Sunniness,
In the place
Where nothing stirs;
Quietly
In quietness;
In the quiet
Of the furze
They stand a while;
They dream;
They lie;
They stare
Upon the roving sky.

If you approach
They run away!
They will stare,
And stamp,
And bound,
With a sudden angry sound,
To the sunny
Quietude:

To crouch again,
Where nothing stirs,
In the quiet
Of the furze.
To crouch them down
Again,
And brood,
In the sunny
Solitude.

III

Were I but
As free
As they,
I would stray
Away
And brood;
I would beat
A hidden way,
Through the quiet
Heather spray

223

To a sunny
Solitude.

And should you come
I'd run away!
I would make an angry sound,
I would stare,
And stamp,
And bound
To the deeper
Quietude;
To the place
Where nothing stirs
In the quiet
Of the furze.

IV

In that airy
Quietness
I would dream
As long as they:
Through the quiet
Sunniness
I would stray
Away
And brood,
All among
The heather spray
In a sunny
Solitude.

V

—I would think
Until I found
Something
—I can never find,
Something
Lying
On the ground,
In the bottom
Of my mind.

The Sloth

THEODORE ROETHKE

In moving-slow he has no Peer.
You ask him something in his Ear,
He thinks about it for a Year;

And, then, before he says a Word
There, upside down (unlike a Bird),
He will assume that you have Heard—

A most Ex-as-per-at-ing Lug.
But should you call his manner Smug,
He'll sigh and give his Branch a Hug;

Then off again to Sleep he goes,
Still swaying gently by his Toes,
And you just *know* he knows he knows.

"THE TIGER" is one of the most striking of Blake's shorter poems. Its very opening lines plunge us into a mysterious and almost fearful world. The tiger burning "in the forests of the night" and the gentle lamb, though two opposing symbols, have been fashioned by the one "immortal hand." The tremendous power of the poem rises from its startling images, and from the cadences that resound like hammer-blows on an anvil.

The Tiger

WILLIAM BLAKE

Tiger, tiger, burning bright
In the forests of the night,
What immortal hand or eye
Could frame thy fearful symmetry?

In what distant deeps or skies
Burnt the fire of thine eyes?
On what wings dare he aspire?
What the hand dare seize the fire?

And what shoulder and what art
Could twist the sinews of thy heart?
And, when thy heart began to beat,
What dread hand and what dread feet?

What the hammer? What the chain?
In what furnace was thy brain?
What the anvil? what dread grasp
Dare its deadly terrors clasp?

When the stars threw down their spears,
And watered heaven with their tears,
Did He smile his work to see?
Did He who made the lamb make thee?

Tiger, tiger, burning bright
In the forests of the night,
What immortal hand or eye
Dare frame thy fearful symmetry?

Grizzly Bear

MARY AUSTIN

If you ever, ever, ever meet a grizzly bear,
You must never, never, never ask him *where*
He is going,
Or *what* he is doing;
For if you ever, ever dare
To stop a grizzly bear,
You will never meet *another* grizzly bear.

THE NEXT POEM is something of a surprise, having been written by Abraham Lincoln. Although there is more poetic worth in Lincoln's brief "Gettysburg Address" than in this over-lengthy bear hunt, its existence adds another side to the complex character of America's remarkable sixteenth president.

The Bear Hunt

ABRAHAM LINCOLN

A wild-bear chase, didst never see?
   Then hast thou lived in vain.
Thy richest bump of glorious glee,
   Lies desert in thy brain.

When first my father settled here,
   'Twas then the frontier line:
The panther's scream, filled night with fear
   And bears preyed on the swine.

But woe for Bruin's short lived fun,
   When rose the squealing cry;
Now man and horse, with dog and gun,
   For vengeance, at him fly.

A sound of danger strikes his ear;
   He gives the breeze a snuff:
Away he bounds, with little fear,
   And seeks the tangled rough.

On press his foes, and reach the ground,
   Where's left his half munched meal;
The dogs, in circles, scent around,
   And find his fresh made trail.

With instant cry, away they dash,
   And men as fast pursue;
O'er logs they leap, through water splash,
   And shout the brisk halloo.

Now to elude the eager pack,
   Bear shuns the open ground;
Through matted vines, he shapes his track
   And runs it, round and round.

The tall fleet cur, with deep-mouthed voice,
   Now speeds him, as the wind;
While half-grown pup, and shorted-legged fi
   Are yelping far behind.

And fresh recruits are dropping in
   To join the merry corps.
With yelp and yell,—a mingled din—
   The woods are in a roar.

And round, and round the chase now goes,
   The world's alive with fun;
Nick Carter's horse, his rider throws,
   And more, Hill drops his gun.

Now sorely pressed, bear glances back,
    And lolls his tired tongue;
When is, to force him from his track,
    An ambush on him sprung.

Across the glade he sweeps for flight,
    And fully is in view.
The dogs, new-fired, by the sight,
    Their cry, and speed, renew.

The foremost ones, now reach his rear,
    He turns, they dash away;
And circling now, the wrathful bear,
    They have him full at bay.

At top of speed, the horse-men come,
    All screaming in a row.
"Whoop! Take him Tiger—Seize-him Drum"—
Bang,—Bang—the rifles go.

And furious now, the dogs he tears.
    And crushes in his ire—
Wheels right and left, and upward rears,
    With eyes of burning fire.

But leaden death is at his heart,
    Vain all the strength he plies—
And, spouting blood from every part,
    He reels, and sinks, and dies.

And now a dinsome clamor rose,
    'Bout who should have his skin;
Who first draws blood, each hunter knows,
    This prize must always win.

But who did this, and how to trace
    What's true from what's a lie,
Like lawyers, in a murder case
    They stoutly argufy.

Aforesaid fice, of blustering mood,
    Behind, and quite forgot,
Just now emerging from the wood,
    Arrives upon the spot.

With grinning teeth, and up-turned hair—
    Brim full of spunk and wrath,
He growls, and seizes on dead bear,
    And shakes for life and death.

And swells as if his skin would tear,
    And growls and shakes again;
And swears, as plain as dog can swear,
    That he has won the skin.

Conceited whelp! we laugh at thee—
    Nor mind, that not a few
Of pompous, two-legged dogs there be,
    Conceited quite as you.

Fice—a small dog

Hunting Song

Samuel Taylor Coleridge

Up, up! ye dames, and lasses gay!
To the meadows trip away.
'Tis you must tend the flocks this morn,
And scare the small birds from the corn.
    Not a soul at home may stay:
      For the shepherds must go
      With lance and bow
    To hunt the wolf in the woods to-day.

Leave the hearth and leave the house
To the cricket and the mouse:
Find grannam out a sunny seat,
With babe and lambkin at her feet.
    Not a soul at home may stay:
      For the shepherds must go
      With lance and bow
    To hunt the wolf in the woods to-day.

COMPOSED BY AN UNKNOWN English minstrel more than a hundred years ago, "The Ballad of the Fox" found its way across the Atlantic and became popular with generations of American ballad lovers.

The Ballad of the Fox

ANONYMOUS

A fox went out in a hungry plight,
And he begged of the moon to give him light,
For he'd many miles to trot that night
      Before he could reach his den, O!

And first he came to a farmer's yard,
Where the ducks and geese declared it hard
That their nerves should be shaken and their rest be marred
      By the visit of Mister Fox, O!

He took the gray goose by the sleeve;
Says he, "Madam Goose, and by your leave,
I'll take you away without reprieve,
      And carry you home to my den, O!"

He seized the black duck by the neck,
And swung her all across his back;
The black duck cried out, "Quack! quack! quack!"
      With her legs hanging dangling down, O!

Then old Mother Slipper-slopper jumped out of bed,
And out of the window she popped her head,—
"John, John, John, the gray goose is gone,
      And the fox is off to his den, O!"

Then John he went up to the hill,
And he blew a blast both loud and shrill.
Says the fox, "This is very pretty music—still
      I'd rather be at my den, O!"

At last the fox got home to his den;
To his dear little foxes, eight, nine, ten,
Says he, "You're in luck; here's a good fat duck,
      With her legs hanging dangling down, O!"

He then sat down with his hungry wife;
They did very well without fork or knife;
They never ate a better goose in all their life,
      And the little ones picked the bones, O!

The Squirrel

ANONYMOUS

Whisky, frisky,
Hippity hop;
Up he goes
To the tree top!

Whirly, twirly,
Round and round,
Down he scampers
To the ground.

Furly, curly
What a tail!
Tall as a feather
Broad as a sail!

Where's his supper?
In the shell,
Snappity, crackity,
Out it fell.

The little animal that gave his life
for the lining of my gloves. . . .
So begins the poignantly moving poem by Joseph Tusiani, gifted
teacher, translator, and poet. Further on in the poem, he recalls
an Aesop fable "about a squirrel minding his own green business"
and then killed so that the killer's hands can be kept warm.
Though the tone of the poem is gentle and compassionate, the
theme makes us aware of many harsh but true things about the
world and ourselves that we overlook.

The Little Animal

JOSEPH TUSIANI

The little animal that gave his life
for the lining of my gloves
wanted to live and love
as I do. When and if

of my brief passing on this earth remain
only the husk of my day
and the cold of my night, in what ways
shall I be one

of the warm useful things beneath the winter
of the sky? Shall I forgive
and follow with my love
Fate's everlasting Sunday?

Saint Aesop, martyr of the truth—
for telling me I kill
something helpless, something small,
Just to own my bit of earth,—

did you think, dying, of your last
fable about a squirrel minding
his own green business, counting
his kernels, and then killed to save from frost

two killing hands? I do not know how many
things with my life I have slain.
I only know I'm one
whose end will make no corner sunny.

O little animal that gave your life
for the lining of my gloves,
if so it had to be, no life receives
on earth a longer spring than it can give.

229

To Miss Georgiana Shipley

On the loss of her American Squirrel, who,
escaping from his Cage, was Killed by a
Shepherd's Dog

BENJAMIN FRANKLIN

London, 26th September, 1772

Dear Miss: I lament with you most sincerely the unfortunate
end of poor Mungo. Few squirrels were better accomplished,
for he had a good education, had travelled far, and seen much
of the world. As he had the honour of being, for his virtues,
your favorite, he should not go, like common skuggs, without an elegy or an epitaph. Let us give him one on the monu-
mental style and measure, which, being neither prose nor
verse, is perhaps the properest for grief; since to use common
language would look as if we were not affected, and to make
rhymes would seem trifling in sorrow.

EPITAPH

Alas! poor Mungo!
Happy wert thou, hadst thou known
Thy own felicity.
Remote from the fierce bald eagle,
Tyrant of thy native woods,
Thou hadst naught to fear from his piercing talons,
Nor from the murdering gun
Of the thoughtless sportsman.

Safe in thy wired castle,
Grimalkin never could annoy thee.
Daily wert thou fed with the choicest viands,
By the fair hand of an indulgent mistress;
But, discontented,
Thou wouldst have more freedom.
Too soon, alas! didst thou obtain it;
and wandering,

Thou art fallen by the fangs of wanton
cruel Ranger!
Learn hence,
Ye who blindly seek more liberty,
Whether subjects, sons, squirrels, or daughters,
That apparent restraint may be real protection,
Yielding peace and plenty
With security.

You see, my dear miss, how much more decent and proper
this broken style is than if we were to say by way of epitaph:
Here Skugg
Lies snug
As a bug
In a rug.

230 Grimalkin—cat
Skugg—squirrel

To a Squirrel at Kyle-na-no

WILLIAM BUTLER YEATS

Come play with me;
Why should you run
Through the shaking tree
As though I'd a gun
To strike you dead?
When all I would do
Is to scratch your head
And let you go.

On a Squirrel Crossing the Road
in Autumn, in New England

RICHARD EBERHART

It is what he does not know,
Crossing the road under the elm trees,
About the mechanism of my car,
About the Commonwealth of Massachusetts,
About Mozart, India, Arcturus,

That wins my praise. I engage
At once in whirling squirrel-praise.

He obeys the orders of nature
Without knowing them.
It is what he does not know
That makes him beautiful.
Such a knot of little purposeful nature!

I who can see him as he cannot see himself
Repose in the ignorance that is his blessing.

It is what man does not know of God
Composes the visible poem of the world.
                    . . . Just missed him!

The Blind Men and the Elephant

JOHN GODFREY SAXE

A Hindoo Fable

It was six men of Indostan
    To learning much inclined,
Who went to see the Elephant
    (Though all of them were blind),
That each by observation
    Might satisfy his mind

The *First* approached the Elephant,
    And happening to fall
Against his broad and sturdy side,
    At once began to bawl:
"God bless me! but the Elephant
    Is very like a wall!"

The *Second*, feeling of the tusk,
    Cried, "Ho! what have we here
So very round and smooth and sharp?
    To me 'tis mighty clear
This wonder of an Elephant
    Is very like a spear!"

The *Third* approached the animal,
    And happening to take
The squirming trunk within his hands,
    Thus boldly up and spake:
"I see," quoth he, "the Elephant
    Is very like a snake!"

The *Fourth* reached out an eager hand,
    And felt about the knee.
"What most this wondrous beast is like
    Is mighty plain," quoth he;
" 'Tis clear enough the Elephant
    Is very like a tree!"

The *Fifth* who chanced to touch the ear,
    Said: "E'en the blindest man
Can tell what this resembles most;
    Deny the fact who can,
This marvel of an Elephant
    Is very like a fan!"

The *Sixth* no sooner had begun
    About the beast to grope,
Than, seizing on the swinging tail
    That fell within his scope,
"I see," quoth he, "the Elephant
    Is very like a rope!"

And so these men of Indostan
    Disputed loud and long,
Each in his own opinion
    Exceeding stiff and strong,
Though each was partly in the right,
    And all were in the wrong!

Moral

So oft in theologic wars,
    The disputants, I ween,
Rail on in utter ignorance
    Of what each other mean,
And prate about an Elephant
    Not one of them has seen!

Brown and Furry

CRISTINA ROSSETTI

Brown and furry
Caterpillar in a hurry
Take your walk
To the shady leaf, or stalk,
Or what not,

Which may be the chosen spot.
No toad spy you,
Hovering bird of prey pass by you;
Spin and die,
To live again a butterfly.

Animal Fair

ANONYMOUS

I went to the animal fair,
The birds and the beasts were there,
The big baboon, by the light of the moon,
Was combing his auburn hair.

The monkey, he got drunk
And sat on the elephant's trunk.
The elephant sneezed and fell on his knees
And what became of the monk, the monk?

Bed-Time Story

MELVILLE CANE

Once there was a spaniel
By the name of Daniel,
And a pig,
Sig,
And a pussy,
Gussie,—
She chased a mouse,
Klaus;
And a squirrel,
Errol,
And a white she–bear,
Claire,
And a Scotch lion,
Ian,
And a very fierce shark,
Mark.

You'll agree, my dear,
They were rather a queer
Assortment
Of temperament and deportment.

And yet,
My pet,
In spite of their diversities
And perversities
Both zoological
And ideological
They all gathered together
One day, when the weather
Was especially frightful, and decided
It wasn't safe to stay divided
Any longer, and that they should,
For their common good,
(Rather than risk another calamity)
Try amity.

And that's the way there began to dawn a
Plan they christened UNITED FAUNA.

. . . .

"And did they live happily ever after, daddy?"
"I'll tell you the rest tomorrow. Good-night, dear."

The Snail

ANONYMOUS

The snail he lives in his hard round house,
  In the orchard, under the tree:
Says he, "I have but a single room;
  But it's large enough for me."

The snail in his little house doth dwell
  All the week from end to end,
You're at home, Master Snail; that's all very well.
  But you never receive a friend

Nursery Snail

RUTH HERSCHBERGER

The garden snail,
moist in its bed,
arises,
tickled by the grass
at its feet
and the new dew.

Snail-paced,
the garden snail
ventures
a shell's length,
and finding you,
withdraws,
snag-toothed,
smoulder-still,
from the sweet grass
and the new dew
and the small
capture-soft
hand of you.

Its horns steal out
for comfort,
finding
moss at the touch
and the new dew.

The Snail

WILLIAM COWPER

To grass, or leaf, or fruit, or wall,
The Snail sticks close, nor fears to fall,
As if he grew there, house and all
    Together.

Within that house secure he hides,
When danger imminent betides
Of storm, or other harm besides,
    Of weather.

Give but his horns the slightest touch,
His self-collecting power is such,
He shrinks into his house, with much
    Displeasure.

Where'er he dwells, he dwells alone,
Except himself has chattels none,
Well satisfied to be his own
    Whole treasure.

Thus hermit-like his life he leads,
Nor partner of his banquet needs,
And if he meets one, only feeds
    The faster.

Who seeks him must be worse than blind
(He and his house are so combin'd)
If, finding it, he fails to find
    Its master.

The Housekeeper

CHARLES LAMB

The frugal snail, with forecast of repose,
Carries his house with him wher'er he goes;
Peeps out,—and if there comes a shower of rain,
Retreats to his small domicile again.
Touch but a tip of him, a horn,—'tis well,—
He curls up in his sanctuary shell.
He's his own landlord, his own tenant; stay
Long as he will, he dreads no quarter day.
Himself he boards and lodges; both invites
And feasts himself; sleeps with himself o' nights.
He spares the upholsterer trouble to procure
Chattels; himself is his own furniture,
And his sole riches. Wheresoe'er he roam,—
Knock when you will,—he's sure to be at home.

Remonstrance with the Snails

ANONYMOUS

Ye little snails,
With slippery tails,
Who noiselessly travel
Along this gravel,
By a silvery path of slime unsightly,
I learn that you visit my pea-rows nightly.
Felonious your visit, I guess!
And I give you this warning,
That, every morning,
I'll strictly examine the pods;
And if one I hit on,
With slaver or spit on,
Your next meal will be with the gods.

I own you're a very ancient race,
And Greece and Babylon were amid;
You have tenanted many a royal dome,
And dwelt in the oldest pyramid;

The source of the Nile!—O, you have been there!
  In the ark was your floodless bed;
On the moonless night of Marathon
  You crawled o'er the mighty dead;
    But still, though I reverence your ancestries,
    I don't see why you should nibble my peas.

The meadows are yours,—the hedgerow and brook,
  You may bathe in their dews at morn;
By the aged sea you may sound your *shells*,
  On the mountains erect your *horn*;
The fruits and the flowers are your rightful dowers,
  Then why—in the name of wonder—
Should my six pea-rows be the only cause
  To excite your midnight plunder?

I have never disturbed your slender shells;
  You have hung round my aged walk;
And each might have sat, till he died in his fat,
  Beneath his own cabbage-stalk:
But now you must fly from the soil of your sires;
  Then put on your liveliest crawl,
And think of your poor little snails at home,
  Now orphans or emigrants all.

Utensils domestic and civil and social
  I give you an evening to pack up;
But if the moon of this night does not rise on your flight,
  To-morrow I'll hang each man Jack up.
You'll think of my peas and your thievish tricks,
With tears of slime, when crossing the *Styx*.

Cast of Characters

Whether the characters in this cast are real or imaginary, the poets have fixed a spotlight on each, have illuminated each one unforgettably. Some are fully developed portraits, some an impression quickly gained, but all become somehow timeless and real.

239

The Village Schoolmaster

OLIVER GOLDSMITH

Beyond yon straggling fence that skirts the way,
With blossomed furze unprofitably gay,
There in his noisy mansion, skilled to rule,
The village master taught his little school;

.   .   .   .

The village all declared how much he knew,
'Twas certain he could write, and cipher too;
Lands he could measure, terms and tides presage,
And e'en the story ran that he could gauge;
In arguing too, the parson owned his skill,
For, e'en though vanquished, he could argue still,
While words of learned length and thundering sound
Amazed the gazing rustics ranged around;
And still they gazed, and still the wonder grew
That one small head could carry all he knew.

The Ballad of William Sycamore

STEPHEN VINCENT BENÉT

My father, he was a mountaineer,
His fist was a knotty hammer;
He was quick on his feet as a running deer,
And he spoke with a Yankee stammer.

My mother, she was merry and brave,
And so she came to her labor,
With a tall green fir for her doctor grave
And a stream for her comforting neighbor.

And some are wrapped in the linen fine,
And some like a godling's scion;
But I was cradled on twigs of pine
And the skin of a mountain lion.

And some remember a white, starched lap
And a ewer with silver handles;
But I remember a coonskin cap
And the smell of bayberry candles.

The cabin logs, with the bark still rough,
And my mother who laughed at trifles,
And the tall, lank visitors, brown as snuff,
With their long, straight squirrel-rifles.

I can hear them dance, like a foggy song,
Through the deepest one of my slumbers,
The fiddle squeaking the boots along
And my father calling the numbers.

The quick feet shaking the puncheon-floor,
And the fiddle squealing and squealing,
Till the dried herbs rattled above the door
And the dust went up to the ceiling.

There are children lucky from dawn till dusk,
But never a child so lucky!
For I cut my teeth on "Money Musk"
In the Bloody Ground of Kentucky!

When I grew tall as the Indian corn,
My father had little to lend me,
But he gave me his great, old powder-horn
And his woodsman's skill to befriend me.

241

With a leather shirt to cover my back,
And a redskin nose to unravel
Each forest sign, I carried my pack
As far as a scout could travel.

Till I lost my boyhood and found my wife,
A girl like a Salem clipper!
A woman straight as a hunting-knife
With eyes as bright as the Dipper!

We cleared our camp where the buffalo feed,
Unheard-of streams were our flagons;
And I sowed my sons like the apple-seed
On the trail of the Western wagons.

They were right, tight boys, never sulky or slow,
A fruitful, a goodly muster.
The eldest died at the Alamo.
The youngest fell with Custer.

The letter that told it burned my hand.
Yet we smiled and said, 'So be it!'
But I could not live when they fenced my land,
For it broke my heart to see it.

I saddled a red, unbroken colt
And rode him into the day there;
And he threw me down like a thunderbolt
And rolled on me as I lay there.

The hunter's whistle hummed in my ear
As the city-men tried to move me,
And I died in my boots like a pioneer
With the whole wide sky above me.

Now I lie in the heart of the fat, black soil,
Like the seed of a prairie-thistle;
It has ashed my bones with honey and oil
And picked them clean as a whistle.

And my youth returns, like the rains of Spring,
And my sons, like the wild-geese flying;
And I lie and hear the meadow-lark sing
And have much content in my dying.

Go play with the towns you have built of blocks,
The towns where you would have bound me!
I sleep in my earth like a tired fox,
And my buffalo have found me.

The Ox-Tamer

WALT WHITMAN

In a far away northern county in the placid pastoral region,
Lives my farmer friend, the theme of my recitative, a famous
    tamer of oxen,
There they bring him the three-year-olds and the four-year-olds to
    break them,
He will take the wildest steer in the world and break him and
    tame him,
He will go fearless without any whip where the young bullock
    chafes up and down the yard,
The bullock's head tosses restless high in the air with raging eyes,
Yet see you! how soon his rage subsides—how soon this tamer
    tames him;
See you! on the farms hereabout a hundred oxen young and old,
    and he is the man who has tamed them,
They all know him, all are affectionate to him;
See you! some are such beautiful animals, so lofty looking;
Some are buff-coloured, some mottled, one has a white line
    running along his back, some are brindled,
Some have wide flaring horns (a good sign)—see you! the bright hides,
See, the two with stars on their foreheads—see the round bodies
    and broad backs,
How straight and square they stand on their legs—what fine
    sagacious eyes!
How they watch their tamer—they wish him near them—how
    they turn to look after him!
What yearning expression! how uneasy they are when he moves
    away from them;
Now I marvel what it can be he appears to them (books, politics,
    poems, depart—all else departs),
I confess I envy only his fascination—my silent, illiterate friend,
Whom a hundred oxen love there in his life on farms,
In the northern county far, in the placid pastoral region.

HERE IS A VIEW of the great Biblical kings David and Solomon somewhat different from that usually presented in Sunday School.

King Solomon and King David

ANONYMOUS

King Solomon and King David
  Led merry, merry lives,
Had many, many lady friends
  And many, many wives.
But when old age crept on them,
  With many, many qualms,
King Solomon wrote the Proverbs,
  And King David wrote the Psalms.

Parson Gray

OLIVER GOLDSMITH

A quiet home had Parson Gray,
  Secluded in a vale;
His daughters all were feminine,
  And all his sons were male.

How faithfully did Parson Gray
  The bread of life dispense—
Well "posted" in theology,
  And post and rail his fence.

'Gainst all the vices of the age
  He manfully did battle;
His chickens were a biped breed,
  And quadruped his cattle.

No clock more punctually went,
  He ne'er delayed a minute—
Nor ever empty was his purse,
  When he had money in it.

His piety was ne'er denied;
  His truths hit saint and sinner;
At morn he always breakfasted;
  He always dined at dinner.

He ne'er by any luck was grieved,
  By any care perplexed—
No filcher he, though when he preached
  He always "took" a text.

As faithful characters he drew
  As mortal ever saw;
But ah! poor parson! when he died,
  His breath he could not draw!

THE IRISH have a long, rich heritage. They cherish, as a part of this heritage, two national characters: the makers of poems—the bards—and the makers of music—the fiddlers, who wandered about making the air sweet with their sounds. It is firmly maintained in Ireland that he who makes the heart merry with song is well worth a place by the fireside and a portion of food and drink. And no Irishman would object to the heavenly reception predicted for the Fiddler of Dooney by the modern Irish bard William Butler Yeats.

The Fiddler of Dooney

WILLIAM BUTLER YEATS

When I play on my fiddle in Dooney
  Folk dance like a wave of the sea;
My cousin is priest in Kilvarnet;
  My brother in Moharabuiee.

I passed my brother and cousin:
  They read in their books of prayers;
I read in my book of songs
  I bought at the Sligo fair.

When we come at the end of time,
  To Peter sitting in state,
He will smile on the three old spirits,
  But call me first through the gate;

For the good are always the merry,
  Save by an evil chance;
And the merry love the fiddle,
  And the merry love to dance:

And when the folk there spy me,
  They will all come up to me,
With "Here is the fiddler of Dooney!"
  And dance like a wave of the sea.

Quoits

MARY EFFIE LEE NEWSOME

In wintertime I have such fun
  When I play quoits with father.
I beat him almost every game.
  He never seems to bother.

He looks at mother and just smiles.
  All this seems strange to me,
For when he plays with grown-up folks,
  He beats them easily.

245

WILLIAM ALLINGHAM, the 19th-century Irish poet has left us
a number of spirited poems dealing with wonder-working elves
and fairies. Here is one of his poems infused with airiness and
charm.

The Lepracaun; or, Fairy Shoemaker

WILLIAM ALLINGHAM

I

Little Cowboy, what have you heard,
  Up on the lonely rath's green mound?
Only the plaintive yellow bird
  Sighing in sultry fields around,
Chary, chary, chary, chee-ee!—
Only the grasshopper and the bee?—
    "Tip tap, rip-rap,
    Tick-a-tack-too!
Scarlet leather, sewn togther,
  This will make a shoe.
Left, right, pull it tight;
  Summer days are warm;
Underground in winter,
  Laughing at the storm!"
Lay your ear close to the hill.
Do you not catch the tiny clamor,
Busy click of an elfin hammer,
Voice of the Lepracaun singing shrill
  As he merrily plies his trade?
    He's a span
    And a quarter in height.
Get him in sight, hold him tight,
    And you're a made
    Man!

II

You watch your cattle the summer day,
Sup on potatoes, sleep in the hay;
  How would you like to roll in your carriage,
  Look for a duchess's daughter in marriage?
Seize the Shoemaker—then you may!

"Big boots a-hunting,
    Sandals in the hall,
White for a wedding-feast,
    Pink for a ball.
This way, that way,
    So we make a shoe;
Getting rich every stitch,
    Tick-tack-too!"
Nine-and-ninety treasure-crocks
This keen miser-fairy hath,
Hid in mountains, woods, and rocks,
Ruin and round-tow'r, cave and rath,
    And where the cormorants build;
        From times of old
        Guarded by him;
        Each of them fill'd
        Full to the brim
        With gold!

III

I caught him at work one day, myself,
    In the castle-ditch, where foxglove grows,—
A wrinkled, wizen'd, and bearded Elf,
    Spectacles stuck on his pointed nose,
    Silver buckles to his hose,
    Leather apron—shoe in his lap—
        "Rip-rap, tip-tap,
        Tick-tack-too!
    (A grasshopper on my cap!
        Away the moth flew!)
    Buskins for a fairy prince,
        Brogues for his son,—
    Pay me well, pay me well,
        When the job is done!"
The rogue was mine, beyond a doubt.
I stared at him; he stared at me;
"Servant, Sir!" "Humph!" says he,
    And pull'd a snuff-box out.
He took a long pinch, look'd better pleased,
    The queer little Lepracaun;
Offer'd the box with a whimsical grace,—
Pouf! he flung the dust in my face,
    And, while I sneezed,
        Was gone!

The Shepherd

WILLIAM BLAKE

How sweet is the Shepherd's sweet lot!
From the morn to the evening he strays;
He shall follow his sheep all the day,
And his tongue shall be filled with praise.

For he hears the lamb's innocent call,
And he hears the ewe's tender reply;
He is watchful while they are in peace,
For they know when their Shepherd is nigh.

Maud Muller

JOHN GREENLEAF WHITTIER

Maud Muller on a summer's day
Raked the meadow sweet with hay.

Beneath her torn hat glowed the wealth
Of simple beauty and rustic health.

Singing, she wrought, and her merry glee
The mock-bird echoed from his tree.

But when she glanced to the far-off town,
White from its hill-slope looking down,

The sweet song died, and a vague unrest
And a nameless longing filled her breast,—

A wish that she hardly dared to own,
For something better than she had known.

The Judge rode slowly down the lane,
Smoothing his horse's chestnut mane.

He drew his bridle in the shade
Of the apple-trees, to greet the maid,

And asked a draught from the spring that flowed
Through the meadow across the road.

She stooped where the cool spring bubbled up,
And filled for him her small tin cup,

And blushed as she gave it, looking down
On her feet so bare, and her tattered gown.

"Thanks!" said the Judge; "a sweeter draught
From a fairer hand was never quaffed."

He spoke of the grass and flowers and trees,
Of the singing birds and the humming bees;

Then talked of the haying, and wondered whether
The cloud in the west would bring foul weather.

And Maud forgot her brier-torn gown,
And her graceful ankles bare and brown;

And listened, while a pleased surprise
Looked from her long-lashed hazel eyes.

At last, like one who for delay
Seeks a vain excuse, he rode away.

Maud Muller looked and sighed: "Ah me!
That I the Judge's bride might be!

"He would dress me up in silks so fine,
And praise and toast me at his wine.

"My father should wear a broadcloth coat;
My brother should sail a painted boat.

"I'd dress my mother so grand and gay,
And the baby should have a new toy each day.

"And I'd feed the hungry and clothe the poor,
And all should bless me who left our door."

The Judge looked back as he climbed the hill,
And saw Maud Muller standing still.

"A form more fair, a face more sweet,
Ne'er hath it been my lot to meet.

"And her modest answer and graceful air
Show her wise and good as she is fair.

"Would she were mine, and I to-day,
Like her, a harvester of hay;

"No doubtful balance of rights and wrongs,
Nor weary lawyers with endless tongues,

"But low of cattle and song of birds,
And health and quiet and loving words."

But he thought of his sisters, proud and cold,
And his mother, vain of her rank and gold.

So, closing his heart, the Judge rode on,
And Maud was left in the field alone.

But the lawyers smiled that afternoon,
When he hummed in court an old love-tune;

And the young girl mused beside the well
Till the rain on the unraked clover fell.

He wedded a wife of richest dower,
Who lived for fashion, as he for power.

Yet oft, in his marble hearth's bright glow,
He watched a picture come and go;

And sweet Maud Muller's hazel eyes
Looked out in their innocent surprise.

Oft, when the wine in his glass was red,
He longed for the wayside well instead;

And closed his eyes on his garnished rooms
To dream of meadows and clover-blooms.

And the proud man sighed, with a secret pain,
"Ah, that I were free again!

"Free as when I rode that day,
Where the barefoot maiden raked her hay."

She wedded a man unlearned and poor,
And many children played round her door.

But care and sorrow, and childbirth pain,
Left their traces on heart and brain.

And oft, when the summer sun shone hot
On the new-mown hay in the meadow lot,

And she heard the little spring brook fall
Over the roadside, through the wall,

In the shade of the apple-tree again
She saw a rider draw his rein;

And, gazing down with timid grace,
She felt his pleased eyes read her face.

Sometimes her narrow kitchen walls
Stretched away into stately halls;

The weary wheel to a spinet turned,
The tallow candle an astral burned,

And for him who sat by the chimney lug,
Dozing and grumbling o'er pipe and mug,

A manly form at her side she saw,
And joy was duty and love was law.

Then she took up her burden of life again,
Saying only, "It might have been."

Alas for maiden, alas for Judge,
For rich repiner and household drudge!

God pity them both! and pity us all,
Who vainly the dreams of youth recall.

For of all sad words of tongue or pen,
The saddest are these: "It might have been!"

Ah, well! for us all some sweet hope lies
Deeply buried from human eyes;

And, in the hereafter, angels may
Roll the stone from its grave away!

One More River

Anonymous

Old Noah once he built the Ark,
And sealed it up with hickory bark,

Chorus: There's one more river to cross,
And that's the river Jordan,
One more river,
There's one more river to cross.

He went to work to load his stock,
He anchored the Ark on a great big rock.   Chorus

The animals went in one by one,
The elephant chewing a caraway bun,   Chorus

The animals went in two by two,
The lion and the kangaroo,   Chorus

The animals went in three by three,
The skunk, the flea and the bumble bee,   Chorus

The animals went in four by four,
Old Noah got mad and yelled for more,   Chorus

The animals went in five by five,
Noah asked when the rain would arrive,   Chorus

The animals went in six by six,
The hyena laughed at the monkey's tricks,   Chorus

The animals went in seven by seven,
Said the rabbit to the elephant, "Who are you a-shovin'?"   Chorus

The animals went in eight by eight,
They came with a rush 'cause it was late,   Chorus

The animals went in nine by nine,
Old Noah hollered "Cut that line!"—   Chorus

The animals went in ten by ten,
The Ark she blew her whistle then,   Chorus

And then the voyage did begin,
Old Noah pulled the gang-plank in.   Chorus

They never knew where they were at,
Till the old Ark bumped on Ararat.   Chorus

251

THE STORY OF Captain John Smith and the Indian maid Pocahontas has fascinated many generations of school-children. It also stirred the imagination of the famous English novelist William Makepeace Thackeray. Here is his version of how Pocahontas, brave daughter of Chief Powhatan, saved the life of John Smith.

Pocahontas

WILLIAM MAKEPIECE THACKERAY

Wearied arm and broken sword
　Wage in vain the desperate fight;
Round him press a countless horde,
　He is but a single knight.
Hark! a cry of triumph shrill
　Through the wilderness resounds,
　As, with twenty bleeding wounds,
Sinks the warrior, fighting still.

Now they heap the funeral pyre,
　And the torch of death they light;
Ah! 't is hard to die by fire!
　Who will shield the captive knight?
Round the stake with fiendish cry
　Wheel and dance the savage crowd,
　Cold the victim's mien and proud,
And his breast is bared to die.

Who will shield the fearless heart?
　Who avert the murderous blade?
From the throng with sudden start
　See, there springs an Indian maid,
Quick she stands before the knight:
　"Loose the chain, unbind the ring!
I am daughter of the king,
And I claim the Indian right!"

Dauntlessly aside she flings
　Lifted axe and thirsty knife,
Fondly to his heart she clings,
　And her bosom guards his life!
In the woods of Powhatan,
　Still 't is told by Indian fires
　How a daughter of their sires
Saved a captive Englishman.

A POEM NEED NOT BE a work of creative excellence to capture the public fancy. One of the most popular but not very distinguished poems of William Wordsworth is "We Are Seven." The poet met a little girl during one of his walking tours, and questioning her about her family, is told that there are seven brothers and sisters. Further questions reveal that though two of the seven have died, the "simple child" insists that "we are seven."

We Are Seven

WILLIAM WORDSWORTH

—A Simple Child,
That lightly draws its breath,
And feels its life in every limb,
What should it know of death?

I met a little cottage Girl:
She was eight years old, she said;
Her hair was thick with many a curl
That clustered round her head.

She had a rustic, woodland air,
And she was wildly clad:
Her eyes were fair, and very fair;
—Her beauty made me glad.

"Sisters and brothers, little Maid,
How many may you be?"
"How many? Seven in all," she said,
And wondering looked at me.

"And where are they? I pray you tell."
She answered: "Seven are we;
And two of us at Conway dwell,
And two are gone to sea.

"Two of us in the church-yard lie,
My sister and my brother;
And, in the church-yard cottage, I
Dwell near them with my mother."

"You say that two at Conway dwell,
And two are gone to sea,
Yet ye are seven!—I pray to tell,
Sweet Maid, how this may be."

Then did the little Maid reply,
"Seven boys and girls are we;
Two of us in the church-yard lie,
Beneath the church-yard tree."

"You run about, my little Maid,
Your limbs they are alive;
If two are in the church-yard laid,
Then ye are only five."

"Their graves are green, they may be seen,"
The little Maid replied,
"Twelve steps or more from my mother's door,
And they are side by side.

"My stockings there I often knit,
My kerchief there I hem;
And there upon the ground I sit,
And sing a song to them.

"And often after sunset, Sir,
When it is light and fair,
I take my little porringer,
And eat my supper there.

"The first that died was sister Jane;
In bed she moaning lay,
Till God released her of her pain;
And then she went away.

"So in the church-yard she was laid;
And, when the grass was dry,
Together round her grave we played,
By brother John and I.

"And when the ground was white with snow,
And I could run and slide,
My brother John was forced to go,
And he lies by her side."

"How many are you, then," said I,
"If they two are in heaven?"
Quick was the little Maid's reply,
"O Master! we are seven."

"But they are dead; those two are dead!
Their spirits are in heaven!"
'T was throwing words away; for still
The little Maid would have her will,
And said, "Nay, we are seven!"

The Watch

MAY SWENSON

When I
took my
watch to the watchfixer I
felt privileged but also pained to
    watch the operation. He
had long fingernails and a
    voluntary squint. He
fixed a magnifiying cup over his
squint eye. He
undressed my
watch. I
watched him
split her
in three layers and lay her
middle—a quivering viscera—in
    a circle on a little plinth. He
shoved shirtsleeves up and
    leaned like an ogre over my
naked watch. With critical
    pincers he
poked and stirred. He
lifted out little private things
    with a magnet too tiny
    for me
to watch almost. "Watch out!" I
almost said. His
eye watched, enlarged, the
    secrets of my
watch, and I
watched anxiously. Because
    what if he
touched her
ticker too rough, and she

gave up the ghost out of pure
    fright? Or put her
things back backward so she'd
run backwards after this? Or he
might lose a miniscule part,
    connected to her
exquisite heart, and mix her
up, instead of fix her.
And all the time,
all the time-
pieces on the walls, on the
    shelves, told the time,
told the time
in swishes and ticks,
swishes and ticks,
and seemed to be gloating, as
    they watched and told. I
felt faint, I
was about to lose my
breath—my
ticker going lickety-split—when
    watchfixer clipped her
three slices together with a
    gleam and two flicks of his
tools like chopsticks. He
spat out his
eye, lifted her
high, gave her
a twist, set her
hands right, and laid her
little face, quite as usual, in its
place on my wrist.

For Children if They'll Take Them

X. J. KENNEDY

The man
With the tan
Hands
Who stands
And scoops up
Hot
Roast
Chestnuts
In cups

Of old
News
Folded
Like perching
Birds

Sold us
A few
New
Words.

Skipper Ireson's Ride

JOHN GREENLEAF WHITTIER

Of all the rides since the birth of time,
Told in story or sung in rhyme,—
On Apuleius's Golden Ass,
Or one-eyed Calender's horse of brass,
Witch astride of a human back,
Islam's prophet on Al-Borák,—
The strangest ride that ever was sped
Was Ireson's, out from Marblehead!
  Old Floyd Ireson, for his hard heart,
    Tarred and feathered and carried in a cart
      By the women of Marblehead!

Body of turkey, head of fowl,
Wings a-droop like a rained-on fowl,
Feathered and ruffled in every part,
Skipper Ireson stood in the cart.
Scores of women, old and young,
Strong of muscle, and glib of tongue,
Pushed and pulled up the rocky lane,
Shouting and singing the shrill refrain:
  "Here's Flud Oirson, fur his horrd horrt,
    Torr'd an' futherr'd an' corr'd in a corrt
      By the women o' Morble'ead!"

Wrinkled scolds with hands on hips,
Girls in bloom of cheek and lips,
Wild-eyed, free-limbed, such as chase
Bacchus round some antique vase,
Brief of skirt, with ankles bare,
Loose of kerchief and loose of hair,
With conch-shells blowing and fish-horns' twang,
Over and over the Maenads sang:
    "Here's Flud Oirson, fur his horrd horrt,
    Torr'd an' futherr'd an' corr'd in a corrt
        By the women o' Morble'ead!"

Small pity for him!—He sailed away
From a leaking ship in Chaleur Bay,—
Sailed away from a sinking wreck,
With his own town's-people on her deck!
"Lay by! lay by!" they called to him.
Back he answered, "Sink or swim!
Brag of your catch of fish again!"
And off he sailed through the fog and rain!
    Old Floyd Ireson, for his hard heart,
    Tarred and feathered and carried in a cart
        By the women of Marblehead!

Fathoms deep in dark Chaleur
That wreck shall lie forevermore.
Mother and sister, wife and maid,
Looked from the rocks of Marblehead
Over the moaning and rainy sea,—
Looked for the coming that might not be!
What did the winds and the sea-birds say
Of the cruel captain who sailed away?—
    Old Floyd Ireson, for his hard heart,
    Tarred and feathered and carried in a cart
        By the women of Marblehead!

Through the street, on either side,
Up flew windows, doors swung wide;
Sharp-tongued spinsters, old wives gray,
Treble lent the fish-horn's bray.
Sea-worn grandsires, cripple-bound,
Hulks of old sailors run aground,
Shook head, and fist, and hat, and cane,
And cracked with curses the hoarse refrain:
    "Here's Flud Oirson, fur his horrd horrt,
    Torr'd an' futherr'd an' corr'd in a corrt
        By the women o' Morble'ead!"

Sweetly along the Salem road
Bloom of orchard and lilac showed.
Little the wicked skipper knew
Of the fields so green and the sky so blue.
Riding there in his sorry trim,
Like an Indian idol glum and grim,
Scarcely he seemed the sound to hear
Of voices shouting far and near:
   "Here's Flud Oirson, fur his horrd horrt,
   Torr'd an' futherr'd an' corr'd in a corrt
     By the women o' Morble'ead!"

"Hear me, neighbors!" at last he cried,—
"What to me is this noisy ride?
What is the shame that clothes the skin
To the nameless horror that lives within?
Waking or sleeping, I see a wreck,
And hear a cry from a reeling deck!
Hate me and curse me,—I only dread
The hand of God and the face of the dead!"
   Said old Floyd Ireson, for his hard heart,
   Tarred and feathered, and carried in a cart
     By the women of Marblehead!

Then the wife of the skipper lost at sea
Said, "God has touched him! why should we!"
Said an old wife mourning her only son,
"Cut the rogue's tether and let him run!"
So with soft relentings and rude excuse,
Half scorn, half pity, they cut him loose,
And gave him a cloak to hide him in,
And left him alone with his shame and sin.
   Poor Floyd Ireson, for his hard heart,
   Tarred and feathered and carried in a cart
     By the women of Marblehead!

The Gardener

ROBERT LOUIS STEVENSON

The gardener does not love to talk,
He makes me keep the gravel walk;
And when he puts his tools away,
He locks the door and takes the key.

He digs the flowers, green, red, and blue,
Nor wishes to be spoken to.
He digs the flowers and cuts the hay,
And never seems to want to play.

Away behind the currant row
Where no one else but cook may go,
Far in the plots, I see him dig,
Old and serious, brown and big.

Silly gardener! summer goes,
And winter comes with pinching toes,
When in the garden bare and brown
You must lay your barrow down.

Well now, and while the summer stays,
To profit by these garden days
O how much wiser you would be
To play at Indian wars with me!

Old Meg

John Keats

Old Meg she was a Gipsy
    And liv'd upon the Moors;
Her bed it was the brown heath turf,
    And her house was out of doors.

Her apples were swart blackberries,
    Her currants, pods o'broom;
Her wine was dew of the wild white rose,
    Her book a churchyard tomb.

Her Brothers were the craggy hills,
    Her Sisters larchen trees—
Alone with her great family
    She liv'd as she did please.

No breakfast had she many a morn,
    No dinner many a noon,
And 'stead of supper, she would stare
    Full hard against the moon.

But every morn, of woodbine fresh
    She made her garlanding,
And, every night, the dark glen Yew
    She wove, and she would sing.

And with her fingers, old and brown,
    She plaited Mats o' Rushes,
And gave them to the cottagers
    She met among the Bushes.

Old Meg was brave as Margaret Queen
    And tall as Amazon;
An old red blanket cloak she wore,
    A chip hat had she on.
God rest her aged bones somewhere!
    She died full long agone!

WHO ARE THE TRULY GREAT people of the world? They need not be rulers or conquerors. To Stephen Spender, they are the people who do not deny their essential natures, who never violate their basic needs for beauty or song or love, who never dishonor themselves by dishonoring another. To Stephen Spender, these are the elect of the earth.

I Think Continually of Those Who Were Truly Great

STEPHEN SPENDER

I think continually of those who were truly great.
Who, from the womb, remembered the soul's history
Through corridors of light where the hours are suns
Endless and singing. Whose lovely ambition
Was that their lips, still touched with fire,
Should tell of the Spirit clothed from head to foot in song.
And who hoarded from the Spring branches
The desires falling across their bodies like blossoms.

What is precious is never to forget
The essential delight of the blood drawn from ageless springs
Breaking through rocks in worlds before our earth.
Never to deny its pleasure in the morning simple light
Nor its grave evening demand for love.
Never to allow gradually the traffic to smother
With noise and fog the flowering of the spirit.

Near the snow, near the sun, in the highest fields
See how these names are fêted by the waving grass
And by the streamers of white clouds
And whispers of wind in the listening sky.
The names of those who in their lives fought for life
Who wore at their hearts the fire's centre.
Born of the sun they travelled a short while towards the sun,
And left the vivid air signed with their honour.

He Bloomed among Eagles

DAVID ROSS

He bloomed among eagles,
The valley boy.
He bloomed with each briefing.
The domed cock-pit
Greenhouse to his growing,
And all flying weathers blowing
April to his leafing.

Over target wheeling
In summergolden sun,
A blight of guns assailing,
Wormed his green age winterwan,
And from the eagle's ceiling
He withered leaflorn down.

Flyer, flyer, in the furrow,
Leveled with the mole
At ceiling zero,
With the dust impounded!
Tap him gently bugles!
O valley boy
For all duration grounded,
Be remembered of eagles.

Anne Rutledge

EDGAR LEE MASTERS

Out of me unworthy and unknown
The vibrations of deathless music;
"With malice toward none, with charity for all."
Out of me the forgiveness of millions toward millions,
And the beneficent face of a nation
Shining with justice and truth.
I am Anne Rutledge who sleep beneath these weeds,
Beloved in life of Abraham Lincoln,
Wedded to him, not through union,
But through separation.
Bloom forever, O Republic,
From the dust of my bosom!

On April 1, 1688, King James II of England imprisoned seven bishops of the Church of England for ignoring instructions he had given. One of the bishops was Sir Jonathan Trelawny, a Cornishman and popular in Cornwall. The following song was printed anonymously in a small newspaper and immediately became popular. "Michael's hold" is a huge rock off the coast of Cornwall; the Tamar and Severn are rivers that mark the boundary between Cornwall and the rest of England.

Song of the Western Men

Robert Stephen Hawker

A good sword and a trusty hand!
　A merry heart and true!
King James's men shall understand
　What Cornish lads can do.

And have they fix'd the where and when?
　And shall Trelawny die?
Here's twenty thousand Cornish men
　Will know the reason why!

Out spake their captain brave and bold,
　A merry wight was he:
"If London Tower were Michael's hold,
　"We'll set Trelawny free!

"We'll cross the Tamar, land to land,
　The Severn is no stay,
With 'one and all,' and hand in hand,
　And who shall bid us nay?

"And when we come to London Wall,
　A pleasant sight to view,
Come forth! come forth, ye cowards all,
　Here's men as good as you!

"Trelawny he's in keep and hold,
　Trelawny he may die;
But here's twenty thousand Cornish bold
　Will know the reason why!"

261

Wight—person

On April 14, 1865, while attending a performance at Ford's Theater in Washington, D.C., President Abraham Lincoln was shot and mortally wounded. He died the following evening. His death, coming at a time of exultation that the terrible Civil War was at last drawing to a close, sent the nation into shocked mourning. One of the most moving elegies, embodying the themes of rejoicing that the War was over and grief at the loss of so great and beloved a leader, is Walt Whitman's "O Captain! My Captain!"

O Captain! My Captain!

WALT WHITMAN

O Captain! my Captain! our fearful trip is done,
The ship has weathered every rack, the prize we sought
  is won,
The port is near, the bells I hear, the people all exulting,
While follow eyes the steady keel, the vessel grim and
  daring;
But O heart! heart! heart!
    O the bleeding drops of red,
        Where on the deck my Captain lies,
          Fallen cold and dead.

O Captain! my Captain! rise up and hear the bells;
Rise up—for you the flag is flung—for you the bugle
  trills,
For you bouquets and ribboned wreaths—for you the
  shores acrowding,
For you they call, the swaying mass, their eager faces
  turning;
Here Captain! dear father!
    This arm beneath your head!
      It is some dream that on the deck
        You've fallen cold and dead.

My Captain does not answer, his lips are pale and still,
My father does not feel my arm, he has no pulse
   nor will,
The ship is anchored safe and sound, its voyage closed
   and done,
From fearful trip the victor ship comes in with object
   won;
Exult O shores, and ring O bells!
     But I, with mournful tread,
       Walk the deck my Captain lies,
       Fallen cold and dead.

Lincoln Was a Tall Man

Elias Lieberman

Lincoln was a tall man,
   Soul and limb;
Never may a small man
   Measure him.

His mind could dig as
   Deep as dearth;
His heart was as big as
   The whole round earth.

He towered and towered
   Beyond all hate;
His love empowered
   Decrees of state.

He broke old chains and
   Man-made bars;
He strode the plains and
   Grasped the stars.

Lincoln was a tall man,
   Soul and limb;
Never may a small man
   Measure him.

IN THE OLD TESTAMENT there is a prophecy concerning
Ishmael, a tender of sheep and goats and son of Abraham and
Hagar. It is foretold that his hand shall be against everyman, and
everyman's hand against him. Here the American poet Genevieve
Taggard etches for us the character of the nomad boy.

Song for Unbound Hair

GENEVIEVE TAGGARD

Oh, never marry Ishmael!
Marry another and prosper well;
But not, but never Ishmael.
What has he ever to buy or sell?
He only owns what his strength can keep,
Only a vanishing knot of sheep,
A goat or two. Does he sow or reap?
In the hanging rocks rings his old ram's bell . . .
Who would marry Ishmael?

What has he to give to a bride?
Only trouble, little beside,
Only his arm like a little cave
To cover a woman and keep her safe;
A rough fierce kiss, and the wind and the rain,
A child, perhaps, and another again—
Who would marry Ishmael?

The arrogant Lucifer when he fell
Bequeathed his wrath to Ishmael;
The hand of every man is set
Against this lad, and this lad's hand
Is cruel and quick,—forget, forget
The nomad boy on his leagues of sand . . .

Marry another and prosper well,
But not, but never Ishmael.

Adventures with My Grandfather

Anne Marx

"Once around is enough," my grandfather said,
plucking me off the merry-go-round.
"We will walk in the park together."
My hand rested in his big one
as I skipped secret steps to equal his stride.
Pipe fragrance lingered long on my mittens.

Years later, we went to watch Westerns,
balcony-exclusive, in nearby movie houses.
At the end, he was always ready.
Parting with pipe, he cleared his throat:
"You will never enjoy it again like the first time.
Once around is enough."
I was still learning to leave when a show was over.

A final day: he beyond Westerns and winter walks,
content at his corner window as on a balcony;
surveying far boundaries of park;
reviewing a merry-go-round parade of people below.
As I wondered out loud:
"Would you like to do it all over again, grandpa?"
he managed the longest smile without removing his pipe—
and I knew the answer.

In 1803, Dorothy Wordsworth accompanied her brother William and their friend Samuel Taylor Coleridge on a tour of Scotland. Dorothy later wrote that it was harvest time and the fields were "enlivened by small companies of reapers." She added that it was quite common to see a single reaper working alone in some lonely fields. This experience inspired her brother to write the following poem—one of the most notable in the English language.

The Solitary Reaper

WILLIAM WORDSWORTH

Behold her, single in the field,
Yon solitary Highland Lass!
Reaping and singing by herself;
Stop here, or gently pass!
Alone she cuts and binds the grain,
And sings a melancholy strain;
O listen! for the Vale profound
Is overflowing with the sound.

No Nightingale did ever chaunt
More welcome notes to weary bands
Of travellers in some shady haunt,
Among Arabian sands:
A voice so thrilling ne'er was heard
In spring-time from the Cuckoo-bird.
Breaking the silence of the seas
Among the farthest Hebrides.

Will no one tell me what she sings?—
Perhaps the plaintive numbers flow
For old, unhappy, far-off things,
And battles long ago:
Or is it some more humble lay,
Familiar matter of to-day?
Some natural sorrow, loss, or pain,
That has been, and may be again?

Whate'er the theme, the Maiden sang
As if her song could have no ending;
I saw her singing at her work,
And o'er the sickle bending;—
I listened, motionless and still;
And, as I mounted up the hill,
The music in my heart I bore,
Long after it was heard no more.

An Old Woman of the Roads

PADRAIC COLUM

O, to have a little house!
To own the hearth and stool and all!
The heaped up sods upon the fire,
The pile of turf against the wall!

To have a clock with weights and chains
And pendulum swinging up and down!
A dresser filled with shining delph,
Speckled and white and blue and brown!

I could be busy all the day
Clearing and sweeping hearth and floor,
And fixing on their shelf again
My white and blue and speckled store!

I could be quiet there at night
Beside the fire and by myself,
Sure of a bed and loth to leave
The ticking clock and the shining delph!

Och! but I'm weary of mist and dark,
And roads where there's never a house nor bush,
And tired I am of bog and road,
And the crying wind and the lonesome hush!

And I am praying to God on high,
And I am praying Him night and day,
For a little house—a house of my own—
Out of the wind's and the rain's way.

Delph—Delft china

Cockles and Mussels

ANONYMOUS (traditional Irish ballad)

In Dublin's fair city,
Where the girls are so pretty,
    I first set my eyes on sweet Mollie Malone.
She wheeled her wheelbarrow
Through streets broad and narrow,
    Crying, "Cockles and mussels, alive, alive, oh!
        "Alive, alive, oh!
        Alive, alive, oh!"
    Crying, "Cockles and mussels, alive, alive, oh!"

She was a fishmonger,
But sure 'twas no wonder,
    For so were her father and mother before.
And they both wheeled their barrow
Through streets broad and narrow,
    Crying, "Cockles and mussels, alive, alive, oh!
        "Alive, alive, oh!
        Alive, alive, oh!"
    Crying, "Cockles and mussels, alive, alive, oh!"

She died of a fever,
And none could relieve her,
    And that was the end of sweet Mollie Malone.
But her ghost wheels her barrow
Through streets broad and narrow,
    Crying, "Cockles and mussels, alive, alive, oh!
        "Alive, alive, oh!
        Alive, alive, oh!"
    Crying, "Cockles and mussels, alive, alive, oh!"

267

In January, 1878, the London papers carried the story that the Ahkond of Swat was dead. Although not many people could identify the Ahkond or locate Swat, the names were sufficiently exotic to capture the public imagination, and Edward Lear was inspired to write this poem. Swat, now a section of East Pakistan, is no longer ruled by an Ahkond.

The Ahkond of Swat

Edward Lear

Who, or why, or which, or *what*,
                Is the Ahkond of Swat?

Is he tall or short, or dark or fair?
Does he sit on a stool or sofa or chair,   or Squat,
             The Ahkond of Swat?

Is he wise or foolish, young or old?
Does he drink his soup and his coffee cold,
                or Hot,
             The Ahkond of Swat?

Does he sing or whistle, jabber or talk,
And when riding abroad does he gallop or walk,
                or Trot,
             The Ahkond of Swat?

Does he wear a turban, a fez or a hat?
Does he sleep on a mattress, a bed or a mat,
                or a Cot,
             The Ahkond of Swat?

When he writes a copy in round-hand size,
Does he cross his t's and finish his i's
                with a Dot,
             The Ahkond of Swat?

Can he write a letter concisely clear,
Without a speck or a smudge or smear   or Blot,
             The Ahkond of Swat?

Do his people like him extremely well?
Or do they, whenever they can, rebel,   or Plot,
             At the Ahkond of Swat?

If he catches them then, either old or young,
Does he have them chopped in pieces or hung,
                or Shot,
             The Ahkond of Swat?

Do his people prig in the lanes or park?
Or even at times, when days are dark,   Garotte?
             Oh, the Ahkond of Swat?

Does he study the wants of his own dominion?
Or doesn't he care for public opinion   a Jot,
             The Ahkond of Swat?

To amuse his mind do his people show him
Pictures, or any one's last new poem,   or What,
             For the Ahkond of Swat?

At night if he suddenly screams and wakes,
Do they bring him only a few small cakes,
                or a Lot,
             For the Ahkond of Swat?

Does he live on turnips, tea or tripe,
Does he like his shawl to be marked with a stripe
                or a Dot,
             The Ahkond of Swat?

Does he like to lie on his back in a boat
Like the lady who lived in that isle remote,
                Shalott.
             The Ahkond of Swat?

Is he quiet, or always making a fuss?
Is his steward a Swiss or a Swede or a Russ,
                or a Scot,
             The Ahkond of Swat?

Does he like to sit by the calm blue wave?
Or to sleep and snore in a dark green cave,
                    or a Grott,
          The Ahkond of Swat?

Does he drink small beer from a silver jug?
Or a bowl? or a glass? or a cup? or a mug?
                    or a Pot,
          The Ahkond of Swat?

Does he beat his wife with a gold-topped pipe,
When she lets the gooseberries grow too ripe,
                    or Rot,
          The Ahkond of Swat?

Does he wear a white tie when he dines with his
     friends,
And tie it neat in a bow with ends,   or a Knot,
          The Ahkond of Swat?

Does he like new cream, and hate mince-pies?
When he looks at the sun does he wink his eyes,
                    or Not,
          The Ahkond of Swat?

Does he teach his subjects to roast and bake?
Does he sail about on an inland lake,
                    in a Yacht,
          The Ahkond of Swat?

          Some one, or nobody knows I wot
          Who or which or why or what
                    Is the Ahkond of Swat!

     Prig—steal

THE POET THOMAS MOORE was a charming, talented, and
popular man of his time. These lines were dedicated to him by
his close friend, Lord Byron.

To Thomas Moore

GEORGE GORDON, LORD BYRON

My boat is on the shore,
   And my bark is on the sea;
But, before I go, Tom Moore,
   Here's double health to thee!

Here's a sigh to those who love me,
   And a smile to those who hate;
And, whatever sky's above me,
   Here's a heart for every fate.

Though the ocean roar around me,
   Yet it still shall bear me on;
Though a desert should surround me,
   It hath springs that may be won.

Were't the last drop in the well,
   As I gasp'd upon the brink,
Ere my fainting spirit fell,
   'Tis to thee that I would drink.

          With that water, as this wine,
             The libation I would pour
          Should be—peace with thine and mine,
             And a health to thee, Tom Moore.

LOVE POEMS

POEMS THAT DEAL WITH LOVE are among the most beautiful in the language—and often they reveal more about the poet than they do about the person described or addressed.

The Bailiff's Daughter of Islington

ANONYMOUS

There was a youth, and a well-belovéd youth,
　And he was an esquire's son,
He loved the bailiff's daughter dear,
　That lived in Islington.

But she was coy, and she would not believe
　That he did love her so,
No, nor at any time she would
　Any countenance to him show.

But when his friends did understand
　His fond and foolish mind,
They sent him up to fair London,
　An apprentice for to bind.

And when he had been seven long years,
　And his love he had not seen;
"Many a tear have I shed for her sake
　When she little thought of me."

All the maids of Islington
  Went forth to sport and play;
All but the bailiff's daughter dear;
  She secretly stole away.

She put off her gown of grey,
  And put on her puggish attire;
She's up to fair London gone,
  Her true-love to require.

As she went along the road,
  The weather being hot and dry,
There was she aware of her true-love,
  At length came riding by.

She stept to him, as red as any rose,
  And took him by the bridle-ring:
"I pray you, kind sir, give me one penny,
  To ease my weary limb."—

"I prithee, sweetheart, canst thou tell me
  Where that thou wast born?"—
"At Islington, kind sir," said she,
  "Where I have had many a scorn."—

"I prithee, sweetheart, canst thou tell me
  Whether thou dost know
The bailiff's daughter of Islington?"—
  "She's dead, sir, long ago."—

"Then will I sell my goodly steed,
  My saddle and my bow;
I will into some far countrey,
  Where no man doth me know."—

"Oh stay, Oh stay, thou goodly youth!
  She's alive, she is not dead;
Here she standeth by thy side,
  And is ready to be thy bride."—

"Oh farewell grief, and welcome joy,
  Ten thousand times and o'er!
For now I have seen my own true-love,
  That I thought I should have seen no more."

Puggish—rough, fit for a tramp.

I Will Make You Brooches

Robert Louis Stevenson

I will make you brooches and toys for your delight
Of bird-song at morning and star-shine at night.
I will make a palace fit for you and me
Of green days in forests and blue days at sea.

I will make my kitchen, and you shall keep your room,
Where white flows the river and bright blows the broom,
And you shall wash your linen and keep your body white
In rainfall at morning and dewfall at night.

And this shall be for music when no one else is near,
The fine song for singing, the rare song to hear!
That only I remember, that only you admire,
Of the broad road that stretches and the roadside fire.

271

John Anderson, My Jo

ROBERT BURNS

John Anderson, my jo, John,
    When we were first acquent,
Your locks were like the raven,
    Your bonnie brow was brent;
But now your brow is beld, John,
    Your locks are like the snow;
But blessings on your frosty pow,
    John Anderson, my jo!

John Anderson, my jo, John,
    We clamb the hill thegither;
And monie a canty day, John,
    We've had wi' ane anither:
Now we maun totter down, John,
    But hand in hand we'll go,
And sleep thegither at the foot,
    John Anderson, my jo.

Jo—sweetheart. Brent—smooth. Beld—bald. Pow—pate. Canty—cheerful.

The Passionate Shepherd to His Love

CHRISTOPHER MARLOWE

Come live with me and be my Love,
And we will all the pleasures prove
That valleys, groves, hills and fields,
Woods or steepy mountain yields.

And we will sit upon the rocks
Seeing the shepherds feed their flocks.
By shallow rivers, to whose falls
Melodious birds sing madrigals.

And I will make thee beds of roses
And a thousand fragrant posies,
A cap of flowers, and a kirtle
Embroidered all with leaves of myrtle.

A gown made of the finest wool,
Which from our pretty lambs we pull,
Fair linèd slippers for the cold,
With buckles of the purest gold.

A belt of straw and ivy buds,
With coral clasps and amber studs:
And if these pleasures may thee move,
Come live with me and be my Love.

The shepherd swains shall dance and sing
For thy delight each May-morning:
If these delights thy mind may move,
Then live with me and be my Love.

Kirtle—long dress

Reply to the Passionate Shepherd

Sir Walter Raleigh

If all the world and love were young,
And truth in every shepherd's tongue,
These pretty pleasures might me move
To live with thee and be thy Love.

But Time drives flocks from field to fold;
When rivers rage and rocks grow cold;
And Philomel becometh dumb;
The rest complains of cares to come.

The flowers do fade, and wanton fields
To wayward Winter reckoning yields:
A honey tongue, a heart of gall,
Is fancy's spring, but sorrow's fall.

Thy gowns, thy shoes, thy beds of roses,
Thy cap, thy kirtle, and thy posies,
Soon break, soon wither—soon forgotten,
In folly ripe, in reason rotten.

Thy belt of straw and ivy-buds,
Thy coral clasps and amber studs,—
All these in me no means can move
To come to thee and be thy Love.

But could youth last, and love still breed,
Had joys no date, nor age no need,
Then these delights my mind might move
To live with thee and be thy Love.

Philomel—the nightingale

Music I Heard with You

Conrad Aiken

Music I heard with you was more than music,
And bread I broke with you was more than bread;
Now that I am without you, all is desolate;
All that was once so beautiful is dead.

Your hands once touched this table and this silver,
And I have seen your fingers hold this glass.
These things do not remember you, belovèd,—
And yet your touch upon them will not pass.

For it was in my heart you moved among them,
And blessed them with your hands and with your eyes;
And in my heart they will remember always,—
They knew you once, O beautiful and wise.

Men at Arms

H<small>UMAN HISTORY</small>, to some extent, has been the history of battles fought and wars waged. As countless poets have shown there is fierce joy in battle as well as inexpressible grief. Battles bring out strong emotions, and sometimes these emotions are extended to the objects used by warriors, as the first selection in this section indicates.

IN THE AUTUMN of 1830, the U.S. Navy declared the gallant warship *Constitution* unseaworthy and recommended that she be destroyed. On reading of this in a Boston paper, Oliver Wendell Holmes protested in the following stanzas. The poem was widely reprinted and blew up so great a storm of patriotic fervor that the Navy rescinded its order and rebuilt the ship. "Old Ironsides" remains to this day open to the public in Boston harbor.

Old Ironsides

OLIVER WENDELL HOLMES

Ay, tear her tattered ensign down!
　Long has it waved on high,
And many an eye has danced to see
　That banner in the sky;
Beneath it rung the battle shout,
　And burst the cannon's roar;—
The meteor of the ocean air
　Shall sweep the clouds no more.

Her deck, once red with heroes' blood,
　Where knelt the vanquished foe,
When winds were hurrying o'er the flood,
　And waves were white below,
No more shall feel the victor's tread,
　Or know the conquered knee;—
The harpies of the shore shall pluck
　The eagle of the sea!

Oh, better that her shattered hulk
　Should sink beneath the wave;
Her thunders shook the mighty deep,
　And there should be her grave;
Nail to the mast her holy flag,
　Set every threadbare sail,
And give her to the god of storms,
　The lightning and the gale!

IN THE BATTLE OF BALACLAVA, during the Crimean War of 1854, a brigade of British soldiers charged a Russian gun position when ordered, although they knew the charge was suicidal. This ill-fated maneuver cost the lives of most of the six hundred members of the brigade and inspired the following famous poem.

The Charge of the Light Brigade

ALFRED, LORD TENNYSON

Half a league, half a league,
  Half a league onward,
All in the valley of Death
  Rode the six hundred.
"Forward, the Light Brigade!
Charge for the guns!" he said;
Into the valley of Death
  Rode the six hundred.

"Forward, the Light Brigade!"
  Was there a man dismayed?
Not though the soldier knew
  Some one had blundered:
Theirs not to make reply,
Theirs not to reason why,
Theirs but to do and die:
Into the valley of Death
  Rode the six hundred.

Cannon to right of them,
  Cannon to left of them,
Cannon in front of them
  Volleyed and thundered;
Stormed at with shot and shell,
Boldly they rode and well;
Into the jaws of Death,
Into the mouth of Hell,
  Rode the six hundred.

Flashed all their sabres bare,
  Flashed as they turned in air,
Sabring the gunners there,
  Charging an army, while
All the world wondered:
Plunged in the battery-smoke,
Right through the line they broke:
Cossack and Russian

Reeled from the sabre-stroke,
    Shattered and sundered.
Then they rode back, but not—
    Not the six hundred.

Cannon to right of them,
    Cannon to left of them,
Cannon behind them
    Volleyed and thundered:
Stormed at with shot and shell,
While horse and hero fell,

They that had fought so well
Came through the jaws of Death
Back from the mouth of Hell,—
All that was left of them,
    Left of six hundred.

When can their glory fade?
O the wild charge they made!
    All the world wondered.
Honor the charge they made!
Honor the Light Brigade,
    Noble six hundred!

ALTHOUGH THE BALLAD doesn't tell us where, how, or why
Bonnie George Campbell failed to return home, it does state that
he went forth his "sword at his knee." Whether or not he drew
it, the ballad doesn't say.

Bonnie George Campbell

ANONYMOUS

High upon Highlands,
And low upon Tay,
Bonnie George Campbell
Rode out on a day;
Saddled and bridled,
And gallant to see;
Home came his good horse,
    But home came not he.

Out ran his mother,
Wild with despair;
Out ran his bonnie bride
Tearing her hair.
He rode saddled and bridled,
A sword at his knee:
Home came his good horse,
    But never came he.

"My meadow lies green,
And my corn is unshorn,
My barn is unbuilt,
And my babe is unborn."
He rode saddled and bridle
And gallant to see:
Home came his good horse
    But never came he.

The Soldier's Dream

THOMAS CAMPBELL

Our bugles sang truce,—for the night-cloud had lowered,
    And the sentinel stars set their watch in the sky;
And thousands had sunk on the ground overpowered,
    The weary to sleep, and the wounded to die.

When reposing that night on my pallet of straw,
  By the wolf-scaring fagot that guarded the slain;
At the dead of the night a sweet vision I saw,
  And thrice ere the morning I dreamt it again.

Methought from the battle-field's dreadful array,
  Far, far I had roamed on a desolate track:
'T was autumn,—and sunshine arose on the way
  To the home of my fathers, that welcomed me back.

I flew to the pleasant fields traversed so oft
  In life's morning march, when my bosom was young;
I heard my own mountain-goats bleating aloft,
  And knew the sweet strain that the corn-reapers sung.

Then pledged we the wine-cup, and fondly I swore,
  From my home and my weeping friends never to part;
My little ones kissed me a thousand times o'er,
  And my wife sobbed aloud in her fulness of heart.

"Stay, stay with us,—rest, thou art weary and worn";
  And fain was their war-broken soldier to stay;—
But sorrow returned with the dawning of morn,
  And the voice in my dreaming ear melted away.

As the Civil War was drawing to a close, Abraham Lincoln spoke of the desperate need for binding up the nation's wounds. Here is a tribute of love and devotion to those soldiers of both North and South who fell in a cause each side thought was right.

The Blue and the Gray

Francis Miles Finch

By the flow of the inland river,
　Whence the fleets of iron have fled,
Where the blades of the grave-grass quiver,
　Asleep are the ranks of the dead:
　　Under the sod and the dew,
　　　Waiting the judgment-day;
　　Under the one, the Blue,
　　　Under the other, the Gray.

These in the robings of glory,
　Those in the gloom of defeat,
All with the battle-blood gory,
　In the dusk of eternity meet:
　　Under the sod and the dew,
　　　Waiting the judgment-day;
　　Under the laurel, the Blue,
　　　Under the willow, the Gray.

From the silence of sorrowful hours
　The desolate mourners go,
Lovingly laden with flowers
　Alike for the friend and the foe:
　　Under the sod and the dew,
　　　Waiting the judgment-day
　　Under the roses, the Blue,
　　　Under the lilies, the Gray.

So with an equal splendor,
　The morning sun-rays fall,
With a touch impartially tender,
　On the blossoms blooming for all:
　　Under the sod and the dew,
　　　Waiting the judgment-day
　　Broidered with gold, the Blue,
　　　Mellowed with gold, the Gray.

So, when the summer calleth,
　On forest and field of grain,
With an equal murmur falleth
　The cooling drip of the rain:
　　Under the sod and the dew,
　　　Waiting the judgment-day;
　　Wet with the rain, the Blue,
　　　Wet with the rain, the Gray.

Sadly, but not with upbraiding,
　The generous deed was done,
In the storm of the years that are fading
　No braver battle was won:
　　Under the sod and the dew,
　　　Waiting the judgment-day;
　　Under the blossoms, the Blue,
　　　Under the garlands, the Gray.

No more shall the war cry sever,
　Or the winding rivers be red;
They banish our anger forever
　When they laurel the graves of our **dead!**
　　Under the sod and the dew,
　　　Waiting the judgment-day;
　　Love and tears for the Blue,
　　　Tears and love for the Gray.

Johnny Has Gone for a Soldier

ANONYMOUS

Sad I sit on Butternut Hill,
  Who could blame me cry my fill?
And every tear would turn a mill,
  Johnny has gone for a soldier.

Me oh my, I loved him so,
  Broke my heart to see him go,
And only time can heal my woe,
  Johnny has gone for a soldier.

I'll sell my clock, I'll sell my reel,
  Likewise I'll sell my spinning wheel,
To buy my love a sword of steel,
  Johnny has gone for a soldier.

Sad I sit on Butternut Hill,
  Who can blame me cry my fill?
And every tear would turn a mill,
  Johnny has gone for a soldier.

Battle-Hymn of the Republic

JULIA WARD HOWE

Mine eyes have seen the glory of
  the coming of the Lord:
He is trampling out the vintage where
  the grapes of wrath are stored;
He hath loosed the fateful lightning of
  his terrible swift sword:
    His truth is marching on.

I have seen him in the watch-fires of
  a hundred circling camps;
They have builded him an altar in
  the evening dews and damps;
I can read his righteous sentence by
  the dim and flaring lamps:
    His day is marching on.

He has sounded forth the trumpet that
  shall never call retreat;
He is sifting out the hearts of men
  before his judgment-seat:
O, be swift, my soul, to answer him!
  be jubilant, my feet!
    Our God is marching on.

In the beauty of the lilies Christ was
  born across the sea,
With a glory in his bosom that
  transfigures you and me;
As he died to make men holy, let us
  die to make men free,
    While God is marching on.

281

IN THE 6TH CENTURY B.C. the people of Rome rose against Tarquin, their Etruscan king, and drove him from the city. The Etruscan king of the neighboring city of Clusium, Lars Porsena, thereupon gathered a vast army—including the Roman turncoat Sextus—to march on Rome and restore Tarquin to his throne. The story of the resulting battle, as handed down in Roman legend, is retold here by the 19th-century English man of letters Thomas Babington Macaulay.

Horatius at the Bridge

THOMAS BABINGTON MACAULAY

Lars Porsena of Clusium
  By the Nine Gods he swore
That the great house of Tarquin
  Should suffer wrong no more.

By the Nine Gods he swore it,
  And named a trysting-day,
And bade his messengers ride forth,
East and west and south and north,
  To summon his array.

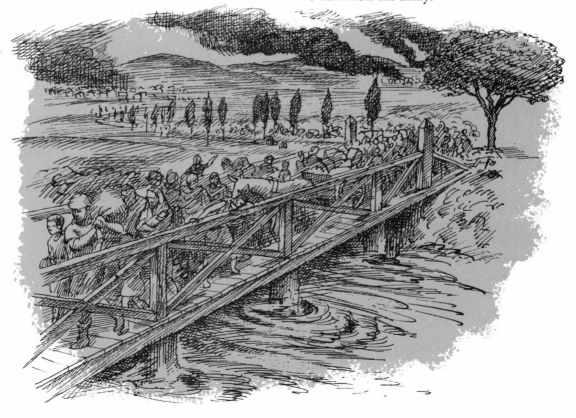

Fast by the royal standard,
  O'erlooking all the war,
Lars Porsena of Clusium
  Sat in his ivory car.
By the right wheel rode Mamilius,
  Prince of the Latian name;
And by the left false Sextus,
  That wrought the deed of shame.

But when the face of Sextus
  Was seen among the foes,
A yell that rent the firmament
  From all the town arose.
On the house-tops was no woman
  But spat towards him and hissed,
No child but screamed out curses,
  And shook its little fist.

But the Consul's brow was sad,
  And the Consul's speech was low,
And darkly looked he at the wall,
  And darkly at the foe:
"Their van will be upon us
  Before the bridge goes down;
And if they once may win the bridge,
  What hope to save the town?"

Then out spake brave Horatius,
  The Captain of the Gate:
"To every man upon this earth
  Death cometh soon or late.
And how can man die better
  Than facing fearful odds
For the ashes of his fathers
  And the temples of his Gods,

283

"And for the tender mother
    Who dandled him to rest,
And for the wife who nurses
    His baby at her breast,
And for the holy maidens
    Who feed the eternal flame,—
To save them from false Sextus
    That wrought the deed of shame?

"Hew down the bridge, Sir Consul,
    With all the speed ye may;
I, with two more to help me,
    Will hold the foe in play.
In yon strait path a thousand
    May well be stopped by three:
Now who will stand on either hand,
    And keep the bridge with me?"

Then out spake Spurius Lartius,—
    A Ramnian proud was he:
"Lo, I will stand at thy right hand,
    And keep the bridge with thee."
And out spake strong Herminius,—
    Of Titian blood was he:
"I will abide on thy left side,
    And keep the bridge with thee."

"Horatius," quoth the Consul,
    "As thou sayest so let it be."
And straight against that great array
    Forth went the dauntless Three.
For Romans in Rome's quarrel
    Spared neither land nor gold,
Nor son nor wife, nor limb nor life,
    In the brave days of old.

Then none was for a party;
    Then all were for the state;
Then the great man helped the poor,
    And the poor man loved the great:
Then lands were fairly portioned;
    Then spoils were fairly sold:
The Romans were like brothers
    In the brave days of old.

Was none who would be foremost
    To lead such dire attack;
But those behind cried "Forward!"
    And those before cried "Back!"
And backward now and forward
    Wavers the deep array;
And on the tossing sea of steel
    To and fro the standards reel,
And the victorious trumpet-peal
    Dies fitfully away.

Yet one man for one moment
    Stood out before the crowd;
Well known was he to all the Three,
    And they gave him greeting loud:
"Now welcome, welcome, Sextus!
    Now welcome to thy home!
Why dost thou stay, and turn away?
    Here lies the road to Rome."

Thrice looked he at the city;
    Thrice looked he at the dead;
And thrice came on in fury,
    And thrice turned back in dread;
And, white with fear and hatred,
    Scowled at the narrow way
Where, wallowing in a pool of blood,
    The bravest Tuscans lay.

But meanwhile axe and lever
    Have manfully been plied;
And now the bridge hangs tottering
    Above the boiling tide.
"Come back, come back, Horatius!"
    Loud cried the Fathers all.—
"Back, Lartius! back, Herminius!
    Back, ere the ruin fall!"

Back darted Spurius Lartius;—
    Herminius darted back;
And, as they passed, beneath their feet
    They felt the timbers crack.
But when they turned their faces,
    And on the farther shore
Saw brave Horatius stand alone,
    They would have crossed once more;

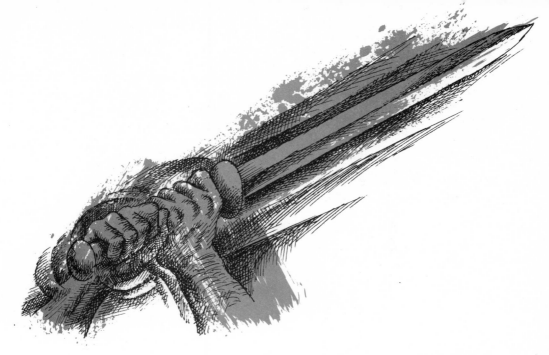

But with a crash like thunder
  Fell every loosened beam,
And, like a dam, the mighty wreck
  Lay right athwart the stream:
And a long shout of triumph
  Rose from the walls of Rome,
As to the highest turret-tops
  Was splashed the yellow foam.

And, like a horse unbroken,
  When first he feels the rein,
The furious river struggled hard,
  And tossed his tawny mane,
And burst the curb, and bounded,
  Rejoicing to be free;
And whirling down, in fierce career,
Battlement, and plank, and pier,
  Rushed headlong to the sea.

Alone stood brave Horatius,
  But constant still in mind,—
Thrice thirty thousand foes before,
  And the broad flood behind.
"Down with him!" cried false Sextus,
  With a smile on his pale face;
"Now yield thee," cried Lars Porsena,
  "Now yield thee to our grace."

Round turned he, as not deigning
  Those craven ranks to see;
Naught spake he to Lars Porsena,
  To Sextus naught spake he;
But he saw on Palatinus
  The white porch of his home;
And he spake to the noble river
  That rolls by the towers of Rome:

"O Tiber! Father Tiber!
  To whom the Romans pray,
A Roman's life, a Roman's arms,
  Take thou in charge this day!'
So he spake, and, speaking sheathed
  The good sword by his side,
And, with his harness on his back,
  Plunged headlong in the tide.

No sound of joy or sorrow
  Was heard from either bank,
But friends and foes in dumb surprise,
With parted lips and straining eyes,
  Stood gazing where he sank;
And when above the surges
  They saw his crest appear,
All Rome sent forth a rapturous cry,
And even the ranks of Tuscany
  Could scarce forbear to cheer.

285

But fiercely ran the current,
  Swollen high by months of rain;
And fast his blood was flowing,
  And he was sore in pain,
And heavy with his armour,
  And spent with changing blows;
And oft they thought him sinking,
  But still again he rose.

Never, I ween, did swimmer,
  In such an evil case,
Struggle through such a raging flood
  Safe to the landing-place;
But his limbs were borne up bravely
  By the brave heart within,
And our good Father Tiber
  Bore bravely up his chin.

"Curse on him!" quoth false Sextus;—
  "Will not the villain drown?
But for this stay, ere close of day
  We should have sacked the town!"
"Heaven help him!" quoth Lars Porsena,
  "And bring him safe to shore;
For such a gallant feat of arms
  Was never seen before."

And now he feels the bottom;
  Now on dry earth he stands;
Now round him throng the Fathers
  To press his gory hands;
And now, with shouts and clapping,
  And noise of weeping loud,
He enters through the River-Gate,
  Borne by the joyous crowd.

When the oldest cask is opened,
  And the largest lamp is lit;
When the chestnuts glow in the embers,
  And the kid turns on the spit;
When young and old in circle
  Around the firebrands close;
When the girls are weaving baskets,
  And the lads are shaping bows;

When the goodman mends his armour,
  And trims his helmet's plume;
When the goodwife's shuttle merrily
  Goes flashing through the loom;
With weeping and with laughter
  Still is the story told,
How well Horatius kept the bridge
  In the brave days of old.

Soldier Rest!

SIR WALTER SCOTT

Soldier, rest! thy warfare o'er
   Sleep the sleep that knows not breaking;
Dream of battled fields no more,
   Days of danger, nights of waking.
In our isle's enchanted hall,
   Hands unseen thy couch are strewing,
Fairy strains of music fall,
   Every sense in slumber dewing.
Soldier, rest! thy warfare o'er,
Dream of fighting fields no more;
Sleep the sleep that knows not breaking,
Morn of toil, not night of waking.

No rude sound shall reach thine ear,
   Armour's clan, or war-steed champing,
Trump nor pibroch summon here
   Mustering clan, or squadron tramping.
Yet the lark's shrill fife may come
   At the day-break from the fallow
And the bittern sound his drum,
   Blooming from the sedgy shallow.
Ruder sounds shall none be near,
Guards nor warders challenge here,
Here's no war-steed's neigh and champing
Shouting clans or squadrons stamping.

Trump—trumpet. Pibroch—bagpipe.

"THE PAPER IN THE MEADOW" is an elegy for the young who died in World War II. The poem is subdued in tone, yet the repetition of "the news is yellowing in the rain" has the ache and throb of a fresh wound. There is grief here, but because it is expressed with grace and compassion it is bearable.

The Paper in the Meadow

OSCAR WILLIAMS

The news is yellowing in the rain,
The paper lies with all the words plain,
There in the meadow the paper lies
Read by the ants' and the stars' bright eyes.

The news is yellowing in the rain,
Not like the leaves, not like the grain,
Not like the flowers or things that grow,
The news is the color of long ago.

The news is yellowing in the rain,
In the midst of green it lies like stain,
The landscapes won and the faces lost,
The news is yellowing at their cost.

Once this paper was as white as truth,
But the blood turns black that came from youth,
And drawn like the face of the Prince of Pain,
The news is yellowing in the rain.

Recollections

RECOLLECTIONS, LIKE GOLDEN BEES, swarm in the mind. Poets particularly express memories and nostalgia, following the statement by William Wordsworth that poetry is "emotion recollected in tranquillity."

The Sands o' Dee

CHARLES KINGSLEY

"O Mary, go and call the cattle home,
    And call the cattle home,
    And call the cattle home,
    Across the sands o' Dee!"
The western wind was wild and dank wi' foam,
    And all alone went she.

The creeping tide came up along the sand,
    And o'er and o'er the sand,
    And round and round the sand,
    As far as eye could see;
The blinding mist came down and hid the land:
    And never home came she.

"O, is it weed, or fish, or floating hair,—
    A tress o' golden hair,
    O' drownèd maiden's hair,—
    Above the nets at sea?
Was never salmon yet that shone so fair,
    Among the stakes on Dee."

They rowed her in across the rolling foam,—
    The cruel, crawling foam,
    The cruel, hungry foam,—
    To her grave beside the sea;
But still the boatmen hear her call the cattle home
    Across the sands o' Dee.

LONDON-BORN THOMAS HOOD (1799–1845), though a man of pronounced gifts, waged a bitter struggle against poverty all his life. Since his serious poems attracted few readers, Hood drew upon his rich store of humor and published light verse to earn his living. In this connection he wistfully punned to the effect that he had to be a lively Hood in order to earn a livelihood. Here is one of his well-loved serious poems, which, in essence, may be summing up his own life.

I Remember, I Remember

THOMAS HOOD

I remember, I remember
The house where I was born,
The little window where the sun
Came peeping in at morn;
He never came a wink too soon
Nor brought too long a day;
But now, I often wish the night
Had borne my breath away.

I remember, I remember
The roses, red and white,
The violets, and the lily-cups—
Those flowers made of light!
The lilacs where the robin built,
And where my brother set
The laburnum on his birthday,—
The tree is living yet!

I remember, I remember
Where I was used to swing,
And thought the air must rush as fresh
To swallows on the wing;
My spirit flew in feathers then
That is so heavy now,
The summer pools could hardly cool
The fever on my brow.

I remember, I remember
The fir-trees dark and high;
I used to think their slender tops
Were close against the sky:
It was a childish ignorance,
But now 'tis little joy
To know I'm farther off from Heaven
Than when I was a boy.

My Early Home

JOHN CLARE

Here sparrows build upon the trees,
    And stock-dove hides her nest;
The leaves are winnowed by the breeze
    Into a calmer rest:
The blackcap's song was very sweet,
    That used the rose to kiss;
It made the paradise complete:
    My early home was this.

The redbreast from the sweetbrier bush
    Dropt down to pick the worm;
On the horse-chestnut sang the thrush,
    O'er the house where I was born;
The moonlight, like a shower of pearls,
    Fell o'er this "bower of bliss,"
And on the bench sat boys and girls:
    My early home was this.

The old house stooped just like a cave,
    Thatched o'er with mosses green;
Winter around the walls would rave,
    But all was calm within;
The trees are here all green agen,
    Here bees the flowers still kiss,
But flowers and trees seemed sweeter then:
    My early home was this.

The Oak and the Ash

ANONYMOUS

A north-country maid up to London had stray'd,
Although with her nature it did not agree;
She wept and she sigh'd, and she bitterly cried,
"I wish once again in the north I could be.

Oh! the Oak, and the Ash, and the bonny Ivy tree,
They flourish at home in my own country.

While sadly I roam I regret my dear home,
Where lads and young lasses are making the hay;
The merry bells ring, and the birds sweetly sing,
And maidens and meadows are pleasant and gay.

Oh! the Oak, and the Ash, and the bonny Ivy tree,
They flourish at home in my own country.

No doubt did I please, I could marry with ease;
Where maidens are fair many lovers will come;
But he whom I wed must be north-country bred,
And carry me back to my north country home.

Oh! the Oak, and the Ash, and the bonny Ivy tree,
They flourish at home in my own country."

Song

ALFRED, LORD TENNYSON

Who can say
Why Today
Tomorrow will be yesterday?
Who can tell
Why to smell
The violet, recalls the dewy prime
Of youth and buried time?
The cause is nowhere found in rhyme.

Martha

WALTER DE LA MARE

"Once . . . once upon a time . . ."
  Over and over again,
Martha would tell us stories,
  In the hazel glen.

Hers were those clear grey eyes
  You watch, and the story seems
Told by their beautifulness
  Tranquil as dreams.

She would sit with her two slim hands
  Clasped round her bended knees;
While we on our elbows lolled,
  And stared at ease.

Her voice and her narrow chin,
  Her grave small lovely head,
Seemed half the meaning
  Of the words she said.

"Once . . . once upon a time . . ."
  Like a dream in the night,
Fairies and gnomes stole out
  In the leaf-green light.

And her beauty far away
  Would fade, as her voice ran on,
Till hazel and summer sun
  And all were gone:

All fordone and forgot;
  And like clouds in the height of the sky,
Our hearts stood still in the hush
  Of an age gone by.

The Little Girl I Used to Be

MARGUERITE HARRIS

The little girl I used to be
Had angels on her Christmas tree:

Ribbands of blue held her golden hair:
She was bounden round with silken care.

She finger-painted on frosty panes:
Thank-Thee'd for victuals in His Name,

And scraping her apple with a silver spoon
On never-ending afternoons,

Never knew, being only seven,
She was a resident of Heaven.

Time, You Old Gipsy Man

RALPH HODGSON

Time, you old gipsy man,
  Will you not stay,
Put up your caravan
  Just for one day?

All things I'll give you
Will you be my guest,
Bells for your jennet
Of silver the best,
Goldsmiths shall beat you
A great golden ring,
Peacocks shall bow to you,
Little boys sing,
Oh, and sweet girls will
Festoon you with may.
Time, you old gipsy,
Why hasten away?

Last week in Babylon,
Last night in Rome,
Morning, and in the crush
Under Paul's dome;
Under Paul's dial
You tighten your rein—

Only a moment,
And off once again;
Off to some city
Now blind in the womb,
Off to another
Ere that's in the tomb.

Time, you old gipsy man,
  Will you not stay?
Put up your caravan
  Just for one day?

Sing Me a Song

ROBERT LOUIS STEVENSON

Sing me a song of a lad that is gone,
    Say, could that lad be I:
Merry of soul he sailed on a day
    Over the sea to Skye.

Mull was astern, Rum on the port,
    Eigg on the starboard bow;
Glory of youth glowed in his soul:
    Where is that glory now?

Sing me a song of a lad that is gone,
    Say, could that lad be I?
Merry of soul he sailed on a day
    Over the sea to Skye.

Give me again all that was there,
    Give me the sun that shone!
Give me the eyes, give me the soul,
    Give me the lad that's gone.

Sing me a song of a lad that is gone,
    Say, could that lad be I?
Merry of soul he sailed on a day
    Over the sea to Skye.

Billows and breeze, islands and seas,
    Mountains of rain and sun,
All that was good, all that was fair,
    All that was me is gone.

Aladdin

JAMES RUSSELL LOWELL

When I was a beggarly boy,
    And lived in a cellar damp,
    I had not a friend nor a toy,
    But I had Aladdin's lamp;
When I could not sleep for the cold,
    I had fire in my brain,
    And builded, with roofs of gold,
    My beautiful castles in Spain!

The Old Song

CHARLES KINGSLEY

When all the world is young, lad,
    And all the trees are green;
And every goose a swan, lad,
    And every lass a queen;
Then hey for boot and horse, lad,
    And round the world away;
Young blood must have its course, lad,
    And every dog his day.

When all the world is old, lad,
    And all the trees are brown;
And all the sport is stale, lad,
    And all the wheels run down;
Creep home, and take your place there,
    The spent and maimed among:
God grant you find one face there,
    You loved when all was young.

My Lost Youth

HENRY WADSWORTH LONGFELLOW

Often I think of the beautiful town
  That is seated by the sea;
Often in thought go up and down
  The pleasant streets of that dear old town,
      And my youth comes back to me.
      And a verse of Lapland song
      Is haunting my memory still:
      "A boy's will is the wind's will,
And the thoughts of youth are long, long thoughts."

I can see the shadowy lines of its trees,
  And catch in sudden gleams,
The sheen of the far-surrounding seas,
  And islands that were the Hesperides
      Of all my boyish dreams.
      And the burden of that old song,
      It murmurs and whispers still:
      "A boy's will is the wind's will,
And the thoughts of youth are long, long thoughts."

I remember the black wharves and the slips,
  And the sea-tides tossing free;
And Spanish sailors with bearded lips,
  And the beauty and mystery of the ships,
      And the magic of the sea.
      And the voice of that wayward song
      Is singing and saying still:
      "A boy's will is the wind's will,
And the thoughts of youth are long, long thoughts."

I remember the bulwarks by the shore,
  And the fort upon the hill:
The sunrise gun, with its hollow roar,
  The drum-beat repeated o'er and o'er,
      And the bugle wild and shrill.
      And the music of that old song
      Throbs in my memory still:
      "A boy's will is the wind's will,
And the thoughts of youth are long, long thoughts."

I remember the sea-fight far away,
  How it thundered o'er the tide!
And the dead captains, as they lay
  In their graves, o'erlooking the tranquil bay,
      Where they in battle died.
      And the sound of that mournful song
      Goes through me with a thrill:
      "A boy's will is the wind's will,
And the thoughts of youth are long, long thoughts."

I can see the breezy dome of groves,
  The shadows of Deering's Woods;
And the friendships old and the early loves
Come back with a Sabbath sound as of doves
      In quiet neighborhoods.
      And the verse of that sweet old song
      It flutters and murmurs still:
      "A boy's will is the wind's will,
And the thoughts of youth are long, long thoughts."

I remember the gleams and glooms that dart
  Across the schoolboy's brain:
The song and the silence in the heart,
  That in part are prophecies, and in part
      Are longings wild and vain.

And the voice of that fitful song
Sings on, and is never still:
"A boy's will is the wind's will,
And the thoughts of youth are long, long thoughts."

There are things of which I may not speak;
There are dreams that cannot die;
There are thoughts that make the strong heart weak,
And bring a pallor into the cheek,
And a mist before the eye.
And the words of that fatal song
Come over me like a chill:
"A boy's will is the wind's will,
And the thoughts of youth are long, long thoughts."

Strange to me now are the forms I meet
When I visit the dear old town:
But the native air is pure and sweet,
And the trees that o'ershadow each well-known street,
As they balance up and down,
Are singing the beautiful song,
Are sighing and whispering still:
"A boy's will is the wind's will,
And the thoughts of youth are long, long thoughts."

And Deering's Woods are fresh and fair,
And with joy that is almost pain
My heart goes back to wander there,
And among the dreams of the days that were,
I find my lost youth again.
And the strange and beautiful song,
The groves are repeating it still:
"A boy's will is the wind's will,
And the thoughts of youth are long, long thoughts."

All That's Past

WALTER DE LA MARE

Very old are the woods;
    And the buds that break
Out of the briar's boughs,
    When March winds wake,
So old with their beauty are—
    Oh, no man knows
Through what wild centuries
Roves back the rose.

Very old are the brooks;
    And the rills that rise
When snow sleeps cold beneath
    The azure skies
Sing such a history
    Of come and gone,
Their every drop is as wise
    As Solomon.

Very old are we men;
    Our dreams are tales
Told in dim Eden
    By Eve's nightingales;
We wake and whisper awhile,
    But, the day gone by,
Silence and sleep like fields
    Of Amaranth lie.

A Memory

WILLIAM ALLINGHAM

Four ducks on a pond,
A grass-bank beyond,
A blue sky of spring,
White clouds on the wing;
What a little thing
To remember for years—
To remember with tears!

Mountain Road

MARY OLIVER

My grandfather kept no
Unicorns in his gray barn,
But hurly-burly slant-eyed goats
That nimbled through the stacks
    of hay
And filled the milk pails
    every day.
My grandmother kept in her
    scriptures
No potions drained from
    the moon,
Kept no recipes in her gray head
To change the shape of men
    or wolves.
But I remember on her shelves
Apple butter and new bread.
Enchantment is a distant time.

Their farm was recent, filled
    with truth,
With buttered bread and milk
    in bowls,
And he and she were
    simple souls.
And yet I say, in all the earth
I have not found a place
    so sweet.
So it may be some charm did lay
Its arm across their small estate.
In any case when it dissolved—
Sank with their age into
    the wind
And woods again—we found
    it was
A story time could not repeat.

OUR ROOTS GO DOWN DEEP in the land, and our memories are haunted by our forebears who once walked upon that land, and laughed, and toiled and loved and had a dream. Those who came after are, in a sense, a continuation of that dream.

Having New England Fathers

JOHN HOLMES

Having New England fathers in my blood,
Thinking I lived but wisely and not well,
I sought ancestral trees for what they tell,
And ripped the long root up, but got no good.

My ghostly counsellors were not set free.
Whose mortal voice is mine the echo of?
Which face of all, now dark, now bright with love,
Springs to attention in the memory?

Who walked in sun, a worshipper of light?
Who caught the snowflake-star upon the sleeve?
Who chose the world for danger? By whose leave
Was lore like this not down in black and white?

And no one answers, yet in every limb
I feel the blood that finds the legend true.
Passionate patience was his wisdom, too,
And every question makes me sure of him.

No living hand remembers now his hand,
And yet my younger brother wears his face.
He is established in a starry place;
In living bodies; in his native land.

He sleeps. He has mountains for a bed.
Vermont has washed him clean with stony streams.
The Berkshire pines are talking in his dreams,
And all his dreams are running through my head.

Jenny Kissed Me

LEIGH HUNT

Jenny kissed me when we met,
    Jumping from the chair she sat in;
Time, you thief! who love to get
    Sweets into your list, put that in:
Say I'm weary, say I'm sad,
    Say that health and wealth have missed me,
Say I'm growing old, but add,—
    Jenny kissed me.

SOME OF TENNYSON'S finest lyrics appear in his long poem *The Princess.* Here appears "Tears, Idle Tears," a poem that dwells upon the past and carries its lyrical burden of grief and regret for "the days that are no more." Tennyson tells us in a memoir that he composed the poem "in the yellowing autumn-tide at Tintern Abbey, full for me of its bygone memories."

Tears, Idle Tears

ALFRED, LORD TENNYSON

Tears, idle tears, I know not what they mean,
Tears from the depth of some divine despair
Rise in the heart, and gather to the eyes,
In looking on the happy autumn fields,
And thinking of the days that are no more.

Fresh as the first beam glittering on a sail,
That brings our friends up from the under-world,
Sad as the last which reddens over one
That sinks with all we love below the verge;
So sad, so fresh, the days that are no more.

Ah, sad and strange as in dark summer dawns
The earliest pipe of half-awakened birds
To dying ears, when unto dying eyes
The casement slowly grows a glimmering square;
So sad, so strange, the days that are no more.

Dear as remembered kisses after death,
And sweet as those by hopeless fancy feigned
On lips that are for others; deep as love,
Deep as first love, and wild with all regret;
O Death in Life, the days that are no more!

Annabel Lee

Edgar Allan Poe

It was many and many a year ago,
In a kingdom by the sea,
That a maiden there lived whom you may know
By the name of Annabel Lee;
And this maiden she lived with no other thought
Than to love and be loved by me.

I was a child and she was a child,
In this kingdom by the sea:
But we loved with a love that was more than love—
I and my Annabel Lee;
With a love that the winged seraphs of heaven
Coveted her and me.

And this was the reason that, long ago,
In this kingdom by the sea,
A wind blew out of a cloud, chilling
My beautiful Annabel Lee;
So that her highborn kinsman came
And bore her away from me,
To shut her up in a sepulchre
In this kingdom by the sea.

The angels, not half so happy in heaven,
Went envying her and me—
Yes!—that was the reason (as all men know,
In this kingdom by the sea)
That the wind came out of the cloud by night,
Chilling and killing my Annabel Lee.

But our love it was stronger by far than the love
Of those who were older than we—
Of many far wiser than we—
And neither the angels in heaven above,
Nor the demons down under the sea,
Can ever dissever my soul from the soul
Of the beautiful Annabel Lee:

For the moon never beams, without bringing me dreams
Of the beautiful Annabel Lee:
And the stars never rise, but I feel the bright eyes
Of the beautiful Annabel Lee;
And so, all the night-tide, I lie down by the side
Of my darling—my darling—my life and my bride,
In the sepulchre there by the sea,
In her tomb by the sounding sea.

With Rue My Heart Is Laden

A. E. Housman

With rue my heart is laden
  For golden friends I had,
For many a rose-lipt maiden
  And many a lightfoot lad.

By brooks too broad for leaping
  The lightfoot boys are laid;
The rose-lipt girls are sleeping
  In fields where roses fade.

Love and Age

Thomas Love Peacock

I play'd with you 'mid cowslips blowing,
  When I was six and you were four;
When garlands weaving, flower-balls throwing,
  Were pleasures soon to please no more.
Through groves and meads, o'er grass and heather,
  With little playmates, to and fro,
We wander'd hand in hand together;
  But that was sixty years ago.

You grew a lovely roseate maiden,
  And still our early love was strong;
Still with no care our days were laden,
  They glided joyously along;
And I did love you very dearly,
  How dearly words want power to show;
I thought your heart was touch'd as nearly;
  But that was fifty years ago.

Then other lovers came around you,
　Your beauty grew from year to year,
And many a splendid circle found you
　The centre of its glittering sphere.
I saw you then, first vows forsaking,
　On rank and wealth your hand bestow;
O, then I thought my heart was breaking!—
　But that was forty years ago.

And I lived on, to wed another:
　No cause she gave me to repine;
And when I heard you were a mother,
　I did not wish the children mine.
My own young flock, in fair progression,
　Made up a pleasant Christmas row:
My joy in them was past expression;
　But that was thirty years ago.

You grew a matron plump and comely,
　You dwelt in fashion's brightest blaze;
My earthly lot was far more homely;
　But I too had my festal days.
No merrier eyes have ever glisten'd
　Around the hearth-stone's wintry glow,
Than when my youngest child was christen'd;
　But that was twenty years ago.

Time pass'd. My eldest girl was married,
　And I am now a grandsire gray;
One pet of four years old I've carried
　Among the wild-flower'd meads to play.
In our old fields of childish pleasure,
　Where now, as then, the cowslips blow,
She fills her basket's ample measure;
　And that is not ten years ago.

But though first love's impassion'd blindness
　Has pass'd away in colder light,
I still have thought of you with kindness,
　And shall do, till our last good-night.
The ever-rolling silent hours
　Will bring a time we shall not know,
When our young days of gathering flowers
　Will be an hundred years ago.

Memory

Thomas Bailey Aldrich

My mind lets go a thousand things,
Like dates of wars and deaths of kings,
And yet recalls the very hour—
'Twas noon by yonder village tower,
And on the last blue moon in May—
The wind came briskly up this way,
Crisping the brook beside the road;
Then, pausing here, set down its load
Of pine-scents, and shook listlessly
Two petals from that wild-rose tree.

HERE, AS IN THE BALLAD "Christmas at Sea," Stevenson had two opposing impulses to contend with. While his whole life was spent seeking adventure, some deep need in him kept harking back to home and the kind faces of old.

Home No More

ROBERT LOUIS STEVENSON

Home no more home to me, whither must I wander?
   Hunger my driver, I go where I must.
Cold blows the winter wind over hill and heather;
   Thick drives the rain, and my roof is in the dust.
Loved of wise men was the shade of my roof-tree,
   The true word of welcome was spoken in the door—
Dear days of old, with the faces in the firelight,
   Kind folks of old, you come again no more.

Home was home then, my dear, full of kindly faces,
   Home was home then, my dear, happy for the child.
Fire and the windows bright glittered on the moorland;
   Song, tuneful song, built a palace in the wild.
Now, when day dawns on the brow on the moorland,
   Lone stands the house, and the chimney-stone is cold.
Lone let it stand, now the friends are all departed,
   The kind hearts, the true hearts, that loved the place of old.

Spring shall come, come again, calling up the moor fowl,
   Spring shall bring the sun and rain, bring the bees and
      flowers;
Red shall the heather bloom over hill and valley,
   Soft flow the stream through the even-flowing hours;
Fair the day shine as it shone on my childhood—
   Fair shine the day on the house with open door;
Birds come and cry there and twitter in the chimney—
   But I go for ever and come again no more.

The Noise That Time Makes

MERRILL MOORE

The noise that Time makes in passing by
Is very slight but even you can hear it,
Having not necessarily to be near it,
Needing only the slightest will to try:

Hold the receiver of a telephone
To your ear when no one is talking on the line

And what may at first sound to you like the whine
Of wind over distant wires is Time's own
Garments brushing against a windy cloud.

That same noise again but not so well
May be heard by taking a small cockle-shell
From the sand and holding it against your head;

Then you can hear Time's footsteps as they pass
Over the earth brushing the eternal grass.

A POPULAR French lyrical verse form is the villanelle, a poem of nineteen lines, consisting of five three-line stanzas followed by a final four-line stanza. By its nature the villanelle is particularly suited to verses of a light and dainty nature, but in the hands of a superb craftsman it can result in a moving poem, as in this villanelle expressing pity and loss.

The House on the Hill

EDWIN ARLINGTON ROBINSON

They are all gone away,
   The House is shut and still,
There is nothing more to say.

Through broken walls and gray
   The winds blow bleak and shrill;
They are all gone away.

    And our poor fancy-play
      For them is wasted skill:
    There is nothing more to say.

    There is ruin and decay
      In the House on the Hill:
    They are all gone away,
      There is nothing more to say.

Nor is there anyone today
   To speak them good or ill:
There is nothing more to say.

Why is it then we stray
   Around that sunken sill?
They are all gone away,

The Time of Roses

THOMAS HOOD

It was not in the Winter
Our loving lot was cast;
It was the time of roses—
We plucked them as we passed!

That churlish season never frowned
On early lovers yet:
O no—the world was newly crowned
With flowers when first we met!

    'Twas twilight, and I bade you go,
    But still you held me fast;
    It was the time of roses—
    We plucked them as we passed.

TARA, THE ANCIENT CAPITAL of Irish kings still has a romantic hold on the imagination—particularly of the Irish imagination. Thomas Moore was born in Dublin in 1779, and many of his songs are still admired for their romantic lyrics and patriotic fervor.

The Harp That Once through Tara's Halls

THOMAS MOORE

The harp that once through Tara's halls
　　The soul of beauty shed,
Now hangs as mute on Tara's walls,
　　As if that soul were fled.—
So sleeps the pride of former days,
　　So glory's thrill is o'er,
And hearts that once beat high for praise,
　　Now feel that pulse no more.

No more to chiefs and ladies bright
　　The harp of Tara swells;
The chord alone, that breaks at night,
　　Its tale of ruin tells.
Thus Freedom now so seldom wakes,
　　The only throb she gives,
Is when some heart indignant breaks,
　　To show that still she lives.

The Tropics in New York

CLAUDE McKAY

Bananas ripe and green, and gingerroot,
　　Cocoa in pods and alligator pears,
And tangerines and mangoes and grapefruit,
　　Fit for the highest prize at parish fairs,

Set in the window, bringing memories
　　Of fruit trees laden by low-singing rills,
And dewy dawns, and mystical blue skies
　　In benediction over nunlike hills.

My eyes grew dim, and I could no more gaze;
　　A wave of longing through my body swept,
And, hungry for the old, familiar ways,
　　I turned aside and bowed my head and wept.

Chapter Two

Winfield Townley Scott

Listen—I'll say you a
Park in the city, a
Park in the dusk just
As the snow is beginning:
The gray-blue, the sweet-cold, the
Whispering rustling.

And

—Do you remember?—
Floor by floor the lights rising
As darkness filled up
The tall wells of the streets
Gigantically ringing the
Small empty park where
The thin snow slid in
As if it would fall
Through the dusk there forever,
Amidst gears', horns' wrangles
Hushing a circle;
The gray-white, the sweet-cold.

Oh

—Now you remember—
How young and unhappy and
Lovely you were
How uselessly in
Love we were; and there
Walking alone in New York in the snow
You had nobody anywhere to see to
Talk to nowhere to go.

Blue Girls

JOHN CROWE RANSOM

Twirling your blue skirts, travelling the sward
Under the towers of your seminary,
Go listen to your teachers old and contrary
Without believing a word.

Tie the white fillets then about your lustrous hair
And think no more of what will come to pass
Than bluebirds that go walking on the grass
And chattering on the air.

Practice your beauty, blue girls, before it fail;
And I will cry with my loud lips and publish
Beauty which all our power shall never establish,
It is so frail.

For I could tell you a story which is true:
I know a lady with a terrible tongue,
Blear eyes fallen from blue,
All her perfections tarnished—and yet it is not long
Since she was lovelier than any of you.

WILLIAM MAKEPEACE THACKERAY, one of the great Victorian novelists, was also a graceful and witty writer of light verse. Here is a hymn of praise to a delicious fish dish which he garnishes with a few tender recollections of the past.

The Ballad of Bouillabaisse

WILLIAM MAKEPEACE THACKERAY

A street there is in Paris famous,
    For which no rhyme our language yields,
Rue Neuve des Petits Champs its name is—
    The New Street of the Little Fields;
And here 's an inn, not rich and splendid,
    But still in comfortable case;
The which in youth I oft attended,
    To eat a bowl of Bouillabaisse.

This Bouillabaisse a noble dish is—
    A sort of soup or broth, or brew,
Or hotchpotch, of all sorts of fishes,
    That Greenwich never could outdo;
Green herbs, red peppers, mussels, saffern,
    Soles, onions, garlic, roach, and dace;
All these you eat at Terré's tavern,
    In that one dish of Bouillabaisse.

Indeed, a rich and savoury stew 'tis;
    And true philosophers, methinks,
Who love all sorts of natural beauties,
    Should love good victuals and good drinks.
And Cordelier or Benedictine
    Might gladly, sure, his lot embrace,
Nor find a fast-day too afflicting
    Which served him up a Bouillabaisse.

I wonder if the house still there is?
    Yes, here the lamp is, as before;
The smiling red-cheek'd écaillère is
    Still opening oysters at the door.
Is Terré still alive and able?
    I recollect his droll grimace;
He'd come and smile before your table,
    And hope you liked your Bouillabaisse.

We enter—nothing's changed or older.
    "How 's Monsieur Terré, waiter,"
The waiter stares and shrugs his shoulder—
    "Monsieur is dead this many a day."
"It is the lot of saint and sinner,
    So honest Terré's run his race!"
"What will Monsieur require for dinner?"
    "Say, do you still cook Bouillabaisse?"

"Oh, oui, Monsieur," 's the waiter's answer;
    "Quel vin Monsieur désire-t-il?"
"Tell me a good one."—"That I can, Sir:
    The Chambertin with yellow seal."
"So Terré 's gone," I say, and sink in
    My old accustom'd corner-place;
"He's done with feasting and with drinking,
    With Burgundy and Bouillabaisse."

My old accustom'd corner here is,
  The table still is in the nook;
Ah! vanish'd many a busy year is,
  This well-known chair since last I took.
When first I saw ye, *cari luoghi*,
  I'd scarce a beard upon my face,
And now a grizzled, grim old fogy,
  I sit and wait for Bouillabaisse.

Where are you, old companions trusty,
  Of early days, here met to dine?
Come, waiter! quick, a flagon crusty—
  I'll pledge them in the good old wine.
The kind old voices and old faces
  My memory can quick retrace;
Around the board they take their places,
  And share the wine and Bouillabaisse.

There 's Jack has made a wondrous marriage;
  There 's laughing Tom is laughing yet;
There 's brave Augustus drives his carriage;
  There 's poor old Fred in the Gazette;
On James's head the grass is growing:
  Good Lord! the world has wagged apace
Since here we set the Claret flowing,
  And drank, and ate the Bouillabaisse.

Ah me! how quick the days are flitting!
  I mind me of a time that's gone,
When here I'd sit, as now I'm sitting,
  In this same place—but not alone.
A fair young form was nestled near me,
  A dear, dear face looked fondly up,
And sweetly spoke and smiled to cheer me
  —There 's no one now to share my cup.

. . . .

I drink it as the Fates ordain it.
  Come, fill it, and have done with rhymes:
Fill up the lonely glass, and drain it
  In memory of dear old times.
Welcome the wine, whate'er the seal is;
  And sit you down and say your grace
With thankful heart, whate'er the meal is.
  —Here comes the smoking Bouillabaisse!

Wisdom

WISDOM HAS MANY FACETS. Whether it be man or the creatures of the earth, each is wise in his own way. The robin sitting on her eggs; the beaver building his dam; the foraging of the bees for nectar; the wisdom of the ant who "Provideth her meat in the summer/and gathereth her food in the harvest." Even the helpless infant comes to the mother's breast with his instinctive nurseling's wisdom. There is also the wisdom acquired by experience, and learned just through living. As the farmer's, and sailor's; that of the woodsman and scientist, and all men who labor in the world who hope and sing and fear and dream a little. And there are poets whose wisdom is shaped by the joyous or brooding imagination and then bodied forth in song and prophesy.

In the centuries that man has had the Bible, he has gone to it time and again for reassurance and solace. Of all its parts, it is certainly the 23rd Psalm of David, the "sweetest singer in Israel," that has been of most comfort in time of sorrow or heartache.

Psalm 23

THE BIBLE

The Lord is my shepherd; I shall not want.

He maketh me to lie down in green pastures: he leadeth me beside the still waters.

He restoreth my soul: he leadeth me in the paths of righteousness for his name's sake.

Yea, though I walk through the valley of the shadow of death, I will fear no evil: for thou art with me; thy rod and thy staff they comfort me.

Thou preparest a table before me in the presence of mine enemies: thou anointest my head with oil; my cup runneth over.

Surely goodness and mercy shall follow me all the days of my life: and I will dwell in the house of the Lord for ever.

The Noble Nature

BEN JONSON

It is not growing like a tree
    In bulk, doth make man better be;
Or standing long an oak, three hundred year,
To fall a log at last, dry, bald, and sear:
    A lily of a day
    Is fairer far in May,
Although it fall and die that night,—
    It was the plant and flower of Light.
In small proportions we just beauties see,
And in short measures life may perfect be.

Lines Written in Early Spring

WILLIAM WORDSWORTH

I heard a thousand blended notes,
While in a grove I sate reclined,
In that sweet mood when pleasant thoughts
Bring sad thoughts to the mind.

To her fair works did Nature link
The human soul that through me ran;
And much it grieved my heart to think
What man has made of man.

Through primrose tufts, in that green bower,
The periwinkle trailed its wreaths;
And 'tis my faith that every flower
Enjoys the air it breathes.

The birds around me hopped and played,
Their thoughts I cannot measure:—
But the least motion which they made
It seemed a thrill of pleasure.

The budding twigs spread out their fan,
To catch the breezy air;
And I must think, do all I can,
That there was pleasure there.

If this belief from heaven be sent,
If such be Nature's holy plan,
Have I not reason to lament
What man has made of man?

Once in a Saintly Passion

JAMES THOMSON

Once in a saintly passion
    I cried with desperate grief,
"O Lord, my heart is black with guile,
    Of sinners I am chief."

Then stooped my guardian angel
    And whispered from behind
"Vanity, my little man,
    You're nothing of the kind."

How Many

CHRISTINA ROSSETTI

How many seconds in a minute?
Sixty, and no more in it.

How many minutes in an hour?
Sixty for sun and shower.

How many hours in a day?
Twenty-four for work and play.

How many days in a week?
Seven both to hear and speak.

How many weeks in a month?
Four, as the swift moon runn'th.

How many months in a year?
Twelve the almanack makes clear.

How many years in an age?
One hundred says the sage.

How many ages in time?
No one knows the rhyme.

317

The Glories of Our Blood and State

JAMES SHIRLEY

The glories of our blood and state
  Are shadows, not substantial things;
There is no armour against fate;
  Death lays his icy hand on kings:
    Sceptre and crown
    Must tumble down,
And in the dust be equal made
With the poor crooked scythe and spade.

Some men with swords may reap the field,
  And plant fresh laurels where they kill;
But their strong nerves at last must yield;
  They tame but one another still:
    Early or late,
    They stoop to fate,
And must give up their murmuring breath,
When they, pale captives, creep to death.

The garlands wither on your brow,
  Then boast no more your mighty deeds;
Upon Death's purple altar now,
  See, where the victor-victim bleeds:
    Your heads must come
    To the cold tomb,
Only the actions of the just
Smell sweet, and blossom in their dust.

Proprietor

A. M. SULLIVAN

We stood beside the rushing stream,
The lad of seven held my hand;
My breast swelled out in self-esteem,
And Pride, the partner in the scheme,
Measured the eye length of the land.

"Who owns the field?" the youngster asked,
He brought to mind the acre's worth.
"I do," I said. Pride was unmasked,
And in my countenance he basked,
A tyrant over the generous earth.

"Who owns beyond," the young man said,
"Where the marsh grows tall and green?"
"I trapped the beaver till they fled
And snakes and birds have heard my tread;
The land is mine, the land is mean."

"You own the water, too?" He turned
And watched the river's crooked spine.
"I own it all," I said, and learned
How a child in conscience spurned
The meaning of what's mine and thine.

"Come," I said, but he would stay;
"The water," he asked with sudden whim,
"Who owns it when it goes away?"
And I was silent all the day,
Nor did I ever answer him.

THE JESTER TRADITIONALLY attached to a king's court was not always the maker of light-hearted quips and japes. Sometimes, beneath the masquerade of cap and bells, the heart of a philosopher reflected the conscience of the time. Such is the case here.

The Fool's Prayer

EDWARD ROWLAND SILL

The royal feast was done; the King
  Sought some new sport to banish care,
And to his jester cried: "Sir Fool,
  Kneel now, and make for us a prayer!"

The jester doffed his cap and bells,
  And stood the mocking court before;
They could not see the bitter smile
  Behind the painted grin he wore.

He bowed his head, and bent his knee
  Upon the monarch's silken stool;
His pleading voice arose: "O Lord,
  Be merciful to me, a fool!

"No pity, Lord, could change the heart
  From red with wrong to white as wool;
The rod must heal the sin: but, Lord,
  Be merciful to me, a fool!

" 'Tis not by guilt the onward sweep
  Of truth and right, O Lord, we stay;
'Tis by our follies that so long
  We hold the earth from heaven away.

"These clumsy feet, still in the mire,
  Go crushing blossoms without end;
These hard, well-meaning hands we thrust
  Among the heart-strings of a friend.

"The ill-timed truth we might have kept—
  Who knows how sharp it pierced and stung?
The word we had not sense to say—
  Who knows how grandly it had rung?

"Our faults no tenderness should ask,
  The chastening stripes must cleanse them all;
But for our blunders—oh, in shame
  Before the eyes of heaven we fall.

"Earth bears no balsam for mistake;
  Men crown the knave, and scourge the tool
That did his will; but Thou, O Lord,
  Be merciful to me, a fool!"

The room was hushed; in silence rose
  The King, and sought his gardens cool,
And walked apart, and murmured low,
  "Be merciful to me, a fool!"

My Mind to Me a Kingdom Is

EDWARD DYER

My mind to me a kingdom is,
Such present joys therein I find,
That it excels all other bliss
That earth affords or grows by kind:
Though much I want which most would have,
Yet still my mind forbids to crave.

No princely pomp, no wealthy store,
No force to win the victory,
No wily wit to salve a sore,
No shape to feed a loving eye;
To none of these I yield as thrall:
For why? My mind doth serve for all.

I see how plenty surfeits oft,
And hasty climbers soon do fall;
I see that those which are aloft
Mishap doth threaten most of all,
They get with toil, they keep with fear;
Such cares my mind could never bear.

Content to live, this is my stay;
I seek no more than may suffice;
I press to bear no haughty sway;
Look, what I lack my mind supplies:
Lo, thus I triumph like a king,
Content with that my mind doth bring.

Some have too much, yet still do crave;
I little have, and seek no more.
They are but poor, though much they have,
And I am rich with little store;
They poor, I rich; they beg, I give;
They lack, I leave; they pine, I live.

I laugh not at another's loss;
I grudge not at another's pain;
No worldly waves my mind can toss;
My state at one doth still remain;
I fear no foe, I fawn no friend;
I loathe not life, nor dread my end.

Some weigh their pleasure by their lust,
Their wisdom by their rage of will;
Their treasure is their only trust;
A cloaked craft their store of skill:
But all the pleasure that I find
Is to maintain a quiet mind.

Patriotism

SIR WALTER SCOTT

Breathes there the man with soul so dead,
Who never to himself hath said,
　"This is my own, my native land!"
Whose heart hath ne'er within him burn'd
As home his footsteps he hath turn'd
　From wandering on a foreign strand?
If such there breathe, go, mark him well;
For him no minstrel raptures swell;

High though his titles, proud his name,
Boundless his wealth as wish can claim;
Despite those titles, power, and pelf,
The wretch, concentred all in self,
Living, shall forfeit fair renown,
And, doubly dying, shall go down
To the vile dust from whence he sprung,
Unwept, unhonour'd, and unsung.

Content

ROBERT GREENE

Sweet are the thoughts that savor of content;
The quiet mind is richer than a crown;
Sweet are the nights in careless slumber spent;
The poor estate scorns Fortune's angry frown:
Such sweet content, such minds, such sleep, such bliss,
Beggars enjoy, when princes oft do miss.
The homely house that harbors quiet rest,
The cottage that affords nor pride nor care,
The mean that 'grees with country music best,
The sweet consort of mirth and modest fare,
Obscured life sets down a type of bliss:
A mind content both crown and kingdom is.

The Character of a Happy Life

SIR HENRY WOTTON

How happy is he born and taught
That serveth not another's will;
Whose armor is his honest thought,
And simple truth his utmost skill!

Whose passions not his masters are;
Whose soul is still prepared for death,
Not tied unto the world by care
Of public fame or private breath;

Who envies none that chance doth raise,
Nor vice; who never understood
How deepest wounds are given by praise;
Nor rules of state, but rules of good;

Who hath his life from rumors freed;
Whose conscience is his strong retreat;
Whose state can neither flatterers feed,
Nor ruin make oppressors great;

Who God doth late and early pray
More of His grace than gifts to lend;
And entertains the harmless day
With a well-chosen book or friend;

—This man is freed from servile bands
Of hope to rise, or fear to fall:
Lord of himself, though not of lands;
And having nothing, yet hath all.

Sweet Content

Thomas Dekker

Art thou poor, yet hast thou golden slumbers?
    O sweet content!
Art thou rich, yet is thy mind perplexed?
    O punishment!
Dost thou laugh to see how fools are vexed
To add to golden numbers, golden numbers?
O sweet content! O sweet, O sweet content!
  Work apace, apace, apace, apace;
  Honest labor bears a lovely face;
Then hey nonny nonny, hey nonny nonny!
Canst drink the waters of the crispèd spring?
    O sweet content!
Swimm'st thou in wealth, yet sink'st in thine own tears?
    O punishment!
Then he that patiently want's burden bears
No burden bears, but is a king, a king!
O sweet content! O sweet, O sweet content!
  Work apace, apace, apace, apace;
  Honest labor bears a lovely face;
Then hey nonny nonny, hey nonny nonny!

Gladness of Heart

Ecclesiasticus

Gladness of heart is the life of man;
And the joyfulness of man
is length of days.
  Love thine own soul
and comfort thy heart;
and remove sorrow from thee,
for sorrow hath destroyed many
and there is no profit therein.
  Envy and wrath shorten a man's days,
and care bringeth old age before the time.
  A cheerful and good heart
will have a care of his meat and diet.

Fetters

LOUIS GINSBERG

Only in fetters
    Is liberty:
Without its banks,
      Could a river be?

WILLIAM ERNEST HENLEY (1849–1903) crippled at the age of twelve, and physically broken for the remainder of his life, was still able to rise above his wounds and sing with unfaltering courage. His poem "Invictus" is a brave song of defiance.

Invictus

WILLIAM ERNEST HENLEY

Out of the night that covers me,
    Black as the pit from pole to pole,
I thank whatever gods may be
    For my unconquerable soul.

In the fell clutch of circumstance
    I have not winced nor cried aloud.
Under the bludgeonings of chance
    My head is bloody, but unbowed.

Beyond this place of wrath and tears
    Looms but the horror of the shade,
And yet the menace of the years
    Finds and shall find me unafraid.

It matters not how strait the gate,
    How charged with punishments the scroll,
I am the master of my fate;
    I am the captain of my soul.

ALEXANDER POPE (1688–1744), born in London, was hunch-backed and stunted to a height of a dwarfish four and a half feet. The deformity prevented him from attending a university, but did not keep him from poring over the books in his father's well-stocked library. As a youngster, Pope showed an extraordinary aptitude for poetry, composing these lines when a mere twelve years of age.

Solitude

ALEXANDER POPE

Happy the man, whose wish and care
A few paternal acres bound,
Content to breathe his native air
    In his own ground.

Whose herds with milk, whose fields with bread,
Whose flocks supply him with attire;
Whose trees in summer yield him shade,
    In winter, fire.

Blest, who can unconcernedly find
Hours, days, and years slide soft away
In health of body, peace of mind;
    Quiet by day,

Sound sleep by night; study and ease
Together mixed, sweet recreation,
And innocence, which most does please
    With meditation.

Thus let me live, unseen, unknown;
Thus unlamented let me die,
Steal from the world, and not a stone
    Tell where I lie.

Ozymandias

PERCY BYSSHE SHELLEY

I met a traveler from an antique land
Who said: Two vast and trunkless legs of stone
Stand in the desert. Near them, on the sand,
Half sunk, a shattered visage lies, whose frown,
And wrinkled lip, and sneer of cold command,
Tell that its sculptor well those passions read
Which yet survive, stamped on these lifeless things,
The hand that mocked them and the heart that fed;
And on the pedestal these words appear:
"My name is Ozymandias, king of kings:
Look on my works, ye Mighty, and despair!"
Nothing beside remains. Round the decay
Of that colossal wreck, boundless and bare
The lone and level sands stretch far away.

To Get Thine Ends

ROBERT HERRICK

To get thine ends, lay bashfulness aside;
Who fears to ask doth teach to be denied.

He who has suffered shipwreck, fears to sail
Upon the seas, though with a gentle gale.

If little labor, little are our gains:
Man's fortunes are according to his pains.

Milk still your fountains and your springs: for why?
The more they're drawn, the less they will go dry.

Success Is Counted Sweetest

EMILY DICKINSON

Success is counted sweetest
By those who ne'er succeed.
To comprehend a nectar
Requires sorest need.

Not one of all the purple host
Who took the flag today
Can tell the definition,
So clear, of victory,

As he, defeated, dying,
On whose forbidden ear   ·
The distant strains of triumph
Break, agonized and clear.

The Road Not Taken

ROBERT FROST

Two roads diverged in a yellow wood,
And sorry I could not travel both
And be one traveler, long I stood
And looked down one as far as I could
To where it bent in the undergrowth;

Then took the other, as just as fair,
And having perhaps the better claim,
Because it was grassy and wanted wear;
Though as for that the passing there
Had worn them really about the same,

And both that morning equally lay
In leaves no step had trodden black.
Oh, I kept the first for another day!
Yet knowing how way leads on to way,
I doubted if I should ever come back.

I shall be telling this with a sigh
Somewhere ages and ages hence:
Two roads diverged in a wood, and I—
I took the one less traveled by,
And that has made all the difference.

The Little Cares

ELIZABETH BARRETT BROWNING

The little cares that fretted me,
    I lost them yesterday
Among the fields above the sea,
    Among the winds at play;
Among the lowing of the herds,
    The rustling of the trees,
Among the singing of the birds,
    The humming of the bees.

The foolish fears of what may happen—
    I cast them all away
Among the clover-scented grass,
    Among the new-mown hay;
Among the husking of the corn
    Where drowsy poppies nod,
Where ill thoughts die and good are born,
    Out in the fields with God.

Abou Ben Adhem

LEIGH HUNT

Abou Ben Adhem (may his tribe increase!)
Awoke one night from a deep dream of peace,
And saw, within the moonlight in his room,
Making it rich, and like a lily in bloom,
An angel writing in a book of gold:—
Exceeding peace had made Ben Adhem bold,
And to the presence in the room he said,

"What writest thou?"—The vision rais'd its head,
And with a look made of all sweet accord,
Answer'd, "The names of those who love the Lord."

"And is mine one?" said Abou. "Nay, not so,"
Replied the angel. Abou spoke more low,
But cheerly still; and said, "I pray thee, then,
Write me as one that loves his fellow men."

The angel wrote, and vanish'd. The next night
It came again with a great wakening light,
And show'd the names whom love of God had blest,
And lo! Ben Adhem's name led all the rest.

Auguries of Innocence

William Blake

A dog starved at his Master's gate
Predicts the ruin of the State.

*   *   *

A horse misused upon the road
Calls to heaven for human blood.

*   *   *

A skylark wounded in the wing,
A cherubim does cease to sing.

*   *   *

He who shall hurt the little wren
Shall never be belov'd by men.

*   *   *

Under every grief and pine
Runs a joy with silken twine.

*   *   *

The child's toys and the old man's reasons
Are the fruits of the two seasons.

*   *   *

If the sun and moon should doubt,
They'd immediately go out.

ACKNOWLEDGEMENTS

The Editor and Publisher gratefully acknowledge the permission granted by the following authors, publishers, and author's representatives to reprint selections from their publications.

"Crickets" and "Music I Heard with You" from *Collected Poems* by Conrad Aiken, copyright 1953 by Conrad Aiken, reprinted by permission of the Oxford University Press, Inc. "Song for Boys and Girls" by Charles Angoff reprinted with the permission of the author. "The Grizzly Bear" and "Neither Spirit nor Bird" from *The Children Sing in the Far West* by Mary Austin, reprinted by permission of the Houghton Mifflin Co. "The Witch's House" by Laura Benét reprinted with the permission of the author. "The Ballad of William Sycamore" from *Ballads and Poems* by Stephen Vincent Benét, copyright 1931 by Stephen Vincent Benét, copyright © 1959 by Rosemary Carr Benét, reprinted by permission of Holt, Rinehart and Winston, Inc., and Brandt and Brandt, Ltd. "Variation on a Sentence" from *Collected Poems: 1923–1953* by Louise Bogan, published by Farrar, Strauss & Giroux, Inc. "Bed-time Story" copyright 1947 by Melville Cane, reprinted from *So That It Flower* by Melville Cane by permission of Harcourt, Brace & World, Inc. "A Vagabond Song" from *Bliss Carman's Poetry* reprinted by permission of Dodd, Mead & Co., New York, and McClelland and Stewart, Ltd., Toronto. "An Old Woman of the Roads" from *Wild Earth and Other Poems* by Padraic Colum reprinted with the permission of the author. "In Just—", copyright 1923, 1951 by E. E. Cummings, reprinted from his volume *Poems 1923–1954* by permission of Harcourt, Brace & World, Inc., and Faber and Faber, Ltd. "Moment of Visitation" and "A Time for Singing" by Gustav Davidson, reprinted with the permission of the author. "Leisure" by W. H. Davies from *The Complete Poems of W. H. Davies* used by permission of Mrs. H. M. Davies and Jonathan Cape, Ltd. "All That's Past," "Autumn," "Martha," and "A Song of Enchantment," used by permission of the Literary Trustees of Walter de la Mare and The Society of Authors. "On a Squirrel Crossing the Road in Autumn, in New England," from *Collected Poems 1930–1960* by Richard Eberhart, © Richard Eberhart, reprinted by permission of the Oxford University Press, Inc., and Chatto and Windus, Ltd. "The Rum Tum Tugger" from *Old Possum's Book of Practical Cats* by T. S. Eliot, copyright 1939 by T. S. Eliot, renewed 1967 by Esme Valerie Eliot, reprinted by permission of Harcourt, Brace & World, Inc., and Faber and Faber, Ltd. "Donkeys," copyright © by Edward Field, reprinted by permission of Grove Press, Inc. "The Road Not Taken" and "Stopping by Woods on a Snowy Evening" from *Complete Poems of Robert Frost* copyright 1916, 1923 by Holt, Rinehart and Winston, Inc., copyright 1944, 1951 by Robert Frost, reprinted by permission of Holt, Rinehart and Winston, Inc., and Jonathan Cape, Ltd. "Fetters" from *The Everlasting Minute* by Louis Ginsberg © 1965 by Louis Ginsberg, reprinted by permission of Liveright Publishers, New York. "The Darkling Thrush" and "The Last Chrysanthemum" reprinted with permission of The Macmillan Company from *Collected Poems* by Thomas Hardy copyright 1925 by The Macmillan Company and by permission of the Trustees of the Hardy Estate, the Macmillan Company of Canada, Ltd., and Macmillan & Co., Ltd., London. "The Little Girl I Used to Be" by Marguerite Harris, reprinted with the permission of the author. "Nursery Snail" from *A Way of Happening* copyright 1948 by Ruth Herschberger and used by permission. "Time, You Old Gypsy Man" reprinted with the permission of The Macmillan Company, from *Poems* by Ralph Hodgson, copyright 1917 by the Macmillan Company, renewed 1945 by Ralph Hodgson and with the permission of Mrs. Hodgson and Macmillan & Co., Ltd., London, and of the Macmillan Company of Canada, Ltd., "Having New England Fathers" from *Address to the Living* by John Holmes copyright Doris Holmes. "Reveille" and "With Rue My Heart Is Laden" from *A Shropshire Lad*—Authorized Edition—from *The Collected Poems of A. E. Housman*, copyright 1939, 1940, © 1959 by Holt, Rinehart and Winston, Inc. Copyright © 1967 by Robert E. Symons. Reprinted by permission of Holt, Rinehart and Winston, Inc., and with the permission of The Society of Authors, literary representatives of the Estate of the late A. E. Housman, and Jonathan Cape, Ltd: "Crow" from the book *Sleep Without Armor* by Frances Minturn Howard, copyright 1953 by Frances Minturn Howard, reprinted by permission of E.P. Dutton & Co., Inc. Lines from "Chamber Music" and "The Noise of Waters" from *Collected Poems* by James Joyce, copyright 1918 by B. W. Huebsch, Inc., renewed 1946 by Nora Joyce, reprinted by permission of The Viking Press, Inc. and The Society of Authors, literary representatives of the Estate of the late James Joyce, and by the Executors of the James Joyce Estate and Jonathan Cape, Ltd. "For Children If They'll Take Them" copyright 1961 by X. J. Kennedy from *Nude Descending a Staircase* by X. J. Kennedy, reprinted by permission of Doubleday & Company, Inc., and Curtis Brown, Ltd. "Our Window Is Stained" from *Puppet Plays* by Alfred Kreymborg, courtesy of Dorothy Kreymborg. "Lincoln Was a Tall Man" by Elias Lieberman from the book *To My Brothers Everywhere* by Elias Lieberman, E. P. Dutton & Co., Inc., 1954, by permission of the author. "The Little Turtle" reprinted with permission of The Macmillan Company from *Collected Poems* by Vachel Lindsay, copyright 1920 by The Macmillan Company, renewed 1948 by Mamie T. Wheless. "Adventures With My Grandfather" by Anne Marx reprinted with the permission of the author. "The West Wind" reprinted by permission of The Macmillan Company from *Poems* by John Masefield, copyright 1912 by The Macmillan Company, renewed 1940 by John Masefield, and by permission of The Society of Authors as literary representatives of the Estate of the late John Masefield. "Anne Rutledge" from *Spoon River Anthology* by Edgar Lee Masters published by The Macmillan Company and used by permission of Ellen C. Masters. "The Tropics in New York" by Claude McKay reprinted by permission of Twayne Publishers, Inc. "The Harp Weaver" by Edna St. Vincent Millay from *Collected Poems* published by Harper and Row, copyright 1923, 1951 by Edna St. Vincent Millay and Norma Millay Ellis and used with permission. "The Noise That Time Makes" from *Case Record of a Sonnetorium* by Merrill Moore by permission of Twayne Publishers, Inc. "Quoits" by Mary Effie Lee Newsome reprinted by permission of Harper and Row, Inc. "The Going of the Snow" from the book *Collected Poems* by Louise Townsend Nicholl, copyright 1953 by E. P. Dutton, Inc., reprinted by permission of the publishers. "Mountain Road" by Mary Oliver copyright 1968 by The New York Times Company and reprinted by permission. "Fourth of July" is reprinted with the permission of Charles Scribner's Sons from *I, Too, Jehovah* by Edmund Pennant, copyright 1952 by Charles Scribner's Sons. "Blue Girls" by John Crowe Ransom, reprinted with permission of Random House, Inc., and Laurence Pollinger, Ltd. "The House on the Hill" from *Children of the Night* by Edwin Arlington Robinson, reprinted with the permission of Charles Scribner's Sons. "The Chair" and "The Sloth" by Theodore Roethke copyright 1950 by Theodore Roethke and reprinted by permission of Doubleday & Company, Inc., and Faber and Faber, Ltd. "Look at Six Eggs" from "Prairie" from *Cornhuskers* by Carl Sandburg copyright 1918 by Holt, Rinehart and Winston, Inc., copyright 1946 by Carl Sandburg, reprinted by permission of Holt, Rinehart and Winston, Inc., and Laurence Pollinger, Ltd. "Four Little Foxes" from *Covenant with Earth: a Selection from the Poems of Lew Sarett* edited and copyright 1956, by Alma Johnson Sarett and published, 1956, by the University of Florida Press, reprinted by permission of Mrs. Sarett. "I Think Continually of Those Who Were Truly Great" from *Collected Poems* by Stephen Spender, used by permission of Random House, Inc., and Faber and Faber, Ltd. "The Goat Paths," "Washed In Silver," and "The Rivals" from *Collected Poems* by James Stephens used by permission of Mrs. Iris Wise, Macmillan & Co., Ltd., the Macmillan Company of Canada, Ltd., and The Macmillan Company, New York. "Villanelle of the Sea" and "The Proprietor" from *Psalms of the Prodigal* by A. M. Sullivan reprinted with the permission of the author. "The Watch," copyright © 1965 by The Hudson Review, Inc., from *Half Sun Half Sleep* by May Swenson, reprinted with permission of Charles Scribner's Sons. "Song for Unbound Hair" from *Words for the Chisel* by Genevieve Taggard reprinted with the permission of Random House, Inc. "First Thanksgiving of All" by Nancy Byrd Turner reprinted with the permission of the author. "The Little Animal" by Joseph Tusiani from *The Fifth Season* © 1964 by Joseph Tusiani, reprinted by permission of Astor-Honor, Inc., 26 East 42nd Street, New York City. "Single Majesty" from *Collected and New Poems: 1924-1963* by Mark Van Doren, copyright © 1963 by Mark Van Doren and reprinted by permission of Mark Van Doren and Hill and Wang, Inc. "Theatre Mouse" from *Nearer the Bone* by Charles Wagner and used by permission of the author. "Seaside Poems: Do Fishes Go to School?" by Ruth Whitman by permission of the author. "The Paper in the Meadow" by Oscar Williams from *That's All That Matters* copyright 1945 by Oscar Williams and used by permission of the Executors of the Estate of Oscar Williams. "The Eagle and the Mole" and "Velvet Shoes" by Elinor Wylie by permission of Random House, Inc. "The Song of Wandering Aengus," "The Fiddler of Dooney," and "To a Squirrel at Kyle-Na-No" reprinted with permission of The Macmillan Company from *Collected Poems* by William Butler Yeats, copyright 1906 by The Macmillan Company, renewed 1934 by William Butler Yeats and also by

permission of Mr. M. B. Yeats and Macmillan and Company, Ltd., London.

A careful effort has been made to trace the ownership of the poems included in this anthology in order to secure permission to reprint copyrighted material and to make full acknowledgement of their use. If any error of omission has occurred, it is purely inadvertent, and will be corrected in subsequent editions, provided written notification is made to the publisher, Grosset & Dunlap, Inc., 51 Madison Avenue, New York, N.Y. 10010.

PICTURE CREDITS

The work of the following illustrators, commissioned especially for this volume, appear on the pages listed below.
BURMAH BURRIS: 2, 4, 5, 6, 13, 16, 17, 19, 25, 26, 30, 95, 116, 123, 153, 214, 218, 238, 240, 248, 258, 272, 291, 310, 331. URSULA LANDSHOFF: 31, 76, 89, 121, 134, 136, 150, 166, 213, 224, 246, 247, 265, 307. ROY McKIE: 34, 49, 80, 110, 136, 137, 139, 149, 159, 164, 174, 178, 180, 181, 182, 185, 192, 199, 203, 207, 211. MEL KLAPHOLZ: 37, 44-45, 53, 56, 60, 79, 91, 102, 104, 107, 109, 145, 242, 256, 277, 282, 283, 285, 286, 296, 298, 312, 314, 319, 325, 329.

The illustrations listed below are used by special arrangement with the copyright holders.

ALLEN, DOUGLAS and SWEET, DARRELL, from *The How and Why Wonder Book of Reptiles*, © 1960 by Wonder Books, Inc., 67. BALDRIDGE, CYRUS LEROY, from *Hans Brinker*, © 1945, by Grosset & Dunlap, Inc., 23, 51, 54, 93. BAUMGARTNER, WARREN, from *The Story of Abraham Lincoln*, copyright, 1952 by Nina Brown Baker, 263. BERSON, HAROLD, from *A Treasury of Mother Goose*, © 1967, by Grosset & Dunlap, Inc., 46. COOPER, MARIO, from *The Story of Pocahontas*, copyright, 1953, by Shirley Graham, 27, 252. Currier & Ives, 279. DOKTOR, IRV, from *The Illustrated Book of American Folklore*, illustrations © 1958, by Grosset & Dunlap, Inc., 151. DOREMUS, ROBERT, from *The How and Why Wonder Book of Ships*, © 1963, by Wonder Books, Inc. 276. ERICKSON, PHOEBE, from *Baby Animal Friends*, copyright, 1954, by Wonder Books, Inc., 215. FALLS, CHARLES B., from *The Story of Davy Crockett*, copyright, 1952, by Enid Lamonte Meadowcroft, 226. FERGUSON, WALTER, from *The How and Why Wonder Book of Wild Animals*, © 1962, by Wonder Books, Inc., 208, 228, 231. FERGUSON, WALTER and SMITH, NED, from *The How and Why Wonder Book of Birds* © 1960, by Wonder Books, Inc., 73, 78, 82, 147. FUJIKAWA, GYO, from *A Child's Book of Poems*, copyright © 1969, by Gyo Fujikawa, 81, 129, 197, 236, 299; from *A Child's Garden of Verses*, © 1957, by Grosset & Dunlap, Inc., 7, 97, 122, 124, 126; from *Mother Goose*, copyright © 1968, by Gyo Fujikawa, 65, 120, 130, 141, 201. GILBERT, W. S., 190. GLANZMAN, LOUIS S., from *Kidnapped*, © 1960, by Grosset & Dunlap, Inc., 38, 42. JAMBOR, LOUIS, from *Little Women*, copyright, 1947, by Grosset & Dunlap, Inc., 14, 40, 86, 294, 301, 306; from *Jo's Boys*, copyright, 1949, by Grosset & Dunlap, Inc., 20, 142, 244, 270, 321, 327. KOEHLER, CYNTHIA ILIFF and ALVIN, from *The How and Why Wonder Book of Wild Flowers*, © 1962, by Wonder Books, Inc., 10; from *The How and Why Wonder Book of Ants and Bees*, © 1962, by Wonder Books, Inc., 63; from *The How and Why Wonder Book of Fish*, © 1963, by Wonder Books, Inc., 66, 68; from *Kittens and Puppies, Horses and Rabbits and Insects, Turtles and Birds*, copyright © 1959, 1960, 1961, 1963, 1964, 1965, 1969 by Grosset & Dunlap, Inc., 67, 70, 71, 73, 75, 212, 216, 220; from *The How and Why Wonder Book of Butterflies and Moths*, © 1963, by Wonder Books, Inc., 83; from *You Can Teach Your Child to Read*, © 1957, by Grosset & Dunlap, Inc., 69, 223. LEAR, EDWARD, from *Nonsense Songs and Stories*, 169. LEASON, PERCY, from *The Big Book of Dogs*, copyright, 1952, by Grosset & Dunlap, Inc., 217. LLOBERA, JOSE, from *The Adventures of Don Quixote, Man of La Mancha*, © 1964 by AFHA—Italia—Milano, 84. LONETTE, REISIE, from *The Five Little Peppers and How They Grew*, illustrations copyright © 1963 by Grosset & Dunlap, Inc., 98.

MAGAGNA, ANNA MARIE, from *Read Me a Poem*, © 1965, by Grosset & Dunlap, Inc., 9, 118, 119, 140, 155, 156. SEIDEN, ART, from *Tom Glazer's Treasury of Folk Songs*, illustrations, © 1964, by Grosset & Dunlap, Inc., 28, 33, 233; from *Famous Myths and Legends of the World*, © 1960, by Grosset & Dunlap, Inc., 132. SHARP, WILLIAM, from *Heidi*, copyright, 1945, by Grosset & Dunlap, Inc., 29, 324. SMITH, NED, from *The Book of Songbirds*, © by Grosset & Dunlap, Inc., 1956, 12. SWEET, DARRELL, from *The How and Why Wonder Book of North America*, © 1962, by Wonder Books, Inc., 225. SZYK, ARTHUR, from *Andersen's Fairy Tales*, copyright MCMXLV by Grosset & Dunlap, Inc., 288. TENNIEL, SIR JOHN, from *Alice in Wonderland & Through the Looking Glass*, 162, 171, 172, 176. VOSBURGH, LEONARD, from *The Family Album of Favorite Poems*, © 1959 by P. Edward Ernest, 112. WARD, LYND, from *The Story of Ulysses S. Grant*, copyright, 1952, by Jeannette Covert Nolan, 280, 281. WEBER, NETTIE and CLEMENT, CHARLES, from *A Child's First Picture Dictionary*, copyright, 1948, by Wonder Books, Inc., 212.

INDEX OF AUTHORS, TITLES, AND FIRST LINES OF POETRY

In this index, author's names have been set in capital letters (AIKEN, CONRAD); titles of poems have been set in italic type (*Abdul Abulbul Amir*); and the first lines of poetry have been set in regular, roman type (A bird came down the walk). When all or part of the first line of the poem has been used as its title, only the first line is used.

A bird came down the walk	76
A Book	86
A Briton who swore at his king	179
A capital ship for an ocean trip	167
A centipede was happy quite	136
A child said What is the grass? fetching it to me with full hands	126
A clergyman told from his text	181
A dog starved at his master's gate	329
A flea and a fly in a flue	179
A fox went out in a hungry plight	
A funny thing about a chair	136
A good sword and a trusty hand!	261
A maiden at college named Breeze	181
A man in the wilderness asked me	139
A milkmaid, who poised a full pail on her head	204
A nightingale that all day long	64
A north-country maid up to London had strayed	292
A quiet home had Parson Gray	244
A sail! A sail! Oh, whence away	44
A simple child	253
A song of enchantment I sang me there	146
A spaniel, Beau, that fares like you	216
A street there is in Paris famous	311
A thing of beauty is a joy forever	133
A voice on the winds	115
A wet sheet and a flowing sea	43
A wild-bear chase didst never see?	226
A yak who was new to the zoo	180
Abdul Abulbul Amir	184
Abou Ben Adhem, may his tribe increase	328
Across the narrow beach we flit	70
Adventures with My Grandfather	265
After Many a Summer	140
After supper	68
Afton Water	157
Ah! what pleasant visions haunt me	42
Ahkond of Swat, The	268
AIKEN, CONRAD	62, 273
Aladdin	295
Alas! Poor Mungo!	230
ALDRICH, THOMAS BAILEY	35, 305
All day I hear the noise of waters	41
All That's Past	299
All ye woods, and trees, and bowers	222
ALLINGHAM, WILLIAM	150, 246, 299
An epicure dining at Crewe	180
An indolent vicar of Bray	179
And I have loved thee, Ocean! and my joy	40
And it came to pass in those days	28
And what is so rare as a day in June?	11
ANGOFF, CHARLES	149
Animal Fair	233
Annabel Lee	303
Anne Rutledge	260
Announced by all the trumpets of the sky	20
Answer to a Child's Question	75
April	9
Ariel's Song	155
ARNOLD, MATTHEW	50
Art thou poor, yet hast thou golden slumber?	322
As a rule, man is a fool	139
As I Float	89
As I was going to Derby	222
As I was going up the stair	141
As I went into the city, clattering chimes	30
At evening when the lamp is lit	88

At night, when all the feet have
  fled 211
Auguries of Innocence 329
AUSTIN, MARY 161, 225
Autumn 16
Avoid the reeking herd 82
Ay, tear her tattered ensign down 276

Baby Seeds 129
Bailiff's Daughter of Islington, The 270
Ballad of Bouillabaisse, The 311
Ballad of Sir Patrick Spens, The 87
Ballad of the Fox, The 228
Ballad of the Harp Weaver, The 107
Ballad of William Sycamore, The 241
Bananas ripe and green, and
  gingerroot 309
BARHAM, RICHARD HARRIS 200
Battle Hymn of the Republic 281
Bear Hunt, The 226
BEAUMONT, FRANCIS 140
Beau's Reply 216
BEDDOES, THOMAS LOVELL 51
Bed-Time Story 234
Behold her, single in the field 266
Behold him, that great solitary 129
BENET, LAURA 111
BENET, STEPHEN VINCENT 241
Between Nose and Eyes a strange
  contest arose 196
Between the dark and the daylight 98
Beyond yon straggling fence that
  skirts the way 240
BICKERSTAFF, ISAAC 195
Black book clapping above a swamp 78
BLAKE, WILLIAM 5, 125, 221,
    225, 248, 329
Blind Men and the Elephant, The 232
Blow, blow, thou winter wind 21
Blue and the Gray, The 280
Blue Girls 311
BOGAN, LOUISE 210
Bonnie George Campbell 278
Book, A 86
Bread and milk for breakfast 21
Breathes there the man with soul
  so dead 320
Brown and furry 233
BROWNING, ELIZABETH BARRETT 327
BROWNING, ROBERT 7, 93
BRYANT, WILLIAM CULLEN 71
Bugle Song 148
BUNNER, HENRY CUYLER 99
BURNS, ROBERT 157, 272
Busy, curious, thirsty fly! 65
By the flow of the inland river 280
By the side of a murmuring stream 202
BYRON, see under GORDON,
  GEORGE, LORD BYRON

CALVERLY, CHARLES STUART 196, 200
CAMPBELL, THOMAS 278
CAMPION, THOMAS 22
CANE, MELVILLE 234
CANNING, GEORGE 202
CARMAN, BLISS 88
CARROLL, LEWIS 171, 172, 175
CARRYL, CHARLES E. 167, 198
Cats of Kilkenny, The 215

Certainly Adam in Paradise had
  not more sweet 132
Chair, The 136
Changed 200
Chapter Two 310
Character of a Happy Life, The 321
Charge of the Light Brigade, The 277
Charm me asleep, and melt me so 158
Chickens, The 70
CHILD, LYDIA MARIA 18
Children's Hour, The 98
Choric Song 156
Christmas at Sea 36
Christmas is a comin' and the
  geese are getting fat 34
Christ's Nativity 28
Chronicle, A 177
City Mouse, The 212
CLARE, JOHN 26, 65, 77, 147, 292
Clear and cool, clear and cool 47
Clock-a-Clay 65
Close by the margin of the brook 69
Clouds 125
Cockles and Mussels 267
COLERIDGE, SAMUEL TAYLOR 75, 100,
    227
COLERIDGE, SARA 4
COLUM, PADRAIC 267
Come live with me and be my love 272
Come play with me 231
Come unto these yellow sands 155
Confession, The 200
CONSTABLE, THOMAS 17
Content 321
CORNWALL, BARRY 45, 74
CORNWELL, HENRY SYLVESTER 94
Counting-out Rhymes 166
Cow, The 221
COWPER, WILLIAM 64, 90, 196,
    216, 235
CRAIK, DINAH MARIA MULOCK 27
CRANE, STEPHEN 86
Crescent Boat, The 96
Crickets 62
Crossing the Bar 41
Crow 78
Crow Doth Sing, The 144
Cuckoo, The 72
CUMMINGS, E. E. 7
CUNNINGHAM, ALLAN 43
Cure for a Pussy Cat 215

Dame Duck's Lecture 69
Dapple Grey 218
Darkling Thrush, The 77
Dashing thro' the snow 31
DAVIDSON, GUSTAV 131, 154
DAVIES, W. H. 130
Day Is Done, The 160
Deacon's Masterpiece, The 193
December Music 30
Deep and dark is ocean's mystery 52
DEKKER, THOMAS 322
DE LA MARE, WALTER 16, 146, 293,
    299
DIBDIN, CHARLES 43
DICKINSON, EMILY 16, 76, 86, 119, 326
Dinkey Bird, The 172
Do not fear to put thy feet 156

Do you ask what the birds say?
  The sparrow, the dove 75
DOBELL, SIDNEY 54
Donkeys 220
Dover Beach 50
DYER, EDWARD 320
Eagle, The 81
Eagle and the Mole, The 82
EBERHART, RICHARD 231
ECCLESIASTICUS 322
Elderly Gentleman, The 202
Eldorado 92
Elegy on the Death of a Mad Dog 218
ELIOT, T. S. 205
EMERSON, RALPH WALDO 20, 125, 151
Epigram 137
Epitaph 137
Epitaph and Reply 138
Epitaph Intended for Sir Isaac
  Newton 138
Epitaph to a Newfoundland Dog 217
Escape at Bedtime 121
Expostulation, An 195

FANSHAWE, CATHERINE 188
Farmer's Boy, A 201
Father William 176
FAWCETT, EDGAR 73
Fetters 323
Fiddler of Dooney, The 245
FIELD, EDWARD 220
FIELD, EUGENE 172
FIELDS, JAMES THOMAS 55
FINCH, FRANCIS MILES 280
First Dandelion, The 128
First Thanksgiving of All 19
FLETCHER, JOHN 156, 222
Flow gently, sweet Afton, among
  thy green braes 157
Flowers that Bloom in the
  Spring, The 159
Follow the Gleam 91
Fool's Prayer, The 319
FOOTE, SAMUEL 165
For Children If They'll Take Them 255
For I will consider my cat, Jeoffry 214
For want of a nail, the shoe was lost 139
Four ducks on a pond 299
Four Little Foxes 6
Fourth of July 12
FRANKLIN, BENJAMIN 230
Friendly Beasts, The 33
Frog, The 67
FROST, ROBERT 24, 327

Garden Year, The 4
Gardener, The 257
Gather round 149
Gay, guiltless pair 78
Gayly bedight 92
Gentle Jenny, called Rosemary 207
George the First was
  always reckoned 186
Georges, The 186
Giant Fisherman, The 139
GILBERT, W. S. 57, 80, 159, 181, 189
GINSBERG, LOUIS 323
Give me the splendid silent sun
  with all his beams full dazzling 132

Gladness of heart is the life of man 322
Gleaming in silver are the hills 120
Glories of Our Blood and State, The 318
Glory be to God for dappled things 130
Goat, The 223
Goat Paths, The 223
God of Sheep, The 222
Going of the Snow, The 4
Golden Vanity, The 52
GOLDSMITH, OLIVER 218, 240, 244
Gone were but the winter 6
Good people all, of every sort 218
GORDON, GEORGE, LORD BYRON 40,
104, 217, 269
Great Panjandrum, The 165
GREENE, ROBERT 321
Grizzly Bear 225
Hail, old October, bright and chill 17
Half a league, half a league 277
Hands of Toil, The 139
Happy the man, whose wish and
care 324
HARDY, THOMAS 15, 77
Harp That Once through Tara's
Halls, The 309
HARRIS, MARGUERITE 294
Hast thou given the horse strength 219
Have you heard of the wonderful
one-hoss shay 193
Having New England fathers in
my blood 300
HAWKER, ROBERT STEPHEN 261
He bloomed among eagles 260
He clasps the crag with hooked hands 81
Heart's Content 44
Height of the Ridiculous, The 203
HENLEY, WILLIAM ERNEST 323
Here lies the body of Mike O'Day 137
Here sparrows build upon the
trees 292
Here we come a-whistling through
the fields so green 29
HERRICK, ROBERT 158, 326
HERSCHBERGER, RUTH 235
High upon highlands 278
Hinty, minty, cutty corn 166
His angle-rod made of sturdy oak 139
Ho, sailor of the sea 54
HODGSON. RALPH 294
Hold my hand, look away 12
HOLMES, JOHN 300
HOLMES, OLIVER WENDELL 179, 191,
193, 203, 276
Home no more home to me,
whither must I wander 306
Home Thoughts from Abroad 93
HOOD, THOMAS 18, 290, 308
HOPKINS, GERARD MANLEY 130
Horatius at the Bridge 282
Horse, The 219
Horses of the Sea, The 68
Housekeeper, The 236
House on the Hill, The 308
HOUSMAN, A. E. 92, 304
HOVEY, RICHARD 93
How falls it, oriole, thou has
come to fly 73
How happy is he born and taught 321
How many seconds in a minute? 317

How pleasant to know Mr. Lear! 189
How sweet is the shepherd's
sweet lot! 248
How's My Boy? 54
HOWARD, FRANCIS MINTURN 78
HOWE, JULIA WARD 281
HUGHES, LANGSTON 161
Human Heart, The 140
HUNT, LEIGH 66, 301, 328
Hunting Song 227

I am fevered with the sunset 93
I am his highness' dog at Kew 137
I am monarch of all I survey 90
I come to work as well as play 9
I had a dove and the sweet dove died 76
I had a little pony 218
I hear America singing 144
I heard a bird at dawn 149
I heard a thousand blended notes 317
I heard the bells on Christmas Day 29
I know a funny little man 197
I know not why my soul is racked 200
I leant upon a coppice gate 77
I Met a Man 141
I met a traveler from an antique
land 325
I play'd with you 'mid cowslips
blooming 304
I remember, I remember 290
I said, "This horse, sir, will you
shoe?" 166
I saw a man pursuing the horizon 86
I saw a peacock with a fiery tail 165
I saw you toss the kites on high 124
I see the moon 120
I think continually of those who
were truly great 259
I think I could turn and live with
animals 210
I, too, sing America 161
I went out to the hazel wood 105
I went to the animal fair 233
I will make you brooches and toys
for your delight 271
I will not change my horse with
any that treads 219
I wish I had a yellow cat 212
I wrote some lines once on a time 203
If all the land were apple pie 137
If all the world and love were young 273
If you ever, ever, ever meet
a grizzly bear 225
I'll tell thee everything I can 175
In a far away northern county, in
the placid pastoral region 243
In a milkweed cradle 129
In an ocean, 'way out yonder 172
In Dublin's fair city 267
In form and feature, face and limb 178
In Just— 7
In marble halls as white as milk 138
In May, when sea-winds pierced
our solitudes 125
In moving-slow he has no peer 224
In the cowslip pips I lie 65
In the Dumps 138
In the hollow tree, in the old
gray tower 74

In winter time I have such fun 245
In Xanadu did Kubla Khan 100
Incidents in the life of My
Uncle Arly 173
Invictus 323
It chanced to be our washing day 191
It is not growing like a tree 316
It is what he does not know 231
It matters not what star I follow 154
It was an old, old, old, old lady 99
It was many and many a year ago 303
It was not in the winter 308
It was six men of Indostan 232
It was the schooner Hesperus 55
It's a warm wind, the west wind,
full of birds' cries 123
Its wicked little windows leer 111
I've watched you now a full half-
hour 83

Jabberwocky 171
JACKSON, HELEN HUNT 16
January brings the snow 4
Jenny kissed me when we met 301
Jesus our Brother, kind and good 33
Jingle Bells 31
John Anderson, My Jo, John 272
Johnny Has Gone for a Soldier 281
JOHNSON, LIONEL 115
Jolly Red Nose 140
JONSON, BEN 316
JOYCE, JAMES 41, 154
Julius Caesar and the Honey-Bee 64
Jumblies, The 168
June 11
Just as the moon was fading 35

KEATS, JOHN 76, 106, 133, 202, 258
KENNEDY, X. J. 255
KING, BEN 215
King Solomon and King David 244
KING, W. 139
KINGSLEY, CHARLES 47, 290, 295
Kitten and the Falling Leaves, The 213
KREYMBORG, ALFRED 24
Kriss Kringle 35
Kubla Khan 100

La belle Dame sans Merci 106
LAMB, CHARLES 236
Lamb, The 221
Land of Story-Books, The 88
LANDOR, WALTER SAVAGE 186
LANG, ANDREW 15
Lars Porsena of Clusium 282
Last Chrysanthemum, The 15
Laughing Song 125
Lean out of the window 154
LEAR, EDWARD 168, 173, 180, 181,
189, 268
LEIGH, HENRY S. 178
Leisure 130
Leprechaun; or, Fairy Shoemaker,
The 246
Let me go where'er I will 151
Let us walk in the white snow 21
LIEBERMAN, ELIAS 263
Light Is Sweet, The 119
LINCOLN, ABRAHAM 226

Lincoln was a tall man 263
LINDSAY, VACHEL 67
Lines to a Young Lady 189
Lines Written in Early Spring 317
Listen—Ill say you a 310
Little Animal, The 229
Little Billee 46
Little Cares, The 327
Little Cowboy, what have you
heard? 246
Little Girl I Used to Be, The 294
Little Lamb, who made thee? 221
Little Orphant Annie's come to
our house to stay 110
Little Turtle, The 67
Long, Long Ago 32
LONGFELLOW, HENRY WADSWORTH 23,
29, 42, 50, 55, 98, 160, 201, 296
Look at six eggs 150
Lord Chancellor's Song 189
Love and Age 304
LOWELL, JAMES RUSSELL 11, 14, 139,
295

MACAULAY, THOMAS BABINGTON 282
Man and the Fish, The 66
Man in the Moon, The 120
Man in the Wilderness, A 139
Man Is a Fool 139
Man of Thessaly, The 141
MARLOWE, CHRISTOPHER 272
Martha 293
MARX, ANNE 265
MASEFIELD, JOHN 123
MASTERS, EDGAR LEE 260
Maud Muller on a summer's day 248
McKAY, CLAUDE 309
Meditation 132
Memory 305
Memory, A 299
Mermaid, The 48
Merry are the bells and merry
would they ring 156
Methuselah ate what he found on
his plate 192
Milkmaid, The 204
MILLAY, EDNA ST. VINCENT 107
MILTON, JOHN 10
Mine eyes have seen the glory of
the coming of the Lord 281
Miracles 118
Moment of Visitation 131
Moon, The 121
Moon Is Up, The 164
MOORE, MERRILL 307
MOORE, THOMAS 309
Morning 119
Morning 196
Mountain Road 300
Mowers, weary and brown, and blithe 15
Mr. Nobody 197
Music 145
Music 151
Music I heard with you was more
than music 273
My bed is like a little boat 89
My boat is on the shore 269
My cat Jeoffry 214
My daddy is dead, but I can't tell
you how 195

My Early Home 292
My father, he was a mountaineer 241
My father left me three acres of land 35
My grandfather kept no 300
My heart leaps up when I behold 129
My Lost Youth 296
My mind lets go a thousand things 305
My mind to me a kingdom is 320

Nature and Nature's laws lay hid
in night 138
Naughty Boy, The 202
Near this spot 217
Neither Spirit nor Bird 161
New Year, The 27
NEWSOME, MARY EFFIE LEE 245
NICHOLL, LOUISE TOWNSEND 4
Nightingale and Glow-worm, The 64
No man is born into the world
whose work 139
No sun—no moon! 18
Noble Nature, The 316
NOEL, THOMAS 32
Noise of Waters, The 41
Noise That Time Makes, The 307
Nose and the Eyes, The 196
Nose, nose, jolly red nose 140
Not of the sunlight 91
November 18
Now the bright morning star,
Daye's harbinger 10
Now winter nights enlarge 22
Nursery Snail 235

O blithe new-comer! I have heard 72
O Captain! My Captain! our fear-
ful trip is done 262
O Mary, go and call the cattle home 290
O to have a little house 267
O, what can ail thee, knight at arms 106
Oak and the Ash, The 292
Ode 146
Of all the rides since the birth
of time 255
Of white and tawny, black as ink 210
Often I think of the beautiful
town 296
Oh! My aged Uncle Arly 173
Oh, never marry Ishmael 264
Oh, to be in England, 93
Old Ironsides 276
Old Man Who Lived in the
Woods, The 206
Old Meg she was a gypsy 258
Old Noah once he built the ark 251
Old October 17
Old Song, The 295
Old winter sad, in snow yclad 32
Old Woman of the Roads, An 267
Old Year, The 26
OLDYS, WILLIAM 65
OLIVER, MARY 300
On a Fly Drinking from His Cup 65
On a Spaniel Called Beau Killing
a Young Bird 216
On a Squirrel Crossing the Road
in Autumn in New England 231
On a tree by a river a little tom-tit 80

On May Morning 10
"Once around is enough," my
Grandfather said 265
Once—but no matter when 177
Once in a saintly passion 317
Once . . . once upon a time 293
Once there was a spaniel 234
Once upon a midnight dreary,
while I pondered weak and weary 112
One cricket said to another 62
One More River 251
One night came on a hurricane 43
One, Two, Three 99
Only in fetters 323
Orpheus with his lute made trees 145
O'SHAUGHNESSY, ARTHUR 146
Our bugles sang truce,—for the
night-cloud had lowered 278
Our Joyful Feast 33
Our window is stained 24
Out of me unworthy and unknown 260
Out of the bosom of the air 23
Out of the night that covers me 323
Over the river and through the wood 18
Owl, The 74
Ox-Tamer, The 243
Ozymandias 325

Paper in the Meadow, The 287
Parson Gray 244
Passionate Shepherd to His Love,
The 272
PATMORE, COVENTRY 127
Patriotism 320
Peace and Mercy and Jonathan 19
PEACOCK, THOMAS LOVE 304
PENNANT, EDMUND 12
Pheasant, The 79
Pied Beauty 130
PIERPONT, JAMES 31
Pippa's Song 7
Ploughboy in Luck, The 195
Pocahontas 252
POE, EDGAR ALLAN 92, 112, 303
POPE, ALEXANDER 79, 137, 138, 324
Poring on Caesar's death with
earnest eye 64
Praise ye the Lord 158
Proprietor 318
Psalm 23 316
Psalm 150 158

Quoits 245

Rain, The 137
RALEIGH, SIR WALTER 273
Ram, The 222
RANSOM, JOHN CROWE 311
Raven, The 112
Remember man that passeth by 138
Remonstrance with the Snails 236
Reply to the Passionate Shepherd 273
Requiem 101
Reveille 92
Rhodora, The 125
Rhyme for a Simpleton 166
Riddle 138
Riddle, A 188
Riddling Knight, The 186

RILEY, JAMES WHITCOMB 110
Ring out, wild bells, to the wild sky 27
Rivals, The 149
Road Not Taken, The 327
Robin Redbreast 82
Robinson Crusoe's Island 198
ROBINSON, EDWIN ARLINGTON 308
ROETHKE, THEODORE 136, 224
ROSS, DAVID 89, 179, 180, 260
ROSSETTI, CHRISTINA 6, 21, 68, 76, 122, 125, 212, 233, 317
Rum Tum Tugger, The 205
Sad I sit on Butternut Hill 281
Said the first little chicken 70
Sailor's Consolation, The 43
SANDBURG, CARL 150
Sandpiper, The 70
Sands o' Dee, The 290
SARETT, LEW 6
SAXE, JOHN GODFREY 63, 95, 232
SCOTT, SIR WALTER 287, 320
SCOTT, WINFIELD TOWNLEY 30, 310
Scythe Song 15
Sea, The 40
Sea, The 45
Sea Gypsy, The 93
Seaside Poems: Do Fishes Go to School? 68
Secret of the Sea, The 42
See! From the brake the whirring pheasant springs 79
See the kitten on the wall 213
September 16
SHAKESPEARE, WILLIAM 21, 23, 144, 145, 155, 219
SHELLEY, PERCY BYSSHE 127, 325
Shepherd, The 248
SHIRLEY, JAMES 318
Should you ask me, whence these stories 152
SILL, EDWARD ROWLAND 319
Simple and fresh and fair from winter's close emerging 128
Sing me a song of a lad that is gone 295
Singing through the forests 95
Single Majesty 129
Sir, I admit your general rule 137
Sir! When I flew to seize the bird 216
Skipper Ireson's Ride 255
Skylark, The 76
Sloth, The 224
Slow, horses, slow 5
SMART, CHRISTOPHER 214
Snail, The 234
Snail, The 235
Snowbound 25
Snow-flakes 23
Snow-storm, The 20
So, now is come our joyful feast 33
So she went into the garden 165
Soldier, rest! Thy warfare o'er 287
Soldier's Dream, The 278
Solitary Reaper, The 266
Solitude 324
Solomon and the Bees 63
"Son," said my mother 107
Song 76
Song 155

Song 156
Song 293
Song for Boys and Girls 149
Song for Unbound Hair 264
Song in the Songless 151
Song of Enchantment, A 146
Song of Hiawatha, The 152
Song of the Wandering Aengus, The 105
Song of the Western Men, The 261
Song—Tell Me Where Is Fancy Bred 155
Song: The Owl 73
Song's Eternity 147
Sound the flute 5
Speak gently, Spring, and make no sudden sound 6
SPENDER, STEPHEN 259
SPRAGUE, CHARLES 78
Spring 5
Spring Night 5
Spring Quiet 6
Squirrel, The 229
Stay near me—do not take thy flight! 83
STEPHENS, JAMES 120, 149, 223
STEVENSON, ROBERT LOUIS 36, 88, 89, 101, 121, 124, 221, 257, 271, 295, 306
Stopping By Woods on a Snowy Evening 24
Stranger pass by and waste no time 137
Success is counted sweetest 326
Suddenly all the sky is hid 14
Suffolk Epitaph 137
SULLIVAN, A. M. 52, 318
Sumer is icumen in 13
Summer is a-coming in 13
Summer is coming! Summer is coming! 11
Summer is coming, summer is coming 12
Summer Storm 14
Sunset and evening star 41
Sunset City, The 94
Sweet are the thoughts that savor of content 321
Sweet content 322
Sweet William, His Wife and the Sheepskin 207
SWENSON, MAY 254
Swing Song, A 150
Swing, swing 150

TAGGARD, GENEVIEVE 264
TAYLOR, JEFFREYS 204
Tears, idle tears 302
Tell me where is fancy bred 155
Tempest, The 55
TENNYSON, ALFRED LORD 12, 27, 41, 48, 73, 75, 81, 91, 140, 148, 277, 293, 302
THACKERAY, WILLIAM MAKEPEACE 46, 252, 311
Thanks to the human heart by which we live 140
Thanksgiving Day 18
That bottle of perfume that Willie sent 179

That Cat 215
THAXTER, CELIA 70
The beginning of eternity 188
The cat that comes to my window sill 215
The city mouse lives in a house 212
The cock is crowing 8
The crocus, while the days are dark 127
The crooked paths 223
The crow doth sing as sweetly as the lark 144
The cuckoo is a pretty bird 72
The day is done, and the darkness 160
The earth was green, the sky was blue 76
The flowers that bloom in the spring 159
The friendly cow, all red and white 221
The frugal snail, with forecast of repose 236
The garden snail 235
The gardener does not love to talk 257
The glories of our blood and state 318
The goldenrod is yellow 16
The harp that once through Tara's halls 309
The horses of the sea 68
The keen stars were twinkling 127
The king sits in Dumferling town 87
The king was on his throne 104
The lights from the parlor and kitchen shone out 121
The little animal that gave his life 229
The little cares that fretted me 327
The little girl I used to be 294
The Lord is my shepherd; I shall not want 316
The man 255
The man in the moon as he sails the sky 120
The moon has a face like the clock in the hall 121
The moon is up, the moon is up! 164
The morns are meeker than they were 16
The news is yellowing in the rain 287
The night was thick and hazy 198
The noise that time makes in passing by 307
The Old Year's gone away 26
The rain it raineth every day 137
The Reverend Henry Ward Beecher 179
The royal feast was done; the King 319
The Rum Tum Tugger is a Curious Cat 205
The sea is calm tonight 50
The sea! the sea! the open sea! 45
The sheets were frozen hard and they cut the naked hand 36
The snail he lives in his hard round house 234
The sons of the prophet are valiant and bold 184
The splendor falls on castle walls 148
The sun that brief December day 25
The tide rises, the tide falls 50
The woods decay, the woods decay and fall 140
The year's at the spring 7

Theatre Mouse 211
There are sounds within this sound 131
There is no frigate like a book 86
There is something in the autumn
  that is native to my blood 88
There is sweet music here that
  softer falls 156
There is wind where the rose was 16
There once was a young man
  named Hall 181
There was a faith-healer of Deal 180
There was a little girl 201
There was a little turtle 67
There was a lofty ship and she
  put out to sea 52
There was a man, now please
  take note 223
There was a man of Thessaly 141
There was a naughty boy 202
There was a young lady from Crete 181
There was a young lady of Niger 180
There was a young woman
  named Bright 180
There was a youth, and a well-
  beloved youth 270
There was an old lady of Steen 180
There was an old looney of rhyme 181
There was an old man from Peru 180
There was an old man from St. Bees 181
There was an old man in a tree 181
There was an old man who lived in
  the woods 206
There was an old man who said,
  "Do 179
There was an old man with a beard 180
There were once two cats of
  Kilkenny 215
There were three sailors of Bristol
  city 46
There were three sisters fair and
  bright 186
There's a city that lies in the
  Kingdom of Clouds 94
There's music in a hammer 151
There's something in a flying
  horse 96
There's somewhat on my breast,
  father 200
They are all gone away 308
They are not silent like workhorses 220
They have no song, the sedges
  dry 151
They strolled down the lane
  together 201
They that go down to the sea in
  ships 40
They went to sea in a Sieve,
  they did 168
Thing of Beauty, A 133
This is the grave of Mike O'Day 137
THOMPSON, FRANCIS 22
THOMSON, JAMES 317
Three Acres of Land 35
Three Wishes 212
Throstle, The 12
Through the open doors 4
Thrush's Nest, The 77
Tide Rises, the Tide Falls, The 50
Tide River, The 47

Tiger, tiger, burning bright 225
Time for Singing, A 154
Time of Roses, The 308
Time, you old gypsy man 294
Tis the hour when white-
  horsed day 196
"'Tis the voice of the lobster,
  I heard him declare 172
Titwillow 80
To a Fish of the Brook 67
To a Snowflake 22
To a Squirrel at Kyle-Na-No 231
To a Waterfowl 71
To an Oriole 73
To get thine ends, lay bashfulness
  aside 326
To grass, or leaf, or fruit, or wall 235
To Jane 127
To Miss Georgiana Shipley 230
To Morfydd 115
To Music to Becalm His Fever 158
To sea! to sea! the calm is o'er 51
To the Cuckoo 72
To Thomas Moore 269
TRAHERNE, THOMAS 132
Tropics in New York 309
Truly the light is sweet 119
TURNER, CHARLES TENNYSON 64
TURNER, NANCY BYRD 19
TUSIANI, JOSEPH 229
Twas a Friday morn when we
  set sail 48
'Twas brillig, and the slithy toves 171
'Twas in heaven pronounced, and
  'twas muttered in hell 188
'Twas on the shores that round
  our coast 57
Twelfth Night Carol 29
Twins, The 178
Twirling your blue skirts, travelling
  the sward 311
Two little clouds one April day 9
Two roads diverged in a yellow wood 327

Under the Greenwood Tree 155
Under the wide and starry sky 101
Up, up! Ye dames and lasses gay 227

Vagabond Song, A 88
VAN DOREN, MARK 129
Variation on a Sentence 210
Velvet Shoes 21
Verses 90
Very old are the woods 299
Village Schoolmaster, The 240
Villanelle of the Sea 52
Vision of Belshazzar 104
Voice of the Lobster, The 172

WAGNER, CHARLES A. 211
Wake! the silver dust returning 92
Walloping Window-Blind, The 167
Washed in Silver 120
Watch, The 254
Ways and Means 175
We all look on with anxious eyes 192
We Are Seven 253
We are the music-makers 146

We stood beside the rushing
  stream 318
We were crowded in the cabin 55
We wish you a merry Christmas 34
Wearied arm and broken sword 252
Welcome Robin with thy greeting 82
We're all in the dumps 138
West Wind, The 123
WESTWOOD, THOMAS 5
Wet Sheet and a Flowing Sea, A 43
What a wonderful bird the frog are 67
What can't be cured 138
What does little birdie say? 75
What heart could have thought you? 22
What is song's eternity? 147
What Is the Grass? 126
What is this life, if full of care 130
What shoemaker makes shoes
  without leather? 138
What stirred the breath 89
When all the world is young, lad 295
When cats run home and light
  is come 73
When Father Carves the Duck 192
When I 254
When I heard the learn'd
  astronomer 122
When I play on my fiddle in
  Dooney 245
When I was a beggarly boy 295
When icicles hang by the wall 23
When late I attempted your pity
  to move 195
When Solomon was reigning in
  his glory 63
When the green woods laugh
  with the voice of joy 125
When you're lying awake with a
  dismal headache and repose is
  tabooed by anxiety 189
Whisky, frisky 229
White sheep, white sheep 125
Whither, midst falling dew 71
WHITMAN, RUTH 68
WHITMAN, WALT 118, 122, 126, 128,
  132, 144, 210, 243, 262
WHITTIER, JOHN GREENLEAF 25, 248,
  255
Who can say 293
Who comes dancing over the snow? 27
Who has seen the wind 122
Who, or why, or which, or what 268
Who would be 48
Whose woods these are I think
  I know 24
Who's that ringing at my doorbell? 215
Why flyest thou away with fear? 67
Why should this flower delay so long 15
Why, who makes much of miracles? 118
WILLIAMS, OSCAR 287
Will there really be a morning? 119
Wind, The 9
Wind, The 124
Winds through the olive trees 32
Winged Worshippers, The 78
Winter 21
Witch's House, The 111
With rue my heart is laden 304
WITHER, GEORGE 33

Within a thick and spreading
    hawthorn bush   77
WOLCOTT, JOHN   67
Wonderful One-Hoss Shay, The   193
WORDSWORTH, WILLIAM 8, 72, 83, 129,
        140, 213, 253, 266, 317
Work is love made visible   140
WOTTON, SIR HENRY   321

Wreck of the Hesperus, The   55
WRIGHT, E. V.   192
Written in March   8
WYLIE, ELINOR   21, 82

Yarn of the "Nancy Bell," The   57
Ye little snails   236
Year, The   127

YEATS, WILLIAM BUTLER 105, 231, 245
"You are old, Father William,"
    the young man said   176
You beat your pate, and fancy
    wit will come   137
You Fancy Wit   137
You strange, astonished-looking,
    angle-faced   66